The Art of Memory

Holocaust Memorials

in History

The Art of Memory

Holocaust Memorials

in History

Edited by James E. Young

With contributions by Matthew Baigell, James Ingo Freed,
Saul Friedländer, Konstanty Gebert, Esther and
Jochen Gerz, Zvi Gitelman, Hans Haacke,
Andreas Huyssen, Claudia Koonz, Jack Kugelmass,
Primo Levi, Peter Novick, Nathan Rapoport,
Stephan Schmidt-Wulffen, George Segal,
Jochen Spielmann, and James E. Young

Prestel

Published on the occasion of the exhibition "The Art of Memory: Holocaust Memorials in History" held at The Jewish Museum, New York, March 13-July 31, 1994.

Further venues: Deutsches Historisches Museum, Berlin, September 8-November 13, 1994
Münchner Stadtmuseum, Munich, December 9, 1994-March 5, 1995

Exhibition staff: James E. Young, guest curator; Susan Chevlowe, exhibition coordinator; Michal Friedlander, exhibition assistant; Mira Goldfarb, exhibition assistant; Julia Goldman, exhibition assistant; L. Breslin Architecture and Design, designer.

Frontispiece: *Monument to the Deported Jews of Kazimierz* (see p. 25) by Tadeusz Augustynek, 1984 (detail). Photo: Monika Krajewska
Front cover: *The Holocaust* by George Segal. Bronze, 1984. Photo: © Ira Nowinski
Back cover: View of *Treblinka Memorial* by Franciszek Duszenko and Adam Haupt, 1964 (plate 4). Photo: Monika Krajewska

Translation from the Italian: Romy Golan (Primo Levi)
Translation from the German: Michal Friedlander (Stephan Schmidt-Wulffen) and Stephen Lindberg (Jochen Spielmann)
Copyedited by Paula von Bechtolsheim

Prestel-Verlag
16 West 22nd Street, New York, NY 10010, Tel. (212) 627 8199; Fax (212) 627 9866 and
Mandlstrasse 26, 80802 Munich, Germany, Tel. (89) 38 17 09-0; Fax (89) 38 17 09-35

Distributed in continental Europe by Prestel-Verlag
Verlegerdienst München GmbH & Co. KG, Gutenbergstrasse 1, 82205 Gilching, Germany, Tel. (81 05) 38 81 17; Fax (81 05) 38 81 00

Distributed in the US and Canada on behalf of Prestel by te Neues Publishing Company, 16 West 22nd Street, New York, NY 10010, Tel. (212) 627 9090; Fax (212) 627 9511

Distributed in Japan on behalf of Prestel by YOHAN Western Publications Distribution Agency, 14-9 Okubo 3-chome, Shinjuku-ku, Tokyo 169, Japan, Tel. (3) 32080181; Fax (3) 32090288

Distributed in the United Kingdom, Ireland, and all remaining countries on behalf of Prestel by Thames & Hudson Limited, 30-34 Bloomsbury Street, London WC1B 3 QP, England
Tel. (71) 6365488; Fax (71) 6361695

Typeset by OK Satz GmbH, Unterschleissheim
Offset lithography by Repro-Center Färber & Co., Munich
Printed by Aumüller Druck KG, Regensburg
Bound by MIB Conzella, Pfarrkirchen

Printed in Germany

ISBN 3-7913-1322-3 (English edition)
ISBN 3-7913-1337-1 (German edition)

Contents

Preface

The recent decade has been a period of great preoccupation with the Holocaust. Remembering and understanding this tragic era has not only been a concern of Jewish people, but also of non-Jews, especially those living in countries where the atrocities took place. There has been an outpouring of books, films, and visual art on the subject as well as the creation of special exhibitions, remembrance ceremonies, and reunions of survivors. On a larger scale, the memory of the Holocaust has inspired the planning or building of many public monuments and institutions. It is these works and the process of their creation which provoked the staff and the Board of Trustees of The Jewish Museum in New York to address "the creation of public memory," as James E. Young has called it.

The project was initiated in May 1988, when a group of people was invited to the Museum Director's office to discuss how best to represent our concerns in the form of an exhibition as well as in a publication. Architects Allan Greenberg and Lynne Breslin, artist George Segal, historian Sybil Milton, and James Young met with the Museum staff to discuss the idea. Dr. Young's involvement began on that day, and since then the overall concept and creation of the project have rested largely on his imaginative and knowledgeable leadership. Professor of English and Judaic Studies at the University of Massachusetts, Amherst, and author of many books and articles, he has served both as guest curator of the exhibition and as a contributor to and editor of this book.

We have chosen to investigate the reasons why memorials have been built, to look at whose memory is being honored, and to examine the responses to these memorials. The creation of an exhibition and the production of this book presented the opportunity for an analytic perspective. In the process, we have neither created another memorial nor have we solely explored the field of Holocaust art. Rather, we have attempted to reveal the nature of the creative process through the discussion of specific examples of a number of memorials, and we have tried to understand their meaning and the reaction to them in the many places where they exist.

Andreas Huyssen's introduction explores the process of memorialization of the past in the postmodern era, while James Young's essay "The Art of Memory" describes the various aspects of this exhibition more specifically. The artists' profiles provide a special insight on the creative process.

In the essays grouped under the heading "The Holocaust in National Memorial Traditions," the authors attempt to answer the questions how and why public memory of the Holocaust shapes and is shaped by different public constituencies. From their respective areas of expertise, the authors describe memory in context. Their individual approaches vary. One such strategy, for example, as in Claudia Koonz's study of Buchenwald, is to focus on the dilemma of how one country remembers the past and which past it chooses to remember. Jochen Spielmann presents one further example of the complexity of memory at a single site in his examination of the various places of remembrance in Auschwitz-Birkenau. As no survey can ever be exhaustive, the number of sites and the number of countries discussed have necessarily been limited.

Finally, Jack Kugelmass examines our role as memory tourists, and, as a coda, Primo Levi is the voice of the survivor reflecting on the memories which remain in the ruins of Auschwitz.

Joan Rosenbaum, Director

Andreas Huyssen

Monument and Memory
in a Postmodern Age

The abundance of real suffering tolerates no forgetting.
Theodor W. Adorno

Only that which does not cease to hurt remains in memory.
Friedrich Nietzsche

I

Remembrance as a vital human activity shapes our links to the past, and the ways we remember define us in the present. As individuals and societies, we need the past to construct and to anchor our identities and to nurture a vision of the future. As readers of Freud and Nietzsche, however, we know how slippery and unreliable personal memory can be, always affected by forgetting and denial, repression and trauma, and, more often than not, serving the need to rationalize and to maintain power. But a society's collective memory is no less contingent, no less unstable, its shape by no means permanent and always subject to subtle and not so subtle reconstruction.

A society's memory is negotiated in the social body's beliefs and values, rituals and institutions, and in the case of modern societies in particular, it is shaped by such public sites of memory as the museum, the memorial, and the monument. Yet the promise of permanence a monument in stone will suggest is always built on quicksand. Some monuments are joyously toppled at times of social upheaval; others preserve memory in its most ossified form, either as myth or as cliché. Yet others stand simply as figures of forgetting, their meaning and original purpose eroded by the passage of time.

Does it even make sense, however, to oppose memory to forgetting, as we so often do, with forgetting, at best, being acknowledged as the inevitable flaw and deficiency of memory itself? Is it not rather that, paradoxically, each and every memory inevitably depends both on distance and forgetting, the very things that undermine its desired stability and reliability but which, at the same time, are essential for the vitality of memory itself? Is it not a constitutive strength of memory that it can be contested from new perspectives, with novel evidence, from the very spaces it had blocked out? Given this selective and permanently shifting dialogue between present and past, we have come to recognize that our present will inevitably have an impact on what and how we remember. The point is to understand that process, not to regret it in the mistaken belief in some ultimately pure, complete, and transcendent memory. It follows that the strongly remembered past will always be inscribed into our present, from feeding our subconscious desires to guiding our most conscious actions. At the same time, this strongly remembered past may turn into mythic memory. It is not immune to ossification and may become a stumbling block to the needs of the present rather than an opening in the continuum of history.

II

While the capacity to remember is an anthropological given, some cultures will value memory more than others. At any rate, the place of memory in any culture is defined by an extraordinarily complex, discursive web of ritual and mythic, historical, political, and psychological factors. Thus, the lament that our postmodern culture suffers from amnesia merely reverses the long-standing trope in cultural criticism which suggests that enlightened modernization liberates us from tradition and superstitions, that modernity and the past are inherently antagonistic to each other, that museums are not compatible with a truly modern culture, that a modern monument is a contradiction in terms, in short, that to be radically modern means to sever all links with the past. Such was the credo of an unself-critical modernity and of many of its avant-gardist aesthetic manifestations earlier in this century. Indeed, modernization was the often unacknowledged umbilical cord that tied the various aesthetic modernisms and avant-gardes to the social and economic modernity of the bourgeois society they so intensely hated and opposed.

Recent decades, however, have witnessed growing skepticism toward such ideologies of progress, as the dark side of modernization has increasingly impressed itself on the public's consciousness in Western societies in the wake of this century's political totalitarianisms, colonial enterprises, and ecological ravages. In most Western accounts of this crisis of memory and modernity, the Holocaust plays a pivotal role. As Primo Levi once wrote, the Third Reich waged an obsessive war against memory, practicing "an Orwellian falsification of memory, falsification of reality, negation of reality."[1] We know that the strategies of denial and repression did not end with the downfall of the Nazi regime. Fifty years after the notorious Wannsee Conference, at which the Final Solution was first given political and bureaucratic shape, the Holocaust and its memory still stand as a test case for the humanistic and universalistic claims of Western civilization. The issue of remembrance and forgetting touches the core of a multifaceted and diverse Western identity.

There have been intensely fought debates on whether we should see Nazi barbarism as a regression and an aberration of Western civilization, of which Germany, after all, was always a part, or if we should put the emphasis on those aspects of National Socialism that tie it, in however extreme and perverted ways, to the modernity of the West. While the thesis that Nazi Germany was an aberration, more often than not, served interests of denial and forgetting, and by no means only in Germany, the notion that Nazism was but the logical outcome of the evolution of the West was compromised by the orthodox Marxist equation of capitalism with fascism. Such reductive explanations, of course, can easily be dismissed. But the question remains a painful one, and it is hard to come up with an unambiguous answer. Thus, it is one thing to acknowledge Auschwitz as the major wound of Western civilization whose tissues have not healed and can never heal. It is quite another thing, however, to claim that the industrialized murder machinery of the Final Solution, with its systematic degradation of human beings and its planned excesses in "useless violence" (in the words of Primo Levi), is inherent in Western civilization itself and represents its logical outcome.

At this juncture, the postmodern debate about amnesia locks in with the memory of the Holocaust. The French philosopher Jean-François Lyotard has gone so far as to equate the postwar Germans' amnesia and repression vis-à-vis the Holocaust with the failure of Western civilization, in general, to practice anamnesis, to reflect on its constitutive inability to accept difference, otherness, and to draw the consequences from the insidious relationship between enlightenment modernity and Auschwitz.[2] In this view, National Socialism is a singular, but not unique, case in which the narcissistic fantasies of omnipotence and superiority that haunt Western modernity have come to the surface. As an antidote to the seductive power of such fantasies, Lyotard and others have argued that recognition of the other as others, with their histories, aspirations, concrete life-worlds, is paramount. This, it seems to me, is the ethical and political core of much postmodern, poststructuralist thought, and it has been powerfully prefigured within modernism itself, particularly in the work of Theodor W. Adorno, who, with great perspicacity, analyzed the dialectic of enlightenment and violence at a time when the death factory in Auschwitz-Birkenau was operating at maximum capacity and with ruthless efficiency. Without memory, without reading the traces of the past, there can be no recognition of difference (Adorno called it "nonidentity"), no tolerance for the rich complexities and instabilities of personal and cultural, political and national identities.

Not everyone, to be sure, would share Lyotard's sweeping indictment of Western modernity, a view that establishes Auschwitz uncompromisingly as the litmus test for any contemporary reading of the history of modernity and that identifies lack of anamnesis, weakness of memory, repression of otherness as symptoms of the fatal disease of the modern condition. Thus some neoconservative German philosophers, for example, Hermann Lübbe and Odo Marquard, have argued that the undisputed erosion of tradition in modernity actually generated compensatory organs of remembrance such as, among others, the humanities, societies for historical preservation, and the museum. In this view, social and collective memory, as paradigmatically organized in the museum, in historiography, or in archaeology, is not the opposite of modernity but, rather, its very product.

Of course, one argument does not exclude the other. Indeed, even as modernity generates its organs and discourses of remembrance, modernity's historical memory may still be deficient when it comes to the specific anamnesis Lyotard finds wanting: the recognition of otherness, the reflection on constitutive reliance, on exclusion and domination, the work of mourning and memory that would move us beyond what Lyotard diagnoses as our "end-of-the-century melancholy." At any rate, despite their opposition in evaluating the status of memory in Western tradition, both views are predicated on the notion that the very structure of memory (and not just its contents) can be seen as strongly contingent upon the social formation that produces it.

III

How, then, do the technological media affect the structure of memory, the ways we perceive and live our temporality? As the visual media invade ever more aspects of political, cultural, and personal life, we may well want to ask what a postmodern memory would look like, memory at a time in which the basic parameters of an earlier self-confident Western modernity have increasingly come under attack, in which the question of tradition poses itself anew precisely because the tradition of modernity itself is lacking in answers for our predicament. What of the institutions and sites that organize our social memory in the age of television?

If we look at memory in the postmodern 1980s, we are immediately struck not by signs of amnesia but, rather, by a veritable obsession with the past. Indeed, one might even speak of a memorial, or *museal*, sensibility that seems to occupy ever larger parts of everyday culture and experience. Lübbe has diagnosed this expansive historicism of our contemporary culture, claiming that never before has a cultural present been obsessed with the past to the same extent as Western culture was in the 1970s and 1980s, when museums and memorials were being built as though there were no tomorrow.[3] If you add to that the historicizing restoration of old urban centers; the creation of whole museum villages and landscapes; the boom of flea markets, "retro" fashions, and nostalgia waves; the obsessive self-memorialization through the camcorder, memoir writing, and confessional literature; and even the widespread artistic practice of quoting and citing, then the museum, in a broad sense, can be said to function as the key paradigm in contemporary postmodern culture. Far from suffering from amnesia, it seems, we suffer from an overload of memories and have too many museums. Even the monument, which after its nineteenth-century excesses in poor aesthetics and shamelessly legitimizing politics and which fell on hard times with the advent of modernism (despite Gropius or Tatlin), is experiencing a revival of sorts, clearly benefiting from the intensity of our memorial culture.

1   Primo Levi, *The Drowned and the Saved* (New York: Vintage International, 1989), p. 31.

2   Jean-François Lyotard, "Ticket to a New Decor," *Copyright* 1 (Fall 1987): 14-15. On the relationship of Holocaust memory to postmodernism and the discourse of mourning, see Eric L. Santner's superb study *Stranded Objects: Mourning, Memory, and Film in Postwar Germany* (Ithaca and London: Cornell University Press, 1990).

3   See Hermann Lübbe, "Zeit-Verhältnisse," in Wolfgang Zacharias, ed., *Zeitphänomen Musealisierung: Das Verschwinden der Gegenwart und die Konstruktion der Erinnerung* (Essen: Klartext Verlag, 1990), pp. 40-50. See also Lübbe, *Die Aufdringlichkeit der Geschichte* (Graz, Vienna, Cologne: Verlag Styria, 1989).

Critics who focus only on the loss of history, of course, would claim that the new museum and memorial culture of recent years betrays any real sense of history and has instead turned to spectacle and entertainment, thus giving only a postmodern gloss and destroying any real sense of time past, present, and future rather than nurturing it. Perhaps the fascination with the past is actually more than merely the compensatory, even fraudulent, side effect of a new, postmodern temporality which hovers between the need for remembering and the fast track of forgetting. Perhaps it is to be taken seriously as a way of slowing down the speed of modernization, as an attempt, however fragile and fraught with contradiction, to cast lifelines back toward the past and to counteract our culture's undisputed tendency toward amnesia motivated by immediate profit and political expediency. The museum, the monument, and the memorial have, indeed, taken on new life after having been declared dead many times during the history of modernism. Their newly acquired prominence in the public's mind and their success in contemporary culture beg for an explanation. It is simply no longer enough to denounce the museum as an elitist bastion of knowledge and power, nor is an older modernist critique of the monument exactly persuasive when monument artists have incorporated that very critique into their creative practices. Boundaries between museum, memorial, and monument have indeed become fluid in the past decade in ways that make the old interpretation of the museum as fortress for the few and of the monument as medium of reification and forgetting strangely obsolete.

Holocaust museums, memorials, and monuments cannot be seen as somehow separate from this postmodern memorial culture. For even as the Holocaust presents intractable problems to any project of memorial representation,[4] the increasing frequency with which Holocaust museums are built and monuments erected in Israel, Germany, and the rest of Europe, as well as in the United States, is clearly part of a larger cultural phenomenon. It should not be attributed only to the increasing generational distance from the event itself, to the attempt, as it were, to go against the unavoidable process of forgetting at a time when the generation of witnesses and survivors is slowly disappearing and new generations are growing up for whom the Holocaust is either mythic memory or cliché.

One reason for the new-found strength of the museum and the monument in the public sphere may have something to do with the fact that both offer something that the television screen denies: the material quality of the object. The permanence of the monument and of the museum object, formerly criticized as deadening reification, takes on a different role in a culture dominated by the fleeting image on the screen and the immateriality of communications. I would like to suggest that it is the material reality of the object in the museum as it shapes and structures memory, the permanence of the monument in a reclaimed public space in pedestrian zones, in restored urban centers, or in preexisting memorial spaces that attracts a public dissatisfied with simulation and television channel switching. This said, the success of any monument will still have to be measured by the extent to which it connects with the multiple discourses of memory provided to us by the very electronic media to which the monument, as solid matter, provides an alternative. Moreover, there is no guarantee that today's monuments, designed and built with great public participation, lively debate, and memorial engagement, will not one day stand, like their predecessors in the nineteenth century, as objects of forgetting. For now, however, an old medium that once had succumbed to the pace of modernization is exploring new-found possibilities in a memorial media culture.

IV

The problem for Holocaust memory in the 1980s and 1990s has not been forgetting but, rather, the ubiquitousness, the excess of Holocaust imagery everywhere in our culture, from the fascination with fascism in film and fiction, which Saul Friedländer has so persuasively criticized,[5] to the proliferation of an often facile Holocaust victimology in a whole variety of political discourses. In fictional and cinematic representations, in particular, the original trauma is often reenacted and exploited in ways that can be deeply offensive, especially, but not only, to the survivors. Certainly, the unchecked proliferation of the trope itself may be a sign of its traumatic ossification and its remaining locked in a melancholic fixation.

If such proliferation, whether in fiction and film or in contemporary politics, actually trivializes the historical event of the Nazi Final Solution, as many would argue, then the building of still more Holocaust memorials and monuments may not offer a solution to the problems of remembrance either. The attempt to counteract apparent trivializations such as the American television series "Holocaust" (1979) by the building of museums and monumental representations may once again just freeze memory into ritualistic images and discourses. The exclusive insistence on the true representation of the Holocaust in its uniqueness, unspeakability, and incomparability may no longer be adequate in light of its multiple representations and its functioning as a ubiquitous trope in Western culture. Popular representations and historical comparisons are ineradicably part of a Holocaust memory which has become fractured and sedimented.

The criterion for representing the Holocaust cannot just be propriety or awe, as would be appropriate in the face of a cult object. Awe and silent respect may be called for vis-à-vis the suffering of the individual survivor, but it is misplaced as discursive strategy toward the historical event, even if that event may harbor something unspeakable and unrepresentable at its core. For if it is our concern and responsibility to prevent forgetting, we have to be open to the powerful effects that a melodramatic soap opera may exert on the minds of viewers today. In fact, the generations that received their primary socialization through television may find their way to testimony, documentary, and historical treatise precisely through a fictionalized and emotionalized Holocaust made for prime-time television. If the Holocaust can be compared to an earthquake that has destroyed all instruments of measurement, as Lyotard has suggested, then there surely cannot be only one way of representing it.

The increasing temporal and generational distance from the actual experience of the Holocaust, therefore, is important in another respect: it has freed memory to focus on more than the facts alone. In general, we have become increasingly conscious of how social and collective memory is constructed through a variety of multilayered discourses and the media. Holocaust historiography, archives, witness testimony, and documentary footage have all collaborated to establish the hard core of facts, and these facts need to be transmitted to the post-Holocaust generations. Without facts, there is no real memory. But we are also free to recognize that the Holocaust has indeed become dispersed and fractured through the very different ways of memorializing it. Obsessive focus on the unspeakable and unrepresentable, as it was compellingly articulated by Elie Wiesel or George Steiner and as it seems to inform the ethical philosophy of Jean-François Lyotard today, blocks that insight. Even in its historically most serious and legitimate form, Holocaust memory is invested differently in the country of the victims from the way it is structured in the country of the perpetrators, and differently again in the countries of the anti-Nazi alliance.[6]

4 See the excellent collection of essays edited and introduced by Saul Friedländer, *Probing the Limits of Representation: Nazism and the "Final Solution"* (Cambridge, Mass.: Harvard University Press, 1992).

5 Idem, *Reflections of Nazism: An Essay on Kitsch and Death* (New York: Harper and Row, 1984).

6 See James E. Young's ground-breaking study, *The Texture of Memory: Holocaust Memorials and Meaning* (New Haven and London: Yale University Press, 1993).

The same facts have generated significantly different accounts and memory. In Germany, the Holocaust signifies an absence of Jews and a traumatic burden on national identity, in which genuine attempts at mourning are hopelessly entangled with narcissistic injury, ritual breast-beating, and repression. Thus in Germany, until recently, there has been little public knowledge of, or interest in, what was actually lost through the destruction. In Israel, the Holocaust became central to the foundation of the state, both as the end point of a disavowed history of Jews as victims, *and* as a starting point of a new history of nation, self-assertion, and resistance. In the Israeli imagination, the Warsaw Ghetto Uprising has thus been invested with the force of a mythic memory of resistance and heroism unfathomable in Germany. The American focus of the Holocaust concentrates on America as liberator of the camps and haven for refugees and immigrants, and American Holocaust memorials are structured accordingly. In the Soviet account, the genocide of the Jews lost its ethnic specificity and simply became part of the story of the Nazi suppression of international communism in general to an extent which now requires a rewriting of the narratives of East European and Soviet memorial sites.

Much of this, of course, is well known, but it may not yet be fully understood in its implications for the debate about remembering, forgetting, and representing. Such multiple fracturing of the memory of the Holocaust in different countries and the multilayered sedimentation of images and discourses, which range from documentary to soap opera, survivor testimony to narrative fiction, and concentration camp art to memorial painting, has to be seen in its politically and culturally enabling aspects as a potential antidote to the freezing of memory into one traumatic image.

V

What, then, of the monument in this larger field of Holocaust representations and discourses? Clearly, the Holocaust monument is not part of the tradition of the monument as heroic celebration and figure of triumph. Even in the case of the monument to the Warsaw Ghetto Uprising, we face a memorial to suffering, an indictment of crimes against humanity. In contrast to the tradition of the legitimizing, identity-nurturing monument, the Holocaust monument must be considered, rather, as a kind of countermonument. The traditional critique of the monument as burying memory and ossifying the past has often been voiced against the Holocaust monument as well. Holocaust monuments have been accused of "topolatry," especially those constructed at the sites of extermination. They have been reproached as betraying memory, with memory thought of as only internal and thus incompatible with the public externality of the monument. As a variation on Adorno, who, rightfully, was wary of the effects of aestheticizing the unspeakable suffering of the victims, it has been claimed that to build a monument to the Holocaust was itself a barbaric proposition: no monument after Auschwitz. Furthermore, in light of Fascist excesses with monumentalization, some have suggested that Fascist tendencies are inherent in all monuments.[7]

All these critiques of the medium itself focus on the monument as object, as permanent reality in stone, as aesthetic sculpture. They do not, however, recognize the public dimension of the monument, what James Young has described as the "dialogical quality of memorial space." Certainly, we would not be well served by the Holocaust monument as death mask or by an aestheticizing of terror. On the other hand, in the absence of tombstones to the victims, the monument can function as a substitute site of mourning and remembrance. How, after all, are we to guarantee the sur-

A retaining wall at the Jewish cemetery in Kraków, Poland, was built using the fragments of desecrated tombstones.

7 For more on the monument's challenge to itself, see idem, "The Counter-Monument: Memory against Itself in Germany Today," *Critical Inquiry* 18 (Winter 1992): 267–96.

vival of memory if our culture does not provide memorial spaces that can help construct and nurture some collective memory of the *Shoah?* Only if we focus on the public function of the monument, embedding it in public discourses of collective memory, can danger of monumental ossification be avoided.

The great opportunity of the Holocaust monument today lies in its intertextuality as but one part of our memorial culture. As the traditional boundaries of the museum, the monument, and historiography have become more fluid, the monument itself has lost much of its nature of permanence and fixity. The criteria for its success could therefore be the ways it allows for a crossing of boundaries toward other discourses of the Holocaust, the way it pushes us toward reading other texts, other stories.

No single monument will ever be able to convey the Holocaust as such. Such a monument might not even be desirable, just as the Great Book about the *Shoah,* in Geoffrey Hartman's words, might "produce a deceptive sense of totality, throwing into the shadows, even into oblivion, stories, details and unexpected points of view that keep the intellect active and the memory digging."[8] There is much to be said to keep Holocaust monuments and memorials site-specific, to have them reflect local histories, dig up local memories, make the Final Solution palpable, not just by focusing on the sites of extermination, but on the life-worlds of those murdered in the camps.

At some level, however, the question of the Holocaust as a whole, as a totality, will reassert itself together with the problem of its unspeakability. After we have remembered, gone through the facts, mourned for the victims, we will still be haunted by that core of absolute humiliation, degradation, and horror suffered by the victims. How do we approach it when even the witnesses had to say: "I could not believe what I saw with my own eyes." No matter how fractured by media, geography, or subject position representations of the Holocaust are, ultimately, it all comes back to this core: unimaginable, unspeakable, and unrepresentable horror. Post-Holocaust generations, it seems to me, can only approach that core by what I would call mimetic approximation, a mnemonic strategy which recognizes the event in its otherness and beyond identification or therapeutic empathy but which physically relieves some of the horror and the pain in the slow and persistent labor of remembrance. Such mimetic approximation can only be achieved if we sustain the tension between the numbing totality of the Holocaust and the stories of the individual victims, families, and communities. Exclusive focus on the former may lead to the numbing abstraction of statistics and the repression of what these statistics mean; exclusive focus on the latter may provide facile, cathartic empathy and may forget the frightening conclusion that the Holocaust as historical event resulted, as Adi Ophir has suggested, from an exceptional combination of normal processes.[9] The ultimate success of a Holocaust monument would be to trigger such a mimetic approximation, but it can achieve that goal only in conjunction with other related discourses operating within the spectator and in the public sphere.

A monument or memorial will take us only one step toward the kind of knowledge Jürgen Habermas has described as an irreversible rupture in human history:

> There [in Auschwitz] something happened, that up to now nobody considered as even possible. There one touched on something which represents the deep layer of solidarity among all that wears a human face; notwithstanding all the usual acts of beastliness of human history, the integrity of this common layer had been taken for granted.... Auschwitz has changed the basis for the continuity of the conditions of life within history.[10]

8 Geoffrey H. Hartman, "The Book of the Destruction," in Friedländer, ed., *Probing the Limits of Representation,* p. 319.

9 Adi Ophir, "On Sanctifying the Holocaust: An Anti-Theological Treatise," *Tikkun* 2/1 (1987): 64.

10 Jürgen Habermas, *Eine Art Schadensabwicklung* (Frankfurt am Main: Suhrkamp, 1987), p. 163.

11 "Ein Buch muß die Axt sein für das gefrorene Meer in uns," taken from a letter to Oskar Pollak, January 27, 1904.

Such knowledge is all too easily forgotten or repressed. To maintain it is all the more urgent since our postmodern, post-Auschwitz culture is fraught with a fundamental ambiguity. Obsessed with memory and the past, it is also caught in a destructive dynamics of forgetting. But perhaps the dichotomy of forgetting and remembering again misses the mark. Perhaps postmodern culture in the West is itself caught in a traumatic fixation on an event which goes to the heart of our identity and political culture. In that case, the Holocaust monument, memorial, and museum could be the tool Franz Kafka wanted literature to be when he said that the book must be the ax for the frozen sea within us.[11] We need the book and the monument to keep the sea from freezing. In frozen memory, the past is nothing but the past. The inner temporality and the politics of Holocaust memory, however, even where they speak of the past, must be the future.

James E. Young

The Art of Memory
Holocaust Memorials in History

Because I was born in 1951, some six years after the end of World War II, I do not remember the Holocaust. All I know of the Holocaust is what the victims have passed down to me in their diaries, what the survivors have remembered to me in their memoirs. I remember not actual events, but the countless histories, novels, and poems of the Holocaust I have read, the plays, movies, and video testimonies I have watched over the years. I remember long days and nights in the company of survivors, listening to their harrowing tales, until their lives, loves, and losses seemed grafted indelibly onto my own life's story.

Finally, like many others, I have begun to remember more and more often my visits to Holocaust memorials—the museums and monuments—that invite me to remember events I never experienced directly. Indeed, the further the Holocaust recedes in time, the more prominent its memorials and museums become. For a number of reasons, both cultural and demographic, Holocaust memory has begun to find its critical mass in something akin to a Holocaust "museum boom." Thousands of monuments, preserved ruins, plaques, museums, and study centers devoted to Holocaust remembrance now dot European, American, and Israeli landscapes. As the last generation of survivors begins to pass on, many seem almost desperate to leave behind a place, an object around which Holocaust memory might live on. Moreover, as other forms of Jewish learning and traditional education wane among an ever more assimilated generation, the vicarious memory of past catastrophe serves increasingly as a center for Jewish identity and knowledge.

The displacement in memory of one thousand years of European Jewish civilization with twelve catastrophic years is not a happy development, to my mind. But instead of merely bemoaning the Holocaust memory boom, we need to recognize its place in contemporary Jewish life, examine it critically, and understand its consequences. Indeed, memorials to martyrdom have always existed and always will. So rather than begging the moot question of whether such memorials should be erected or not, we turn to examine how the "art of memory" is being created, what kind of understanding it evokes, and to what social ends.

Depending on where these memorials are constructed and by whom, these sites recall the past according to a variety of national myths, ideals, and political needs. Some commemorate war dead, others resistance, and still others the Holocaust. Each reflects both the past experiences and current lives of their communities, as well as the state's memory of itself. On a more specific level, each also reflects the temper of the memory artists' time, their place in contemporary aesthetic discourse, their media and materials.[1]

The reasons for Holocaust memorials and the kinds of memory they generate vary as widely as the sites themselves. Some are built in response to traditional Jewish injunctions to remember, others according to a government's need to explain a nation's past to itself. Where the aim of some memorials is to educate the next generation and to inculcate in it a sense of shared experience and destiny, other memorials are intended to attract tourists. In addition to traditional Jewish memorial iconography, every state has its own institutional forms of remembrance. As a result, Holocaust memorials inevitably mix national and Jewish figures and political and religious imagery.

The aim of our inquiry into Holocaust memorials, therefore, is not just to survey the many faces of public memory, but also to examine precisely *how* and *why* public memory of this era is being shaped by the museums and monuments created to

Traditional Jewish mourning motifs carved on gravestones, such as a broken column, candle, or flower, symbolize life cut short. Here a gravestone in a Jewish cemetery in Sieniawa, Poland, depicts a broken branch.

memorialize events. Instead of concentrating on finished or monolithic memory, we examine the process by which public memory of the Holocaust is constructed. We ask who creates this memory, under what circumstances, and for which audience? Which events are remembered, which forgotten, and how are they explained? What are these monuments' places in national and religious commemorative cycles? What is the contemporary artist's role in public memory? Finally, we ask what the aims and consequences of Holocaust memorialization are and why memory and monuments matter.

In this context, we are reminded that the roles monuments and museums play in historical consciousness have long borne the ire and skepticism of philosophers and cultural critics. "Away with the monuments!" Nietzsche declared in his blistering attack on nineteenth-century German historiography, which he regarded as a petrified version of the past that buried the living.[2] Lewis Mumford echoed this scorn when he pronounced the death of the monument in its seeming incompatibility with his sense of modern architectural forms. "The notion of a modern monument is veritably a contradiction in terms," he wrote. "If it is a monument, it is not modern, and if it is modern, it cannot be a monument."[3]

After World War II, Theodor Adorno recalled that the German term *museal* (museum-like) "described objects to which the observer no longer has a vital relationship and which are in the process of dying."[4] More recently, the late German historian, Martin Broszat, has suggested that monuments to the Fascist era may not recall events so much as bury them beneath layers of national myths and explanations.[5] The art historian, Rosalind Krauss, finds that the modernist period produced monuments unable to refer to anything beyond themselves as pure marker or base.[6] Others, including the French cultural historian Pierre Nora and contemporary artists, have warned that memorials may not concentrate memory so much as displace it altogether, relieving a community of its own, interior memory work.[7] This exhibition aims to examine the many aspects of Holocaust memorials, their power, and their limitations.

While it is true that many memorials are shaped by political agendas, we do not make the resulting distortions the focus of this inquiry. For to do so might also suggest that some memorials are universally true to memory. Rather, we aim to show that the memorials of every community organize public memory of the Holocaust according to a particular understanding of events. In some places, this means that the Jewish experience seems to be hidden or forgotten; in other places, this means that the non-Jewish experience of the Holocaust has been left out. This exhibition hopes to reveal all of these dimensions in the memorial process, to show how every memorial is a result of its particular time and place, its historical and political context.

Toward this end, we have attempted to discuss the interwoven political, religious, and aesthetic dimensions of Holocaust monuments. We compare, for example, monuments erected at the sites of destruction with those built at geographical remove. In addition, we examine the place of these monuments in contemporary artistic and political discourse, the meanings memorials take in new regimes, and how materials and media influence a memorial's conception. We ask how memorials blend traditional religious and national iconography with more contemporary forms such as performance and conceptual art, how artists balance the needs of viewers against the occasionally obscure sensibilities of contemporary art—all of which may depend on the funding of state institutions.

These questions lead us, in turn, to refine the distinctions between high and low and public and popular art in our evaluation of Holocaust memorials. It may no longer be sufficient, for example, merely to identify the traditions and forms out of which memory is constructed, or to ask whether or not these monuments reflect past history, or whether they do so accurately or fashionably. This is not to make public monumental art immune to aesthetic judgment and evaluation but to suggest that other criteria now be considered as well. Rather than dismissing a monument because of its mass appeal or its kitschiness, we examine all parts of its performance as a memorial, the many ways its figures continue to suggest themselves as the bases for political, religious, and communal action.

Through a critical showing of the conception, construction, and reception of these monuments, this exhibition tries to reveal the activity of Holocaust memorialization that takes place first between events and memorials, then between memorials and viewers, and, finally, between viewers and their lives in light of the memorialized past. In this view, the performance of Holocaust monuments encompasses not just the activity that brings them into being, but also the viewers' response to them. Before visitors leave this exhibition, therefore, we remind them that they necessarily complete the memorial act, that with their visit they animate the memorial. In this way, we hope to illustrate the fundamentally dialogical, interactive nature of all memorials and exhibitions.

The Art of Memory: Holocaust Memorials in History

For our purposes, the Holocaust is defined as the calculated mass murder and internment of Jews and other groups (including Poles, the tribes of Sinti and Rom, Soviet prisoners of war, political prisoners, and homosexuals) by the German Nazi state during World War II. Because every nation, every culture, recalls events according to its own traditions, experiences, and political understanding, however, we have opened this exhibition with a comparative look at the very names by which this period is remembered in different lands. That is, before *re*calling events, national groups had to call events something: what is remembered as *Shoah Vegvurah* (catastrophe and heroism) in Israel was remembered in the Soviet Union as the Great Patriotic War; what is called the *Nazi-Zeit* in Germany is recalled as an era of national martyrdom in Poland. By highlighting differences among the literal, plastic shapes of the words themselves, we introduce a verbal iconography of Holocaust memory that is as disparate and various as the memorials themselves.

Jewish Memorial Traditions

Within this context of several, occasionally competing, national memorial traditions, we then turn to the very centrality of memory itself, to Jewish faith, tradition, and identity. Indeed, having defined themselves as a people through the commemorative recitations of their past, the Jews now depend on memory for their very existence as a nation. Throughout the Torah, the Jews are enjoined not only to remember their history, but to observe the rituals of faith through remembrance: "Remember the days of old, consider the years of ages past" (Deut. 32:7); "Remember what Amalek did to you" (Deut. 25:17); "Remember this day, on which you went free from Egypt, the house of bondage, how the Lord freed you from it with a mighty hand" (Exod. 13:3). In memory of either destruction or joyous freedom lay the source of the Jews' covenant with their God of history.

1 For a more comprehensive discussion of these and related issues, see my *The Texture of Memory: Holocaust Memorials and Meaning* (New Haven and London: Yale University Press, 1993). This catalogue essay draws on material first explored in *The Texture of Memory.*

2 Friedrich Nietzsche, *The Use and Abuse of History*, trans. Adrian Collins (New York: Macmillan Publishing Company, 1985), pp. 14-17.

3 Lewis Mumford, *The Culture of Cities* (New York: Harcourt, Brace, Jovanovich, 1938), p. 438.

4 Theodor W. Adorno, "Valéry Proust Museum," in *Prisms*, trans. Samuel and Shierry Weber (Cambridge, Mass.: MIT Press, 1981), p. 175.

5 For the full, much more complex, context of Broszat's remarks, see his series of letters to Saul Friedländer and Friedländer's excellent replies printed first in *Vierteljahreshefte für Zeitgeschichte* 36/2 (April 1988): 339-72, subsequently translated and reprinted as "Martin Broszat/Saul Friedländer: A Controversy about the Historicization of National Socialism," in *Yad Vashem Studies* 19 (Fall 1988): 1-47; also reprinted in *New German Critique* 44 (Spring-Summer 1988): 85-126. The exchange between Broszat and Friedländer was initially sparked by Friedländer's response to Broszat's "Plädoyer für eine Historisierung des National-sozialismus" [Plea for a historization of National Socialism], *Merkur* 39 (1985): 373-85.
Broszat's specific reference to monuments comes in his comments on "mythical memory," which he distinguishes from "scientific insight" (*New German Critique* 44 [Spring-Summer 1988]: 90-91).

6 Rosalind Krauss, *The Originality of the Avant-Garde and Other Modernist Myths* (Cambridge, Mass. and London: MIT Press, 1988), p. 280.

7 Pierre Nora, "Between Memory and History: *Les lieux de mémoire*," trans. Marc Roudebush, *Representations* 26 (1989): 13, reprinted from Pierre Nora, "Entre mémoire et histoire," *Les lieux de mémoire*, Vol. 1, *La république* (Paris: Gallimard, 1984), p. xxvi.

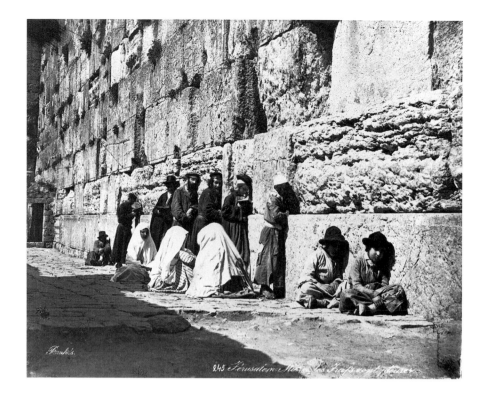

The Western Wall, a surviving fragment of the Second Temple in Jerusalem destroyed in 70 C. E., evokes the memory of communal catastrophe and mourning. Photographed by La Maison Bonfils, 1867-ca. 1907, albumen print. Collection of The Jewish Museum, New York.

When thinking specifically of the Holocaust, however, we need also to distinguish between the rituals and memorial iconography marking personal loss from those commemorating communal catastrophe, that is, to differentiate individual from collective mourning. Among emblems of individual mourning, for example, are sitting *shiva* on a short stool, a rent garment, a covered mirror, the *Jahrzeit* candle and *Yizkor* blessing, and the figures of broken candlesticks emblazoned on a tombstone. We might compare these images to memorial responses drawn from the liturgy and calendar commemorating collective destruction, specifically the destructions of the First and Second Temples: for example, public fast days (the 9th of Av, 10th of Teveth), verses from Lamentations. Other, more folkloristic, responses include a burnt piece of the Sabbath *challah* or a piece of wall left unpainted—both daily reminders of Hurban. In addition, we can compare the text-centered mourning rituals of men to the more performative, household mourning rituals traditionally observed by women.

We also find that in keeping with the bookish, iconoclastic side of Jewish tradition, the first memorials to the Holocaust period came not in stone, glass, or steel, but in narrative. The *Yizkor Bikher*, "memorial books," recalled both the lives and the destruction of European Jewish communities according to the most ancient of Jewish memorial media: the book. Indeed, as the preface to one of these books suggests: "Whenever we pick up the book we will feel we are standing next to [the victims'] grave, because even that the murderers denied them." [8] The shtetl scribes hoped that when read, the *Yizkor Bikher* would turn the site of reading into memorial space. In response to what has been called "the missing gravestone syndrome," the first sites of memory created by survivors were thus interior, imagined grave sites.

Over time, we find many of these traditional memorial motifs repeated in Poland's broken tombstone monuments, in Israel's day of remembrance, in the disjointed angles and architecture of various Holocaust museums. Some traditional images are still used in Holocaust memorials, others abandoned, and still others creatively subverted.

While in operation, the death camps and the destruction of people wrought there were one and the same: site and events were bound to each other in their simultaneity. But with the passage of time, site and events were gradually estranged from each other. While the sites of killing remained ever present, all too real in their physical setting, time subtly interposed itself between the site and its past: events that occurred in another time seemed increasingly to belong to another world altogether. Only a deliberate act of memory could reconnect them, reinfuse the sites with a sense of their historical past.

For, by themselves, the sites of destruction lack what Pierre Nora has called "the will to remember."[9] That is, without a people's intention to remember, the ruins remain little more than inert pieces of the landscape, unsuffused with the meanings and significance created by our visits to them. Without "the will to remember," Nora suggests, the place of memory, "created in the play of memory and history... becomes indistinguishable from the place of history."[10] Nora's observations cut two ways for our understanding of the "memorial camps" in Poland, such as Majdanek and Auschwitz. On the one hand, we are reminded that it was the state's initial move to preserve these ruins — its will to remember — that turned historic sites of destruction into "places of memory." On the other hand, we find that these sites also begin to take on lives of their own, often as resistant to official memory as they are emblematic of it.

The very first monuments to the Holocaust were the places of destruction themselves: in July 1944, the Soviets thus turned Majdanek into the first memorial and museum of its kind (plate 1). In 1947 the Polish parliament declared that the ruins at Auschwitz-Birkenau would be "forever preserved as a memorial to the martyrdom of the Polish nation and other peoples."[11] Recalling that the Germans used 250 Jews from Oświęcim to build the camp there, we realize that, in effect, this memorial was built by the very victims it would later commemorate.

Though both camps are actually much changed in the last fifty years, they seem to have been preserved almost as the Russians found them. Guard towers, barbed wire, barracks, and crematoria — mythologized elsewhere — here stand palpably intact. In contrast to memorials located away from the sites of destruction, the remnants here tend to negate the distinction between themselves and what they evoke. Crumbling crematoria and barracks invite visitors to mistake remnants of the past for

Ruins of the gas chambers and crematoria complex at Auschwitz-Birkenau, Poland, with fences and a guard tower in the background.

8 From "Forwort," in *Sefer Yizkor le-Kedoshei ir (Przedecz) Pshaytask Khurbanot ha'shoah*, p. 130, as quoted in Jack Kugelmass and Jonathan Boyarin, eds. *From a Ruined Garden: The Memorial Books of Polish Jewry* (New York: Schocken Books, 1983), p. 11.

9 Pierre Nora, "Between Memory and History: *Les lieux de mémoire*," p. 19.

10 Ibid.

11 From Kazimierz Smolen, ed. *KL Auschwitz* (Warsaw: Krajowa Agencja Wydawnicza, 1980), p. 16.

events themselves. If, as was the case until recently at Auschwitz-Birkenau, it is engraved in stone that "4 million people suffered and died here," then this is what the ruins tend to confirm (plate 2). In the rhetoric of their ruins, these memorial sites seem not merely to gesture to past events but would now suggest themselves as fragments of events, inviting us to mistake the debris of history for history itself.

We would do well, therefore, to ask precisely what is remembered by the ruins of crematoria at Auschwitz: the killing process or the attempted destruction of evidence by the Germans, an acknowledgment of their guilt? To what extent do the bins of artifacts at Auschwitz and Majdanek — the eyeglasses, hair, toothbrushes, suitcases — represent the absence of those who once animated them? Or to what extent do they remember the victims as the Nazis would have remembered them to us?

The Auschwitz Memorial Competition

At first mention, the notion of a Holocaust "memorial competition" makes one squirm. But, in fact, Holocaust memory is always contested as long as more than one group or individual remembers. Not only does an open memorial competition make such competing memories palpable, but it also brings into relief the complex, nearly impossible questions facing every artist or architect attempting to conceive such a monument. Among the dilemmas for contemporary Holocaust monument-makers are how to remember horribly real events in the abstract gestures of geometric forms, how to create a focal point for remembrance among ruins without desecrating the space itself, and how to embody remembrance without seeming to displace it.

These questions and others arose with the very first open competition for a memorial at Auschwitz-Birkenau in 1957 and have tended to repeat themselves in all subsequent contests. As head of the internationally acclaimed design jury assembled for the Auschwitz memorial competition, Henry Moore wrote:

> The choice of a monument to commemorate Auschwitz has not been an easy task. Essentially, what has been attempted here has been the creation — or, in the case of the jury, the choice — of a monument to crime and ugliness, to murder and to horror. The crime was of such stupendous proportions that any work of art must be on an appropriate scale. But apart from this, is it in fact possible to create a work of art that can express the emotions engendered by Auschwitz?[12]

In Moore's opinion, a very great sculptor — a Michelangelo or Rodin — might have been up to the task. As for the 426 submissions his jury reviewed, however, none was fully satisfactory. Many of the works were brilliant, Moore conceded, but none satisfied the criteria of all the jury, which included artists, architects, critics, and — the most critical judges of all — survivors. For artists working in the period of abstract expressionism, earthworks, and neo-Geo, and for architects answerable to postmodern and deconstructivist design, their public is clear. Artists, critics, and curators generally applaud such designs — and run up immediately against a wall of survivors' outrage. For survivors, the searing reality of their experiences demands as literal a memorial expression as possible. "We weren't tortured and our families weren't murdered in the abstract," survivors complain. Or in the words of Nathan Rapoport, who once asked plaintively, "Could I have made a rock with a hole in it and said 'Voila! The heroism of the Jews'?"

Instead of being paralyzed by the tug and pull of so many competing constituencies, Henry Moore's jury finally decided to compromise. They chose what they judged to be the three strongest teams and asked them to collaborate on one final submission, either taking the best parts of their separate submissions or arriving at a new design altogether. The result was finally unveiled at the end of the railroad tracks at Auschwitz-Birkenau in 1967. But the process remains uniquely instructive of the conundrum at the heart of this tormented "art of memory" (see also pp. 171-73).

The Warsaw Ghetto Monument

Nathan Rapoport's *Warsaw Ghetto Monument*, 1948 (detail).

Of the thousands of Holocaust memorials around the world, Nathan Rapoport's *Warsaw Ghetto Monument* emerges as possibly the most widely known, celebrated, and controversial of all (plate 3). It was the first memorial after the war to mark both the heroism of Jewish resistance to the Nazis and the complete annihilation of the Jews in Warsaw. But in its use of the broadest of cultural archetypes, i. e., the lumbering mytho-proletarian figures of the Stalinist era and the typological image of Jews in exile as they passed through the Arch of Titus on their way to Samuel Hirszenberg's *Golus*,[13] the *Warsaw Ghetto Monument* has found little critical consensus.

Hailed by war-scarred critics at its unveiling (April 19, 1948, the fifth anniversary of the Warsaw Ghetto Uprising) in all its heroic splendor, it was subsequently scorned by curators as kitsch figuration and by "cold warriors" as proletarian pap. In its forty-five-year life, the *Warsaw Ghetto Monument* has endured as a kind of screen across which the projected shadows of a world's preoccupations continue to flicker and dance. Since its maker's hand initially animated its cold, amnesiac clay, the monument has been revitalized by the parade of public figures marching past it and by the ceremonies conducted at its base.

With the state's blessings, it is now as much a gathering place for Polish war veterans as for Jews; to the former Polish government's consternation, the square where the monument stands was also a gathering place for Solidarity and other dissident groups, who turned it into a place for protests. The monument has been extravagantly visited by touring presidents, prime ministers, and even the pope. Everyone memorializes something different here, of course; each creates different meaning in the monument. Its individual figures are echoed in dozens of other monuments to this era throughout Europe and Israel, its images exported as distinctly Jewish martyrological and heroic icons. The monument has been recast and nationalized in Israel, it is pictured on both Polish and Israeli postcards and stamps, and it has been animated to the halftones of Schoenberg's choral work *A Survivor from Warsaw* (1947) in a short Polish film.

By keeping in mind the monument's evolution from a clay maquette fashioned by the sculptor during his wartime exile in Novosibirsk, to its plaster casts from the foundry in Paris, to its unveiling amid the rubble of the Ghetto's destruction, to its political life in the mind of its community over time, we might reinvigorate the monument with memory of its own origins. Thus can we return the monument to its place in history and show the reciprocal relationship between it and its visitors, between history and memory, all of which can be said to constitute this—or any—monument's total aesthetic performance.[14]

Broken Tombstone Monuments

Despite its slightly reductive premise, the question inevitably asked is: "Which is the greatest of all Holocaust memorials?" Despite the risk of oversimplifying, an answer

12   Henry Moore, "The Auschwitz Competition," booklet published by the State Museum of Auschwitz, 1964, unpaginated.

13   By his own admission, Rapoport clearly recalls Hirszenberg's painting *Golus* (also called *Exile*), ca. 1895, which depicts Jews being forced out of their homes during a pogrom.

14   For an exhaustive history of this monument and the events it commemorates, see my article "The Biography of a Memorial Icon: Nathan Rapoport's Warsaw Ghetto Monument," *Representations* 26 (Spring 1989): 69-106.

Memorial at the Treblinka extermination camp, Poland, by Franciszek Duszenko and Adam Haupt, 1964. 17,000 granite stones surround a central obelisk.

springs immediately, if awkwardly, to mind: the memorial at Treblinka in Poland, where some 850,000 Jews were murdered by the Nazis between 1942 and 1944 (plate 4). Upon arriving now at Treblinka, visitors walk for 200 meters through dense woods along a path of concrete railroad ties laid to symbolize the tracks that fed this death camp. These tracks once led to barracks, mass graves, and gas chambers, but all traces of the camp itself were destroyed, plowed under, and planted over by the Germans. At the end of the line now, visitors step onto a huge expanse of open land enclosed by trees. A great obelisk stands in its center, surrounded by a symbolic graveyard of over 17,000 jagged, granite stones set in concrete, several hundred of them bearing the names of Jewish communities in Poland destroyed during the Holocaust.

In this horribly magnificent site, Polish sculptor Franciszek Duszenko and architect Adam Haupt have attempted, in their words, "to suggest iconographically the greatest of all genocidal cemeteries."[15] After direct narrative reference to Jewish victims at the entrance of the memorial, the Jewish character of this memorial grows more subtle: a menorah is carved into the cap of the obelisk on its reverse side. The obelisk itself is cleaved, top to bottom. Jumbled together and protruding in all direc-

Tadeusz Augustynek's memorial to the deported Jews of Kazimierz-Dolny, near Lublin, Poland, 1984. Carved limestone fragments set in mortar.

15   See M. Chmielewski, "Mauzoleum Mycienstwa w Treblince," *Trybuna ludu* 322 (1960): 1.

tions, the densely packed stones bear striking resemblance to the ancient Jewish cemeteries of Eastern Europe. The themes of absence and brokenness found in traditional Jewish funerary motifs reemerge here as two of the predominant motifs by which the Poles have begun to remember their lost Jewish communities.

Indeed, such a precedent in memorial motifs was set by Jewish survivors themselves on their return to Poland just after the war. For when many of the 270,000 returning Polish Jews went out to their cemeteries to mourn lost brethren, they found that even the mourning places had been destroyed by the Germans. Almost all of Poland's Jewish cemeteries had been vandalized, their tombstones broken into pieces and carted off by the Germans to pave roads. Before the survivors could mourn, they had to rebuild the memorial sites, often out of the broken shards of their destroyed cemeteries. In places such as Kazimierz on the Vistula, Lukow, Sandomierz, Siedlce, and the cemeteries in Warsaw and Kraków, survivors gathered the fragments of shattered *matzevoth* into great memorial cairns, obelisks, and retaining walls. Even after survivors left these towns in the face of anti-Jewish pogroms a few years later, many of these memorials remained to commemorate both the shattered communities and the destruction of traditional memory sites themselves.

Unofficial Soviet Memorials

Until recently, almost all memory of the Holocaust in the Soviet Union was included in the state's official history of the great destruction wrought in the Soviet Union during the war. As Zvi Gitelman makes so clear in his essay in this volume, a combination of ideological and political forces assured that the approximately 2 million Jews murdered by the Nazis in the Soviet Union would not be commemorated separately from the altogether 20 million Soviets who died during World War II. All would be remembered as having been martyred in the name of the Soviet motherland during what was called the Great Patriotic War. As a result, when Jewish survivors and families visited the sites of mass executions of Jews by the SS *Einsatzgruppen*, they often erected small, homespun memorials of their own. Over the years, hundreds of these unofficial memorials sprouted in the killing fields and forests outside Riga, Vilna, and Minsk and came to stand in sharp contrast to their state-inspired counter-

One of the many unofficially marked mass grave sites for Jews murdered in the former Soviet Union. Here in Kaunas, Lithuania.

A homemade, wooden Star of David nailed to a tree,
100 meters from a mass grave in the Rumbuli Forest, Latvia.

Site of the mass grave of 8,000 Holocaust victims in Telsiai,
Lithuania.

part at Babi Yar. Occasionally, these unofficial memorials would consist of cast sculpture and reconstructed tombstones. More often, they appeared as simple wooden tablets nailed to a tree with names inscribed on them, or as a pile of stones set in a clearing, or as a grassy burial mound. Because many of these family memorials were discovered and then torn down by local authorities, all that remains of many of them are their images, captured in hundreds of family photographs, mostly yellowing snapshots, deposited in Yad Vashem's archives by recently arrived Soviet immigrants in Israel.

In these photographs, victims' kin, wearing their Sunday best, stand around a grassy burial mound, a pile of stones, or a wooden tablet. In several photos, family members look into an empty clearing: nothing is there. Yet it is written on the back of one of these photographs that this is the site where 8,000 Jews were murdered. These photographs of now-absent memorials begin to function over time as memorials themselves.

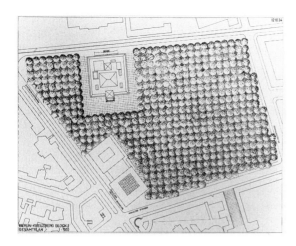

Master plan of proposed memorial at the former site of the
Gestapo headquarters, Berlin, by Jürgen Wenzel and Nikolaus
Lang, 1984. Cast-iron plates with replicas of Nazi documents
and a gridlike chestnut tree forest.

Gestapo-Gelände

In addition to the memorials located at former concentration camps in Poland and
the killing fields in the Baltic States, other sites continue to generate their share of
memory in Germany, Holland, and other European countries. The story of Dachau's
evolution from a World War I munitions factory, to a concentration camp in 1933, to
an exemplary memorial in 1964 is extremely instructive.[16] As explored by Claudia
Koonz in this volume (p. 111), the changing of the memorial guard at Buchenwald can
only hint at the complicated and self-interrogative kinds of memory constantly under-
way in Germany and Austria. Well-known memorial complexes at Bergen-Belsen,
Neuengamme, Ravensbruck, and Mauthausen (among dozens of other sites) all reveal
different sides of Germany's multi-dimensional memorial legacy.[17]

At the same time, however, other less well known sites of destruction have also
functioned in the German phrase as *Steine des Anstoßes* (stumbling blocks). The very
heart of Berlin, for example, former site of the Gestapo headquarters, remains a great,
gaping wound, as politicians, artists, and various committees forever debate the most
appropriate memorial for this site.

What had once been the administrative heartland of the SS-state — a magnificent
complex of palatial buildings and museums — was gutted by Allied firebombs during
the war and later demolished by city planners. Scraped clean, but for a great weed-
choked mountain of rubble, for many years the *Gestapo-Gelände* primarily recalled
the absence of memory here, the destruction of telltale ruins, the nation's memorial
struggle with itself. In fact, many feared that if left as a historical marker, the ruins of
the *Gestapo-Gelände* might even be readopted by former SS soldiers as a rallying
point, a memorial not to what they had perpetrated but to what they had lost.

Between 1982 and 1984 a competition chaired by German president Richard von
Weizsäcker was held to find a memorial design for the site. The 194 proposals submitted to the jury cut a wide swath through the fields of contemporary art and
architecture, drawing on plastic, performative, conceptual, and architectural media.
In April 1984 the jury awarded first prize to the most radically conceptual and inno-
vative design of the competition, submitted by a team headed by the Berlin landscape
architect Jürgen Wenzel and the Bavarian artist Nikolaus Lang (plates 21, 22). In their
design, Wenzel and Lang proposed to seal over the entire area with great plates of cast
iron, broken only by round holes large enough for a tight and orderly grid of chest-

View of the recently excavated ruins of the Gestapo prison
cellar, here laid with wreaths, 1986. After discovery of the
ruins, plans for a memorial on the site were canceled.

16 See Harold Marcuse, "Das ehemalige Konzentrationslager
    Dachau: Der mühevolle Weg zur Gedenkstätte, 1945-1968,"
    Dachauer Hefte 6 (November 1990): 182-205. See also my
    chapter "Dachau: History of a Memorial," in *The Texture of
    Memory*, pp. 60-72.

17 Because this publication divides memorials between those lo-
    cated at the sites of destruction and those removed from these
    sites, discussion of the many memorials in Germany has itself
    been divided between "sites of destruction" and the "aesthetic
    interrogation of the monument." This is why we focus on the
    ways contemporary artists in Germany continue to wrestle
    with Holocaust memory, rather than merely surveying the me-
    morials *in situ* at places like Buchenwald and Dachau. For a
    survey of the many memorials in Germany, see Ulrike Puvogel,
    ed. *Gedenkstätten für die Opfer des Nationalsozialismus: Eine
    Dokumentation* (Bonn: Schriftenreihe der Bundeszentrale für
    politische Bildung, 1987).

nut trees, hundreds planted in rows so that from the sky the area would appear covered. On several thousand of these cast-iron plates, precise copies of actual documents from the SS files would be emblazoned. It was to be an iron-floored forest, a cold landscape, sealed against the possibility of anything ever growing there again.

In the meantime, the basement area of the Gestapo headquarters was unearthed in a "memorial dig," which rendered moot the many objections to the winning design that had begun to pour in. The memorial to the *Gestapo-Gelände* has thus remained unbuilt, with a small document house in its place and a quasi-permanent exhibition entitled "The Topography of Terror." Since then, the memorial debate itself has become a kind of memory work by which the Germans continue to wrestle with how to remember, whom to remember, and for which audience.

Memorials in Holland

One of the most widely visited memorials in Europe is not a site of destruction per se, but rather one of courage and, ultimately, betrayal: the two sides of Holland's memory of their unofficial patron saint, Anne Frank. For reasons explored at greater length in my essay on the Anne Frank House in this volume (pp. 131-37), the memorial canonization of Anne Frank in Holland reflects the deeply mixed Dutch self-perception as traditional refuge, on the one hand, and as a nation of passive bystanders,

Karin Daan created the *Homomonument* for homosexual victims of Nazism, dedicated in Amsterdam in 1987. The monument has also come to serve as a memorial site for those who have died of AIDS.

The commemoration triangle (right) bears an inscribed text from a poem by Jacob Israel de Haan: "NAAR VRIENDSCHAP ZULK EEN MATELOOS VERLANGEN" (Such a boundless longing for friendship).

Heleen Levano's *Gypsy Monument — Memorial of War* with inscription in Rom and Dutch, 1978. This memorial to the Sinti and Rom victims of the Holocaust is located in the Museumplein in Amsterdam.

on the other. Though cleared of the original furniture, the annex at Prinsengracht 263 in Amsterdam, where Anne went into hiding with her family and friends, has been preserved and is still accessible to visitors through the entry behind the false bookshelf. Since the opening of the museum on the ground floor in 1960, the Anne Frank House has become a center for public memory in Amsterdam and a locus for related remembrance as well.

Just around the corner, for example, the community has built a stunningly understated memorial to the homosexuals interned and killed by the Nazis during the war (plates 10, 11). The *Homomonument*, as it is called in Dutch, consists of a large marble triangle traced into the ground: one corner is raised, another flush with the surrounding cobblestones, and the third juts out slightly over the edge of a nearby canal. By its placement, the triangle is located at the center of a memorial matrix: one of its three axes pointing to the Anne Frank House, another to the local Gay Coalition offices, and one to the National Monument. This, along with several dozen other memorial sites throughout Amsterdam, ensures that present life is lived as a constant negotiation with memory of the past.

Memorials Removed from the Sites of Destruction

Israel

Young people from many nations gather at Yad Vashem, the Holocaust memorial in Jerusalem.

Like the Holocaust memorials of other lands, those in Israel reflect both the past experiences and current lives of their communities, as well as the state's memory of itself. Like any state, Israel remembers the past according to its national myths and ideals, its current political needs. Unlike European memorials, however, often anchored in the very sites of destruction, those in Israel are necessarily removed from the "topography of terror." Where European memorials located in situ often suggest themselves rhetorically as the extension of events they would commemorate, those in Israel must gesture abstractly to a past removed in both time and space. In this sense, memorials removed from the sites of destruction in both Israel and America seem not to be anchored in history so much as in the ideals generating them in the first place.

On the one hand, Israel's early founders, such as David Ben-Gurion, regarded the Holocaust as the ultimate fruit of Jewish life in exile. As such, it represented a Diaspora that deserved not only to be destroyed, but also forgotten. On the other hand, however, the state also recognized its perverse debt to the Holocaust; it had, after all, seemed to prove the Zionist dictum that without a state and the power to defend themselves, Jews in exile would always be vulnerable to just this kind of destruction. As Saul Friedländer shows in his essay in this volume, the early leaders found little reason to recall the Holocaust beyond its direct link to the new state.

Finally, prodded by relatives of the murdered and by comrades of the Warsaw Ghetto fighters, however, Israel's parliament first passed the Day of Remembrance Resolution in 1951 and then the National Memorial Authority Act in 1953, which mandated the construction of Yad Vashem in Jerusalem (plates 5-7). Though the destruction of European Jewry was still regarded by many as both incompatible with Israel's vision of the "new Jew" and as too recent and raw an experience to assimilate culturally, small memorials and plaques did begin to appear across Israel's rough landscape. In keeping with Israel's plan to make the desert bloom, forests were planted in memory of the victims and whole *kibbutzim* established. The state itself would become, in the words of a *Davar* editorial in 1951, "the one suitable monument to the memory of European Jewry."

To some extent, the essential paradox between remembering the Holocaust and forgetting it was resolved in Israel by the ubiquitous joining of martyrs with heroes in Israel's memorial iconography. In this mixed figure, the victims are memorable primarily for the ways they demonstrate the need for fighters, who, in turn, are remembered for their part in the state's founding. When placed against the traditional paradigmatic backdrop of destruction and redemption, the memorial message in this dialectic comes into sharp relief: as the destruction of the martyrs is redeemed by those who fought, the *Shoah* itself is redeemed by the founding of the state.

Ze'ev Ben-Zvi's memorial *To the Children of Exile*, dedicated at Kibbutz Mishmar Ha'emek in 1947, was Israel's first Holocaust memorial.

In Israeli museums at *kibbutzim* such as Beit Lohamei Hageta'ot, Tel Yitzhak, Givat Haim, and Yad Mordechai, Jewish life before, during, and after the Holocaust is given first priority (plate 8). Although, as one stands in a corner of the museum at Yad Mordechai and glances between the grainy images of death and destruction in exile and the bright sunlight flooding in through a window through which one views the green gardens and children playing outside, it would be difficult to misread the implicit message: death is there in exile, life and freedom here in Israel (see p. 153).

At Yad Vashem, Israel's national Holocaust memorial, the Holocaust marks not so much the end of Jewish life as it does the end of viable life in exile. Indeed, the Baal Shem Tov's words remind visitors as they leave the museum, "Forgetting lengthens the period of exile. In remembrance lies the secret of deliverance." In the narrative created by Holocaust Remembrance Day's placement on the national calendar (i. e., following Passover and preceding Independence day) the end of the *Shoah* came not with the liberation of the camps, but with the survivors' return to and redemption in the land of Israel. In all cases, the Holocaust is integrated into a long view of Jewish history: it may be a turning point, a confirmation of Zionist ideology, but it is linked, nevertheless, to a millennium of Jewish life in Europe before the war and to Jewish national rebirth afterwards. The subject of the Holocaust in Israel's national memory is further elaborated in this volume by Saul Friedländer.[18]

America

As the shape Holocaust memory takes in Europe and Israel is constrained by political, aesthetic, and religious coordinates, that in America is no less guided by American ideals and experiences of this period. The motives for memory of the Holocaust in America are as mixed as the population at large, the reasons variously lofty and cynical, practical and aesthetic. Some communities build memorials to remember lost brethren, others to remember themselves (plates 25-29). Some build memorials as community centers, others as tourist attractions. Some survivors remember strictly according to religious tradition, while others recall the political roots of their resistance. Veterans' organizations sponsor memorials to recall their role as camp liberators. Congressmen support local monuments to secure votes from among their Jewish

Louis I. Kahn's original model for a proposed *Memorial to the Six Million Jewish Martyrs* in Battery Park, New York City, 1966-72, which was never built.

constituency. Even the national memorial to the Holocaust recently opened in Washington, D.C., was proposed by then-president Jimmy Carter to placate Jewish supporters angered by his sale of F-15 fighter planes to Saudi Arabia (plates 27, 28). All such memorial decisions are made in political time, contingent on political realities.[19]

In this context, therefore, we explore not only the pluralistic definitions of the Holocaust in America (which Holocaust?, whose Holocaust?), but also the ways in which other American ideals and facts of life—such as liberty and immigration—constitute the central memorial motifs here. Situated adjacent to the National Mall and within sight of the Washington Monument to the right and the Jefferson Memorial across the Tidal Basin to the left, the U.S. Holocaust Memorial Museum is a neighbor of the National Museum of American History and the Smithsonian Institution. It will, by dint of its placement, enshrine not just the history of the Holocaust, but American democratic and egalitarian ideals as they counterpoint the Holocaust.

Similarly, a Holocaust memorial designed by the architect Louis I. Kahn was to be placed at the foot of Manhattan at the Battery, within sight of the Statue of Liberty and Ellis Island (plate 24). Had it been funded and erected, it would have become part of a geographical triad commemorating liberty, immigration, and tolerance.

Site of the proposed New England Holocaust Memorial in Union Street Park (the traffic island, lower center), Boston.

18   See also Tom Segev, *The Seventh Million: The Israelis and the Holocaust*, trans. Haim Watzman (New York: Hill and Wang, 1993).

19   For more on the political dimension of memorials, see Michael Berenbaum, "On the Politics of Public Commemoration of the Holocaust," *Shoah* (Fall-Winter 1981-82): 9. See also Berenbaum's collection of essays, *After Tragedy and Triumph: Modern Jewish Thought and the American Experience* (Cambridge and New York: Cambridge University Press, 1991), pp. 3-16.
     For further details on the controversy surrounding the establishment of the U.S. Holocaust Memorial Commission, see Judith Miller, *One, by One, by One: Facing the Holocaust* (New York and London: Simon and Schuster, 1990), pp. 255-66.

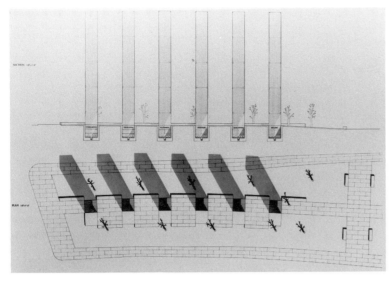

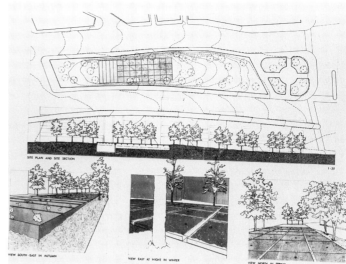

Above left: Winning entry in the competition for the New England Holocaust Memorial by Stanley Saitowitz, 1990.

Above right: Finalist entry board in the competition for the New England Holocaust Memorial by Hali Weiss. Stage I, 1990.

Across the river, Nathan Rapoport's monument *Liberation* stands in Jersey City's Liberty State Park, also within sight of the Statue of Liberty and Ellis Island. This large statue of an American soldier carrying a helpless concentration camp victim emblematizes America's self-idealization as rescuer and refuge for the world's "huddled masses" (see p. 158).

Yet another Holocaust memorial to be built in downtown Boston will in effect become one more stop on the Freedom Trail, two stops after the Paul Revere House on a trail wending its way from the Boston Common to the Bunker Hill Monument (plate 25). No matter what shape the memorial here finally takes, it will be located both spatially and metaphysically in the continuum of American revolutionary history, integrated into the very myth of American origins. In all cases, memorials in the United States will necessarily "Americanize the Holocaust," in the words of Michael Berenbaum, project director of the U.S. Holocaust Memorial Museum.

Other memorials and museums in America, both those built and forever unbuilt, have been accountable to a broad cross section of American civic groups. When a large memorial designed by Nathan Rapoport for a site in Riverside Park to commemorate the Warsaw Ghetto Uprising was rejected by the City Arts Commission in 1965 as too depressing and for seeming to refer to foreign, not American, history, survivors wondered just how American they were. In keeping with its civic mandate, and

A plaque laid in Riverside Park, New York City, in 1947 marks the site of a planned Holocaust memorial never built.

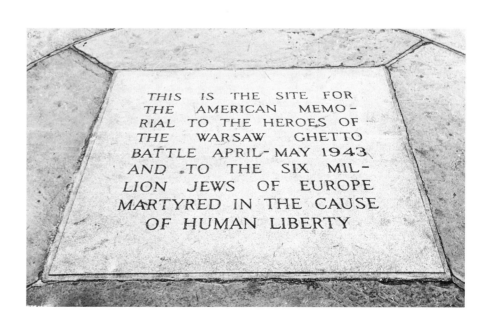

THIS IS THE SITE FOR THE AMERICAN MEMORIAL TO THE HEROES OF THE WARSAW GHETTO BATTLE APRIL-MAY 1943 AND TO THE SIX MILLION JEWS OF EUROPE MARTYRED IN THE CAUSE OF HUMAN LIBERTY

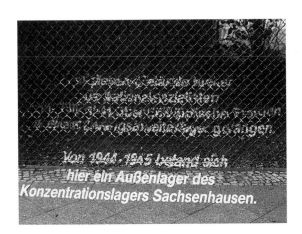

The German artist Norbert Radermacher used slide projections to focus attention on a site of Nazi violence. Pedestrians who walk by trip a light-beam trigger, which in turn flicks on a high-intensity slide projection of a written text relating the historical details of the site's now invisible past. The slide projections here refer to a forced labor camp, which later became one of Sachsenhausen's satellite camps. Conceived in 1989 and to be installed in the Neukölln district in Berlin, 1994.

20 See the catalogue for this exhibition, edited by Werner Fenz, *Bezugspunkte 38/88* (Graz: Steirischer Herbst Veranstaltungs-gesellschaft, 1988).

21 For insights into this project by both the artist and the curator, see Hans Haacke, "Und ihr habt doch gesiegt, 1988," pp. 77-81 below (reprinted from *October* 48 [Spring 1989]: 79-87), and Werner Fenz, "The Monument is Invisible, the Sign Visible," in *October* 48 (Spring 1989): 75-78.

22 See Albert Elsen, "What We Have Learned about Modern Public Sculpture: Ten Propositions," *Art Journal* 48/4 (Winter 1989): 291; see also idem, *Rodin's "Thinker" and the Dilemmas of Modern Public Sculpture* (New Haven: Yale University Press, 1985).

In this context, without intending to be facetious, we might speculate on what a monument to the Holocaust by video artist Nam June Paik might look like. Would it be a single video loop, replaying over and over images set in a concentration camp or deportation site? Or would he make an all-purpose monument, a chunk of marble, inset with a video monitor that played any memorial loop we wanted to insert? Depending on the day and location, this stone and video might commemorate Auschwitz, Hiroshima, or World War I — not to mention any number of future catastrophes.

now answerable to the large African-American, Hispanic, and Asian communities nearby, the Simon Wiesenthal Center's *Beit HaShoah*-Museum of Tolerance in Los Angeles examines the history of all social and ethnic prejudice and its consequences in America. In the words of a promotional brochure, "The museum's main exhibit area is organized in two sections: the history of racism and prejudice within the American experience... and then the story of the most quintessential example of man's inhumanity to man — the Holocaust."

The Aesthetic Interrogation of the Monument

For contemporary artists working in decidedly unmonumental media, the art of the monument cuts at least two ways. When invited to conceive of a Holocaust memorial, contemporary artists turn reflexively to their chosen medium, style, and forms. For, like their generational counterparts in literature and music, most of the contemporary artists commissioned to design memorials remain answerable to both art and memory. In a hypothetical grave marker they designed for the Anne Frank House in Amsterdam, for example, the twin brothers Doug and Mike Starn have overlaid sepia-tinted automat photographs of Anne onto an enlarged page of her diary (plate 9). Instead of segmenting these photographs, they have left them in two strips of three, paired side-by-side, almost twinlike. The diary page, her last, is dated and so recalls the dates of a tombstone, her epitaph self-inscribed.

Hans Haacke, as he has done so effectively with the icons of big business, resurrected a Nazi memorial in Austria, in the town of Graz, in order to remind all of the site's complicitous past (plate 20). In *Bezugspunkte 38/88* (Points of reference 38/88), a city-wide installation, the artist duplicated the Nazis' draping of the town's patron saint in swastika-emblazoned banners in order to turn the image of Nazism against itself.[20] Haacke's "point of reference" was itself turned inside out when neo-Nazis torched the monument, an act which the artist then incorporated into the text of the memorial by adding the inscription: "During the night of November 9, 1938, all synagogues in Austria were looted, destroyed, and set on fire. And during the night of November 2, 1988, this memorial was destroyed by a firebomb."[21]

Sol LeWitt's black cube set in the square of a former palace in Germany, in the town of Münster, recalled both the absent Jews of Münster and his own geometrical forms — before the monument itself was dismantled by town authorities and reconstructed in front of the town hall in Hamburg-Altona (plate 15).

When commissioned to create a monument for San Francisco, George Segal turned to his white plaster figures, using a survivor then living in Israel as his primary model (plates 29, 30). If part of the brilliance in Segal's earlier plaster sculpture was its formalization of pedestrian moments, what happens when his medium is applied to the least pedestrian of subjects? As Albert Elsen reminds us, for many contemporary artists, it will be the needs of art, not the public or memory, that come first.[22]

At the same time, a new generation of artists in Germany has begun to wonder whether the monument itself is more an impediment than an incitement to public memory. Ethically certain of their duty to remember, but aesthetically skeptical of monumental forms still redolent of a Nazi past, artists such as Jochen and Esther Gerz, Horst Hoheisel, and Norbert Radermacher have begun to probe the limits of both their artistic media and the very notion of a memorial. They have posed an essentially German conundrum: how does a nation build a new and just state on the bedrock memory of its crimes? And they have responded with a series of stunning and

Horst Hoheisel's *Denk-Stein-Sammlung* (Memorial Stone Collection), 1989-93. School children in Kassel each dedicated a palm-sized stone to a Jewish victim of their city whose fate they had learned from the book depicted here. The stones were wrapped in paper with a personal message. This campaign, initiated by Horst Hoheisel in 1989, was aimed at preserving the martyrs from anonymity. The 1,007 stones collected were placed in a glass baggage trolley and installed on platform 3, the boarding area for the deportation trains at the train station in Kassel, Germany.

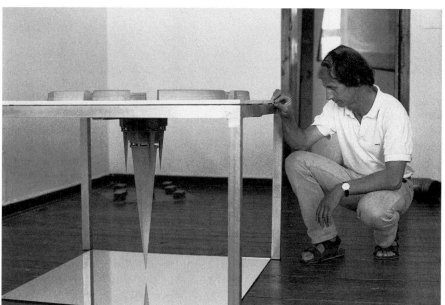

Horst Hoheisel's *"Negative-Form" Monument to the Aschrott-Brunnen*, Kassel, 1987. At right, the artist with a model of the monument, designed as an inverted replica of a fountain built by a Jewish businessman and destroyed by the Nazis. In the finished work (below right) the replica was sunk twelve meters into the ground; passersby can observe the flow of water as it plunges downward.

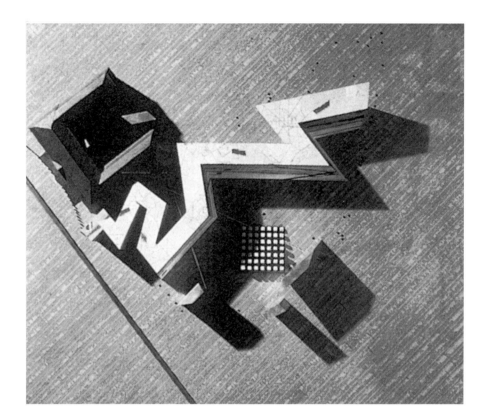

Daniel Libeskind's model of names for the Extension of the Berlin Museum with the Jewish Department, 1989. This conceptual model entered in the competition for an extension to the Berlin Museum incorporates the names of the German Jewish victims of the Holocaust.

provocative public installations — antimonuments — conceived to challenge the very premises of their being.[23]

How does the monument interrogate itself? Jochen and Esther Gerz's Harburg *Monument against Fascism*, a twelve-meter tall, lead-covered column, invited visitors to inscribe their names on it before it vanished into the ground over time (plate 12). A subsequent memorial by Jochen Gerz in Saarbrücken, entitled *2,146 Stones — Monument against Racism*, remains invisible to the eye altogether (plates 13, 14). The model and drawings for Horst Hoheisel's "negative-form" monument in Kassel illustrate the ways that a monument built into the ground forces visitors to shoulder memory themselves, to become, in essence, the monument (plates 16, 17). Slide projections by Shimon Attie and Norbert Radermacher bathe otherwise forgetful sites in Berlin with images and narratives of their recent pasts (plates 18, 19). In his brilliant and disturbing design for the extension of the Berlin Museum with the Jewish Museum, architect Daniel Libeskind suggests that even our contemporary houses of memory must now reflect a discontinuity of form, a futility in reconciling past and present (plate 23). Once challenged in these ways, the idea of the monument — Holocaust or otherwise — will never quite be the same.

The Visitors' Role in the Art of Memory

As the antimonument-makers show so well, by themselves memorials remain inert and amnesiac, mere stones in the landscape without life or meaning. For their memory, these memorials depend completely on the visitor. Only we can animate the stone figures and fill the empty spaces of the memorial, and only then can monuments be said to remember anything at all. In this way, we recognize the essentially dialogical character of Holocaust memorials, the changing faces of memory different visitors bring to them. Given the inevitable variety of competing memories, we may never actually share a common memory at these sites but only the common place of memory, where each of us is invited to remember in his own way.

23 For more on this phenomenon, see my article "The Counter-monument: Memory against Itself in Germany Today," in *Critical Inquiry* 18 (Winter 1992): 267-96 and expanded further in *The Texture of Memory*, pp. 17-48.

We might ask, for example, how survivors remember differently than the second generation, how local inhabitants remember differently than tourists on a memorial pilgrimage. Indeed, as Jack Kugelmass asks later in this volume, what role does the Holocaust tourist play in all this? How do we even discuss the touristic consumption of Holocaust memorials? Guest books from Dachau, Auschwitz, and the Anne Frank House illustrate an unexpected variety of responses to memory, with comments such as "Hitler war richtig!," "Never forget, never forgive!," and "Jesus forgives." Such passages show how other visitors' responses become part of our own memorial experience. Like visitors to the memorial sites themselves, even as our exhibition-goers stand face to face with the tourist kiosk recreated here—replete with memorabilia, pennants, buttons, and postcards—they will have to recognize their own place in the tourist equation, their own part in a Holocaust memorial economy.

In all of this, we recognize that the art of memory neither begins with a monument's ground-breaking nor ends with the ceremonies conducted at its base. Rather, this art consists in the ongoing activity of memory, in the debates surrounding these memorials, in our own participation in the memorial's performance. For, in the end, we must also realize that the art of memory remains incomplete, an empty exercise, until visitors have grasped—and then responded to—current suffering in the world in light of a remembered past.

Plates

1 Wiktor Tolkin and Janusz Dembek: *Monument of Struggle and Martyrdom*, 1970. Majdanek, Poland.

2   Some of the twenty memorial plaques at Auschwitz-Birkenau, Poland, photographed in April 1993.
After the fall of Poland's Communist government the monument's original inscriptions, exaggerating the
number of deaths at the camp, were removed.

3   Nathan Rapoport: *Warsaw Ghetto Monument*, 1948. Warsaw, Poland.

4   Franciszek Duszenko and Adam Haupt: *Treblinka Memorial*, 1964. Treblinka, Poland.

5   Tourists on the Avenue of the Righteous Gentiles at Yad Vashem, Jerusalem, Israel.

6   Buky Schwartz: *Tower of Valor*, 1968-70. Yad Vashem, Jerusalem, Israel.

7   Lipa Yahalom and Dan Zur: Valley of the Communities, 1983-93. Yad Vashem, Jerusalem, Israel.

8   Ze'ev Ben Zvi: *To the Children of Exile*, 1947. Kibbutz Mishmar Ha-Emek, Israel.

9   Doug and Mike Starn: *Anne Frank Grave Marker*, 1989.
Collection Cornelis Suijk, Anne Frank Center, U.S.A.

10   Karin Daan: *Homomonument*, 1987. Westermarkt, Amsterdam, Holland. Detail.

11   Karin Daan: *Homomonument*, 1987. Westermarkt, Amsterdam, Holland.

12   Jochen Gerz and Esther Shalev-Gerz: *Monument against Fascism*, 1986-93.
Harburg, Germany. Photographed in 1990.

13, 14   Jochen Gerz: *2,146 Stones—Monument against Racism*, 1991. Saarbrücken, Germany. A cobble stone (left) from the square in front of Saarbrücken's palace, a former Gestapo headquarters, was inscribed with the name of a German Jewish cemetery and replaced with the inscribed side face down.

15   Sol LeWitt: *Memorial to the Missing Jews*, 1989. Platz der Republik, Hamburg-Altona, Germany.

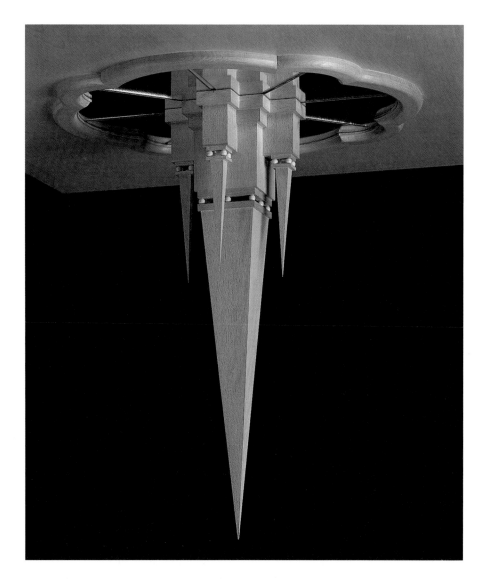

16   Horst Hoheisel: *"Negative-Form" Monument to the Aschrott-Brunnen*, 1987.
Kassel, Germany. Scale model, detail.

17   Horst Hoheisel: *"Negative-Form" Monument to the Aschrott-Brunnen*, 1987. Kassel, Germany.

18   Shimon Attie: *Joachimstraße 2, Slide Projection of Former Jewish Resident, Berlin, 1991 (ca. 1930)*, 1991. Berlin, Germany.

19   Shimon Attie: *Almstadtstraße 43, Slide Projection of Former Hebrew Bookstore, Berlin, 1991 (1930)*, 1991. Berlin, Germany.

20   Hans Haacke: *Und ihr habt doch gesiegt* (And You Were Victorious after All), 1988.
Installation for *Bezugspunkte 38/88* during the cultural festival Steirischer Herbst in Graz, Austria.

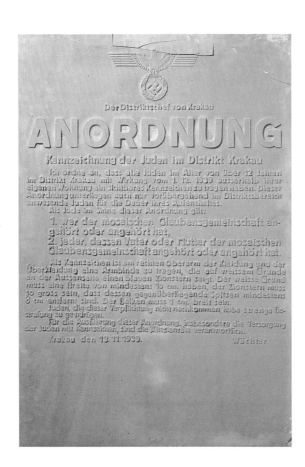

21, 22   Jürgen Wenzel and Nikolaus Lang: Winning entry in the competition for a memorial on the former site of Gestapo, SS, and Reichsicherheitshauptamt on the Prinz-Albrecht-Terrain (*Gestapo-Gelände*), Berlin, ca. 1984. Great plates of cast iron, inscribed with Nazi documents, were to seal over the entire area, broken only by holes large enough for an orderly grid of chestnut trees. One of the iron plates (left) bears the replica of a document prescribing armbands for the Jews of Kraków.

23   Daniel Libeskind: Extension of the Berlin Museum with the Jewish Museum Department. Realistic zinc model, 1989.

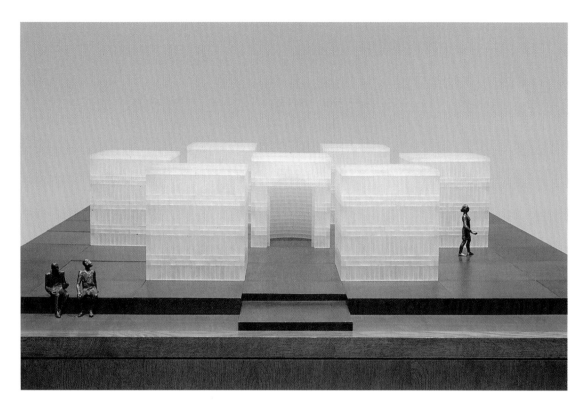

24   Louis I. Kahn: *Memorial to the Six Million Jewish Martyrs*. Battery Park, New York City, 1966-72 (not built).
Scale model. Louis I. Kahn Collection, Architectural Archives of the University of Pennsylvania. Commissioned by the
Museum of Contemporary Art, Los Angeles.

25   Stanley Saitowitz: Model for the New England Holocaust Memorial, Boston, 1990.

26   Ami Shamir: Holocaust Memorial at the Jewish Community Center of Tucson, Arizona, 1988.

27   James Ingo Freed/Pei Cobb Freed & Partners: Exterior rooftop view of the United States Holocaust Memorial Museum, Washington D.C., with the Washington Monument visible in the background.

28   The United States Holocaust Memorial Museum's three-story Tower of Faces contains more than 1,300 photo album pictures taken of the Jewish residents of Ejszyszki, Lithuania, during the 1920s and 1930s. In a two-day period in September 1941, 90 percent of the town's Jewish community of 3,000 people were murdered by Nazi killing squads.

29   George Segal: *The Holocaust*, 1984. Lincoln Park, San Francisco.

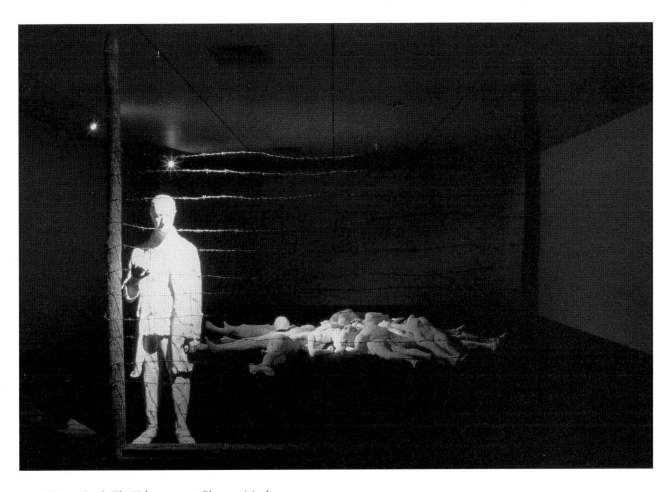

30   George Segal: *The Holocaust*, 1982. Plaster original.
The Jewish Museum, New York. Museum purchase with funds provided by the Dorot Foundation.

The Artist as Monument-maker
Five Profiles

Stephan Schmidt-Wulffen

The Monument Vanishes
A Conversation with Esther and Jochen Gerz

In 1983, the local council of Hamburg Harburg decided that a monument against fascism, war, and violence would be the first priority of their "public art" project. Six artists were invited to participate in a closed competition: Lothar Baumgarten, Jochen Gerz, Jochen Hiltmann, Siegfried Neuenhausen, H. D. Schrader, and Timm Ulrichs. In the end, Esther and Jochen Gerz's plan was selected from the entries submitted (plate 12). They built a twelve-meter high, four-sided column in the bustling center of Harburg. Local inhabitants and passersby could carve their names into the soft lead-covered surface of the steel column and so register their anti-Fascist attitudes. Whenever a one and one-half-meter section filled up, the entire column would be sunk by that much into the ground, until it would eventually disappear completely.* One would be able to see one section of the column through a window in the deep pedestrian underpass, however. A sign (in seven languages) next to the sculpture explained the idea behind the building of the monument and encouraged people to add their signatures:

> We invite the citizens of Harburg and visitors to the town to add their names here to ours. In doing so, we commit ourselves to remain vigilant. As more and more names cover this 12-meter tall lead column, it will gradually be lowered into the ground. One day, it will have disappeared completely and the site of the Harburg monument against fascism will be empty. In the end, it is only we ourselves who can rise up aganst injustice.

...On October 10, 1986, the work was handed over to the public, which has since struggled to come to terms with this "stumbling block [to memory]." I spoke to Esther and Jochen Gerz about the conception and effect of this unusual example of engaged political art.

S. W.:   Your works usually have personal, biographical backgrounds. Is that also true of this anti-Fascist monument, or is it "simply" a commission?

J. G.:   I was particularly impressed by what the city wanted: no leaping deer, no mere representational image; they wanted something that brought social issues into play and displayed them.

I should add that my wife and I met in Israel at the time, and that strengthened my feeling that there is never a time for forgetting. It would have been more natural for me not to feel personally responsible any longer — just as the French say to beggars, "j'ai déjà donné": I gave already. The attitude in Germany [toward this period] often amounted to this: there are no reasons for us to continue facing the past.

That is why I sought out this site. The city wanted to erect the monument in a "creative corner," in a park or somewhere. But there happened to be this ugly spot in Harburg which is packed with buildings, a heavily trafficked central crossing.

S. W.:   So was this very topical reference to Fascist elements in our time planned by the city from the beginning?

J. G.:   Yes, exactly! It is a monument against fascism, not a memorial to fascism.

S. W.:   What immediately fascinated me when I heard about this monument was that anticipated reactions to public art were incorporated into the work itself, for example, the writing of names, spray [painting]. Did such considerations play a role?

* Editor's note: The *Monument against Fascism* was lowered for the eighth and last time on November 11, 1993.

Jochen Gerz and Esther Shalev-Gerz photographed in front of their *Monument against Fascism*, which stood above ground from 1986 to 1993.

J. G.: Certainly, experiences are to be found in this work that can be found only through art: first, the disappearance of the object, its withdrawal. The issue is made more immediate because [the monument] is brought close to disappearing.

When the thing has sunk, it will be visually more expansive. Towards the end, when it has almost completely disappeared, it will stand there like a table. This change interested me a great deal. And then there's the [process of] signing. With your signature, you as the artist usually take everyone else's place away. With our work, we have handed over authorship and so share it with other people; such matters don't actually have much to do with public art directly but with art in general.

S. W.: So what has been the response of the people of Harburg? Has this kind of participation helped to prevent the usual attacks on art?

J. G.: Because the surface is lead, everything that you do with the stylus remains. Unlike graffiti, it can't be removed. By contrast, spray paints don't adhere at all. The lead won't take on any color because it is so greasy. It becomes completely colorless.* What happens instead, and this is a much more clever response by people in the context of this work, is that they cross out the signatures.

When first installed in 1986, the lead-surfaced, steel column stood twelve meters high at a busy intersection in Harburg, an industrial suburb of Hamburg. Passersby were invited to etch their signatures into the lead surface to show their solidarity with the victims of injustice. The column was gradually lowered into the ground.

E. G.: *Der Spiegel* wrote about all the senseless scribble and scrawl. But that [scribble and scrawl] is also a political statement. You don't do that on the subway. One does that when one knows that a statement against fascism is being made here. If you are a Fascist, you come and do the opposite [of signing]. That is a completely political act.

S. W.: So the intelligence shown here by the public asks for a new definition of the concept of vandalism.

J. G.: I agree with you there, and also their ability to understand, which isn't obvious if one only calls it senseless scribble and scrawl.... If someone approaches the column now and sees that signatures have been obliterated—ours, those of Werner Hofmann, of Frau Schuchardt [then director of the Hamburg Art Museum and Minister of Culture, Hamburg], authority has been attacked (which is all right in itself)—that person may be afraid to add his or her signature.

* Editor's note: This was true at the time of the interview. Eventually, however, the monument was covered with spray-painted graffiti, which adhered all too well.

The column in 1990.

S. W.:   But from a certain standpoint, one could also say the work is so open that even this event is a documentation of the way the community thinks. How open was the original concept?

E. G.:   The concept was like a sponge. We also explained that to the commission, that it really is a sponge. And they agreed.

J. G.:   We said the monument is a social test tube. Of course, people from the city government asked what would happen in terms of vandalism. We talked about that. And we said if no one signs, then it's a very normal monument.... Or it gets signed and thus disappears. Because both possibilities exist. The concept was open.

A photograph of the column shortly before it disappeared into the ground in 1993.

At the lowering of the column in 1992.

Detail of the column.

* Editor's note: This refers to an unfinished monument at the Dammtor in Hamburg.

One imagines possible reactions, but imagining doesn't help. On the one hand, one sees people, a particular generation, who all have their heads in the sand, but they come nevertheless. Or they stand around and say it is much too expensive: what are they doing with our tax money? And then really tough political issues turn up for which one can never be properly prepared.

E. G.: There's the monument by [Alfred] Hrdlicka, which cost a lot more, but no one says anything about such trivial matters.* But here it seems as though people are looking for issues so that they won't have to confront the actual topic.

S. W.: Do you think that there is a correlation between this specific kind of monument and the reactions to it? Hrdlicka's has obviously been assimilated, whereas your work is simply unclassifiable. It cannot be digested, which is positive.

J. G.: Three arguments emerge here concerning displacement or repression in art. First, one can say that it's not art, there's nothing to it. This "de-occupation" of the space is actually deeply disturbing, and, of course, there is the challenge that now individuals have to do this by themselves. You don't have the barrier ropes of the museum separating you from the work, telling you here I am and there is the art. Actually, that's the most satisfying thing: [the visitor's] astonishment.

The second repression is a financial one. For that amount of money half an old-age home could have been built or a kindergarten . . . and so on. The third thing is that one regrets that something like this may not be possible [without vandalism]: we already know in advance how it will turn out . . . .

S. W.: Aren't there any political issues here in a narrower sense?

J. G.: No. The argument that we knew what was coming and so we couldn't be *for* it was the official CDU party line.

Even the anti-Fascist resistance organizations say that it's not a memorial against fascism, that it doesn't honor the victims. No one can see that there is also a present moment where decisions are still possible.

E. G.: Many people just say we want a monument with the names of the victims. We want to turn toward the past. But in no way do we want to be confronted with fascism as a reality in the present. They'd like to say that fascism is only in the past.

J. G.: The work provides no information, pro or con. One can't say, I'm on the side of the monument. The monument takes no sides. It is completely indifferent, so much so that one can't even get emotional. People want to deal with this theme in ways that bring peace and reconciliation; they want a tool which works for unity. People seem to find it unbearable that the monument does not fulfill this function. Something seems to be fundamentally lacking in this work insofar as it does not respond to this desire for harmony. In ethnology it is said that when a population seeks harmony, they actually seek death, the end of time. Thus, the perfect solution can only be beyond time. I believe that this is also a society that has no way to respond to reality other than through culture. Everything has to be sublimated. For all reality is hostile.

S. W.: In your opinion, is the idea of culture itself compensatory?

J. G.: Yes, it has to be. Culture functions according to the notion of a court where the king is missing. Everyone is a victim, and no one is responsible.

E. G.: That's why [the Germans are] working so hard at it even now.

S. W.: Can political art still be made today? Years ago it still seemed clear: a clear message for the right people. Such certainties have been done away with. Today we have paradoxical situations.

J. G.: Political art is always a chance hit. To want political art is ridiculous. There are situations which touch the individual heart, and it is an achievement of society that one can be affected so personally. Or to put it more nastily, if there hadn't been National Socialism, there wouldn't have been the monument. That is a personal experience which does not necessarily lead to being mute as well. But it borders on speechlessness. It is a small confrontation of meaning where everything is always written quite small. And I would no more make a program out of political art than out of abstract art.

A pedestrian etches his signature into the lead surface of the column. Photographed in 1986.

Detail showing graffiti etched into the lead surface.

The polemic surrounding this work is ultimately a polemic about political art, about art and political art. Everyone thinks that they understand something about art, even though they don't involve themselves with it. If people go to a stadium, they know what "offside" means, but if people talk about art, they have no interest in knowing anything about it. Everyone has an inner compulsion to understand art. In this connection, political art must be simple, crystal clear, and must project a clear conscience.

S. W.:   A compensatory function.

J. G.:   Yes. We saw Chinese children, Turkish families that came straight over and signed. People who did not have the problem [with art] understood. Those who were well acquainted with the [monument's] history could not understand. If you cannot accept the political, you ascribe it to art in the sense that you can doubt it and say: that isn't art . . . .

So what is it then for someone to sign this monument? In a sense, it is not a political act. One could reproach [the signatory] and say that instead of making a major statement, one only has to give one's name. But your name is important when it appears somewhere. Language reduces itself to a signature, a very simple metaphor. Anyway, it is an element of language that has many consequences. I can be imprisoned as a result of a signature. And then there is writing in a public space, where people are watching as you write. Somehow it is all very strange. Those are matters that somehow really need courage, as stupid as it sounds. It is a declaration.

S. W.:   There must have been an idea as to how the chasm between art and public life could be breached. Now it seems to be acknowledged that as an artist, one should stay out of public life.

J. G.:   Even if public life does not function, it can still function as art. That is just the way it is with contemporary art. On the other hand, it can also function as the *Dorflinde*, or the "village tree," if there is no artistic concept. Thus, people who are able to function either innocently or within known rituals, they also sign. The people aren't inside the museum; yet the art still functions. The *Dorflinde* and contemporary art can be very similar, and one can layer one over the other until they are unrecognizable. And exactly then comes the moment where our society may simply be incapable of communicating. Society can only function when it keeps all these areas separate.

S. W.: Capitalistic or German society?

J. G.: Of course not every people has a past where such explosive devices can be found. Perhaps that's why with the Germans, one finds this highly developed, intellectualized capacity for repression. In my opinion, German society is unbelievably well prepared [one is reared and educated] for such processes but completely inexperienced and immersed in self-censorship. Everyone can talk the way we are talking now. It's amazing, they all talk like books. Except there is absolutely no exchange or differentiation. They really all say mostly the same thing.

The column no longer offers this consolation. It seems that the emptiness of the column is unbearable because, in fact, there is nothing else there.

S. W.: The repression is blocked. Is it also a monument for a repression that no longer functions?

J. G.: Exactly. In the end, it is a duel with repression.

Editor's note: This article was originally published in German under the title "Duell mit der Verdrängung: Ein Gespräch mit Esther und Jochen Gerz," *Kunstforum International* 1 (January 1987): 318-21. Reprinted by permission of the publisher.

Hans Haacke

Und ihr habt doch gesiegt, 1988

Every fall since 1968, a cultural festival known as the Styrian Autumn has been held in Graz, the capital of the Austrian province of Styria. The festival presents concerts, theater, and opera productions, film showings, symposia by writers, and art exhibitions. Although constituted as an independent organization, its director is chosen by a board on which representatives of the provincial and the city governments play an important role. In 1988, the board was chaired by Professor Kurt Jungwirth, the deputy governor of Styria and a prominent member of the conservative party (ÖVP). Graz was represented by its social democratic mayor, Alfred Stingl (SPÖ), and its commissioner of culture Helmut Strobl (ÖVP). The festival is funded by the province, the city of Graz, and the Austrian government.

Dr. Peter Vujica, the director of the Styrian Autumn in 1988, chose for the twentieth anniversary of the festival the motto "Guilt and Innocence of Art" and suggested that reference be made to Hitler's annexation of Austria in 1938. The *Anschluss* was the theme of a number of public events in Austria in the year of its fiftieth anniversary. Inevitably, the enthusiastic welcome Hitler received when his troops marched into Austria became the subject of agitated public debate. That debate was further fueled by the controversy surrounding the role the recently elected Austrian president, Kurt Waldheim, had played as a *Wehrmacht* officer in the Balkans during World War II.

Dr. Vujica commissioned Dr. Werner Fenz, the curator of the city's Neue Galerie, to organize the visual arts section for 1988. Dr. Fenz invited artists from various countries to produce works for temporary installation in selected public places in Graz. He chose as *Points of Reference 38/88* locations that had played a significant role during the Nazi regime, such as the police/Gestapo headquarters, city hall, squares where Nazi rallies had been held, the Hitler Youth headquarters, the bishop's palace, and so forth.

One of the city's older monuments, the *Mariensäule* (Column of the Virgin Mary), rises in a square at the south end of Herrengasse, the most prominent street of Graz. A fluted column on a massive base, crowned by a gilded statue of the Virgin on a crescent moon, it was erected late in the seventeenth century to commemorate the victory over the Turks. It has been a popular landmark ever since.

When Hitler conferred on Graz the honorary title *Stadt der Volkserhebung* (City of the People's Insurrection), the ceremony on July 25, 1938, was held at the foot of the *Mariensäule*. Graz had earned this title as an early and vital Nazi stronghold in Austria. Weeks before the *Anschluss*, 15,000 Nazis had paraded down Herrengasse in a torchlight parade, the swastika flag had been hoisted from the balcony of city hall, and Jewish shop windows had been smashed.

For the 1938 celebration, the *Mariensäule* had been hidden under an enormous obelisk, draped in red fabric, and emblazoned with the Nazi insignia and the inscription *UND IHR HABT DOCH GESIEGT* (And You Were Victorious after All) (plate 20). This claim of ultimate triumph referred to the failed putsch in Vienna on July 25, 1934, four years earlier, during which the Austro-Fascist chancellor, Dr. Engelbert Dollfuss, had been murdered by Nazis. The obelisk was topped by a fire bowl.

Fenz designated the *Mariensäule* and its surroundings as one of the sixteen "points of reference." According to photographs of its transformation into a Nazi victory column, I had its appearance of July 25, 1938, reconstructed for the Styrian Autumn. The only difference from the original was an addition around the base. Listed, white on black ground in the fractura typeface preferred by the Nazis, were "The Vanquished of Styria: 300 Gypsies killed, 2,500 Jews killed, 8,000 political prisoners killed or died in detention, 9,000 civilians killed in the war, 12,000 missing, 27,900 soldiers killed."

Hans Haacke's installation *Und ihr habt doch gesiegt* (And You Were Victorious after All) at the twentieth anniversary of the Styrian Autumn Festival, whose motto was "Guilt and Innocence of Art," Graz, Austria, 1988.

Column of the Virgin Mary, a popular seventeenth century memorial in Graz.

Facing the obelisk, on a spot where, in 1938, a wall of large swastika flags served as a backdrop for the Nazi dignitaries addressing their uniformed audience, I had a billboard erected to hold sixteen posters. With a swastika in the center of each, the posters carried, in white fractura on a red ground, the inscription "Graz — City of The People's Insurrection." Pasted into the middle of the swastikas were facsimile reproductions of documents from 1938. Among them were several classified advertisements from the local newspapers announcing the Aryan ownership or recent "Aryanization" of local shops and the fact that Nazi paraphernalia was in stock. In others, "Aryans" were looking for jobs or marriage partners. One warned the public that he would have anybody prosecuted who spread rumors he might not be "Aryan." Also included were the university law school's catalogue page with the listing of courses on the new race laws and Germanic legal doctrine, as well as the congratulatory telegram

In 1938 Hitler conferred on Graz the honorific title "City of the People's Insurrection," rewarding it for its role as an early Nazi stronghold. A ceremony took place around the Column of the Virgin Mary which was draped in red flags and bore the banner *UND IHR HABT DOCH GESIEGT.*

the university president had sent to Hitler. There were, as well, reproductions of the prayer with which the city's pastor welcomed the new Nazi era and ads by employees publicly thanking their employers for having granted them a bonus on the occasion of the *Anschluss*. Also represented was the local newspaper's jubilant report of the burning of the synagogue: "For Graz the problem of the provocative presence of a Jewish temple has now been unequivocally solved by the will of the people." And there was a facsimile of the Gestapo list of motor vehicles confiscated from local Jews.

When asked to provide a statement to accompany the proposal for my piece, *Und ihr habt doch gesiegt*, in the catalogue of *Points of Reference 38/88*, I wrote: "'And you were victorious after all', the Nazis proclaimed, full of pride, on the red fabric with their eagle and the swastika, which decorated the *Mariensäule* in Graz on July 25, 1938. They were referring to themselves. Fifty years later, I hope we can make sure that their cheering will turn out to have been premature."

As soon as the obelisk was covered with the red drapery carrying the inscriptions and the Nazi eagle and it became clear why the statue of the Virgin had been encased, there was commotion at the site. Throngs of people gathered and engaged in heated

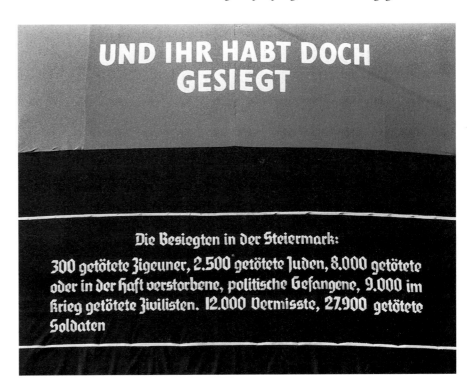

Haacke's 1988 installation recreated the Nazi victory column but transformed it into a memorial to the victims of Nazism by adding: "The Vanquished of Styria: 300 Gypsies killed, 2,500 Jews killed, 8,000 political prisoners killed or died in detention, 9,000 civilians killed in the war. 12,000 missing, 27,900 soldiers killed."

debate over whether, after fifty years, one should stir up the Nazi past again. Some of the opposition was clearly motivated by anti-Semitic sentiments. While most people of retirement age were incensed, the local T.V. also showed several passionate supporters of the idea that they must confront and come to terms with their ugly past. Among them was an old woman commenting, while the camera was rolling, "I wonder why these people are so upset. They must feel guilty." The reaction of those who, due to their age, could not have been implicated in the Nazi period, was very mixed, ranging from hostility, indifference, and incomprehension to enthusiastic approval of the Styrian Autumn's project. In their opening address, both the mayor of Graz and the deputy governor stressed the need for more education about recent history, particularly for the young. And they also stressed that any exhibition of art in public places inevitably has political connotations. No art dealers or critics from outside the region attended the opening. Local media coverage was generous and for the most part decidedly favorable.

Detail of one of the sixteen posters showing a newspaper printed in 1938.

Opposite the column, Haacke constructed a wall with posters and facsimile documents from the Nazi period.

The sixteen posters with documents from 1938 were torn down frequently and had to be replaced. But they also attracted attentive readers, including an occasional class of schoolchildren under the guidance of their teacher. Other works in the exhibition were vandalized, too, probably more out of aggression against what the vandals perceived as offensive to their notions of art or as a prank than for political reasons. An audio piece by the Californian Bill Fontana, in which powerful loudspeakers boomed the sounds of Hamburg foghorns and the mating calls of exotic animals, particularly incurred the population's ire, and it was eventually turned off. From the beginning, a guard was posted at the obelisk every night.

Out of the view of the guard, about a week before the closing of the exhibition, on the night of November 2, my memorial to the victims of the Nazis in Styria was firebombed. Although the fire department was able to extinguish the flames soon, much of the fabric and the top of the obelisk were burned, and the statue of the Virgin was severely damaged when the soldered joints of the copper sculpture melted.

The local, the national, and also the West German press reported the firebombing, some relating it to the hostile reactions to the Burgtheater's premiere of *Der Heldenplatz* by the Austrian playwright Thomas Bernhard. Many headlines now referred to the ruin of the *Mahnmal* (memorial) as *Schandmal* (monument of shame), strongly condemning the arson and the suspected political motivation behind it. An exception was the *Neue Kronen Zeitung*, the largest and most conservative Austrian daily tabloid, which had been the strongest supporter of Kurt Waldheim. The Graz editor used the occasion to accuse the leaders of the Catholic Church of having permitted the encasement of the *Mariensäule* and the politicians of having squandered tax money for such a "shameful" purpose.

Following the arson, Richard Kriesche, an artist from Graz, called for a fifteen-minute demonstration of silence at the ruin to take place at noon on the next Saturday. About 100 people from the local art community joined him and discussed the meaning of the event with the crowd of Saturday shoppers that had gathered around. For days afterwards, inspired by the *Katholische Aktion* (Lay Apostolate), leftist political groups, and students, people demonstrated, deposited flowers, and, at night, lit candles at the foot of the burned obelisk. Kriesche, the mayor, and some local news-

View of the inscription added to the poster wall as a commemoration of *Kristallnacht* after the monument was firebombed in 1988. "On the night of November 9, 1938, all synagogues in Austria were looted, destroyed, and set on fire. And during the night of November 2, 1988, this memorial was destroyed by a firebomb."

The Haacke installation, and the statue of the Virgin Mary it covered, suffered major damage from a firebombing one week before the exhibition closed.

papers and others proposed to leave the ruin in place, as a memorial, beyond the time of the exhibition, until Christmas. But the conservative party (ÖVP) and pressure from Graz merchants eventually defeated this plan.

In commemoration of *Kristallnacht*, the Styrian Autumn covered the billboard of sixteen posters with the inscription: "During the night of November 9, 1938, all synagogues in Austria were looted, destroyed, and set on fire. And during the night of November 2, 1988, this memorial was destroyed by a firebomb."

With the help of a police sketch and descriptions from two people who had seen him from afar, the arsonist was arrested out of the crowd lining the streets of Graz during the silent march commemorating *Kristallnacht*. He was identified as an unemployed thirty-six-year-old man who had been traveling in neo-Nazi circles. The instigator of the firebombing was also arrested. He is a well-known sixty-seven-year-old Nazi.

Reports from Graz suggest that the events surrounding *Points of Reference 38/88* may have served as a catalyst for a critical examination of the local political culture. Stefan Karner, a professor for contemporary social and economic history at the University of Graz and author of a book entitled *Styria during the Third Reich, 1938-1945*, wrote about his observations:

> I can assure you that many people in Graz have been deeply affected, particularly by the damage done to the artwork. And they suddenly realized how important it is to deal with this period, including in artistic terms, and how problematic this subject still seems to be in Graz. I believe many of the reactions give reason to take heart and to be optimistic.

Editor's note: This article has been reprinted by permission of the author from *October* 48 (Spring 1989): 79-87.

Matthew Baigell

George Segal's Holocaust Memorial
An Interview with the Artist

George Segal agreed to let me interview him about his multifigured sculpture *The Holocaust*, a memorial to the victims of the Holocaust, on March 18, 1983. His initial remarks were so heartfelt that further discussion seemed unnecessary. With his approval, I then edited the tape minimally.

The original plaster for *The Holocaust* is in the collection of The Jewish Museum, New York, and was first shown there in April, 1983 (plate 30). It is now on view in the Museum's permanent exhibition, *Culture and Continuity: The Jewish Journey*. The sculpture was also cast in whitened bronze and permanently installed in Lincoln Park in San Francisco (plate 29). It was commissioned by Mayor Dianne Feinstein's Committee for a Memorial to the Six Million Victims of the Holocaust. My interview with the artist follows below.   M. B.

At first, I did not want to make this piece. I was asked months ago, and for half a year I turned it down. I turned down the idea of dwelling with all that death. After all, it happened forty years ago.

When I was younger, helping my father work on his chicken farm, I remember him sending me over to the farm of a couple that had survived Auschwitz, and my job was to teach them how to use machinery, how to feed the chickens properly, and when to collect the eggs.

They were fragile people with bad hearts, who told me in mild, benign voices of all the awful things that happened — of police dogs trained to leap, to tear a baby out of its mother's arms, to murder the child savagely. I heard these stories firsthand in 1947, but we had heard about these stories during the war.

My father came from Russian Poland; he was a Zionist and something of a Socialist. He and his friends made up about 50 percent of the Jewish chicken-farmer community. The other 50 percent were German Jews who had had the brains, insight, and nerve to leave Germany early enough, after they had been beaten up in the streets where they had grown up for simply being Jews.

The statistics were horrifying. Every member of my mother's and father's families who had stayed behind in Europe were gone, as far as we knew. The Yiddish papers made this news more appallingly clear than the English-language American papers did during the war. In 1945, when the Allied armies swept through Germany and there was the torrent of photographs of the survivors of the German death camps, it was an awful drenching, and the only response for Jews was to work incessantly for the establishment of the State of Israel.

Now, this is very strong subject matter. I have spent years in the civilian art world, U.S.A., and, I must add, happily — happily — civilian. The history of the New York art world has to do with the applause and celebration of formal invention — the sheer pleasure and sensual delight taken in the quality of a mark, the thickness of a stroke of paint, or the drag of a brush through a wash. The pleasures of aesthetics and art are somewhat akin to the pleasures of gourmet eating or to the visual delights of architecture, to gorgeous natural landscape and incredibly attractive man-made landscape, and once the disasters of war are put behind us, there is a huge temptation to lose yourself in the joys of the art world.

I found myself rejecting the whole idea of dwelling with death, thinking I'd long since left that behind. The people of San Francisco kept calling me and saying, "At least stop and see the site." I said, "Yes, I would." Helen [Segal] and I were coming back from Tokyo where I had been installing a show — again, the pleasures of the art world — and it was simple to stop off in San Francisco on the way home.

The plaster original of George Segal's *The Holocaust*, with its eleven life-sized figures (detail). Collection of The Jewish Museum, New York, purchased with funds provided by the Dorot Foundation.

83

While in Tokyo, we saw on television the reports of the Israeli invasion of Lebanon. We couldn't make out any details. The Japanese knew very little about the invasion and were essentially unconcerned, it being on the other side of the world, and I couldn't blame them. We landed in San Francisco and checked into a hotel. When I turned on the T.V. set, I was horrified for the first time in my life to hear anti-Semitic words tumbling out of the tube. It was a strange, critical reporting of Israeli behavior in Lebanon. I've been to Israel four or five times. I know many Israelis on intimate terms, and I was disturbed at the tone of the reporting because it didn't jibe with what I had heard to be the real behavior of the P.L.O., which was far from innocent—which was brutal and domineering; and the P.L.O. was the hidden government of Lebanon.

In that moment, I decided I had to do the Holocaust piece. It was a multilevel decision. It seemed precisely the wrong moment for me to abandon my support of the State of Israel and my fellow Jews, despite my objections to Begin and Sharon. I didn't like the chauvinism. I didn't like the militarism; yet I'd been there and visited

The dedication of Segal's installation in San Francisco, 1984.

there and was perfectly aware of the Arabs' implacable hatred and resentment of the Israelis. The overwhelming feeling was one of anguish over the inevitability of this increasingly hard standoff. After five wars, the sensation of a metallic taste in your mouth when you visit the area increases. For me it is always a relief to leave the area and stop off in civilian Rome for the joys and pleasures of shellfish at 10:00 P.M. in the Trastevere.

I felt I had to make the sculpture. I was introduced to the representatives of a large committee of forty people, who represented an older, established Jewish-American community whose ancestors, ironically, had come generations ago from Germany, arriving in San Francisco during Sutter's gold rush. They had prospered enormously, become well educated, and tended toward complete American identification; but they had also finally acknowledged the presence of a small, vigorous Jewish community made up literally of survivors of the camps. These survivors, ranging from fifty to seventy, had themselves been silent about their experiences for years, wanting to bury them; but of late, convinced that they were the last surviving witnesses of this awful occurrence, they were demanding some recognition of it—of the Holocaust.

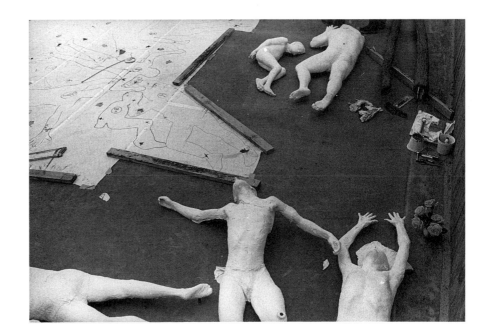

The Holocaust photographed during installation at Lincoln Park. A sketch on the floor indicates the placement of the figures.

After I got home, I went to two libraries but could find none of the pictures I remembered so vividly from 1945. The third library I went to, the Rutgers Library, had a six-foot shelf of books but, again, no pictures. My greatest memory of the Holocaust was my horror at the photographs in *Life* magazine that appeared at the time of the uncovering of the camps. I had to go to a Zionist library in New York, one that's locked up tight with security, to find a cache of photographs. I must have examined thousands of them. I kept being struck by one single horrifying fact. The German determination to kill the Jews was a determination made by a modern, sophisticated industrial state that had all kinds of sophisticated bureaucracy and power to implement that kind of decision. It meant the careful, precise, Germanic construction of places and buildings and the teams of men for the systematic eradication of a selected race. The Jews were held arbitrarily to be responsible for Germany's problems. If you were born Jewish, you could be tabbed for murderous wipeout by the insane logic of a modern political leader — any modern political leader. The dissident mentality that we grew up with, "Hell, no, I won't go," served the Jews no protection.

Plaster version (detail).

A visitor ventures behind the barbed wire fence in Lincoln Park, San Francisco.

Plaster version.

The one visual hook I uncovered was the arrogant contempt displayed by the Germans in their chaotic heaping of corpses. In any culture, if a human being dies, there's an elaborate, orderly ritual that accompanies the burial. The body is laid out in a straight line. Hands are crossed. There's a burial case and a prescribed, almost immoveable succession of events that involve the expression of grief of the family, the expression of love, the expression of the religious beliefs in whatever civilization. It's a prescribed order, and if a modern state turns that order topsy-turvy and introduces this kind of chaos, it is an unthinkable obscenity. I determined that I would have to make a heap of bodies that was expressive of this arrogance and disorder.

One member of the committee who was himself a survivor said, "Forget all those intellectual ideas you have, George. A memorial like this has to make you cry." I decided I had to go for my own emotional jugular. This was the central core of the piece. It meant that I had two options. I could deal with skeletal remains, or I could ask live friends to pose, which meant that I couldn't get — with modern American nutrition—the superthin survivors (or nonsurvivors) true to the photographs. I decided, since I had reread the literature, that the trains delivered enormous crowds of Jews who were tricked into the disinfecting showers and were then gassed. There could be bodies, I reasoned, that were of normal size as well as thin. This made it easier. It meant that I didn't have to go to New York hospitals and make casts of corpses of Bowery victims. I could simply ask friends of mine to pose and tell them what it was for. That was bad enough but not quite as bad as it would have been to make castings of corpses. Each person who posed went into a long free association with his or her ideas of death, so I got that from eleven different people. I must have transmitted my own, as well. Not very pleasant, not very exalting....

Editor's note: Reprinted by permission of the author from *Art in America* 71 (Summer 1983): 134-36. Baigell has rewritten his introductory remarks to allow for the time elapsed since the article first appeared.

James Ingo Freed

The United States
Holocaust Memorial Museum

When we were asked whether we would be interested in doing a Holocaust Memorial Museum, my first response was one of ambivalence. I felt intuitively that this was an emotional building, not an intellectual building, and I didn't know whether it was possible to do it.

Most art that I've seen that deals with the Holocaust has been bad art. The Holocaust as subject matter has prevented both the artist and the viewer from addressing aesthetic issues. Looking over your shoulder, you were always aware of the specter of this thing, these millions of bodies. The art could be kitsch and yet somehow have validation because it dealt with this impossible subject. On the other hand, good art that has dealt with the Holocaust seems to do so by distancing, by making it more abstract. In the last few years, some better art has begun to appear. There is a new interest in the Holocaust, coming from the people who did not live it. Christian Boltanski's work, for instance, deals less with the evocation of the event itself and more with the possibility of memory as an objective means of recalling events. Memory is a fading of events, an abstracting of events. Because of this, the new art that has come out of the subject of the Holocaust speaks as much of art as it does of the Holocaust and is thus able to deal with it; whereas for the older generation of people who lived it, who actually made art while they were in the camps, the art was secondary, a sort of reportage. And when they tried to aestheticize it, they turned it into the worst kind of sentimental kitsch. If there is one thing that the Holocaust is not, that is sentimental. It's a brutal thing. So much I knew about it.

On the Conditions

The site has turned out to be one of the most controversial places in Washington. And, in fact, the Holocaust Memorial is one of the three most controversial monuments ever to be proposed here. The first was the FDR monument, which still isn't built. The second was the Vietnam [Veterans] Memorial, which was thought to give too little monumental weight to the issue. And the third is this one. Now I choose to call it a memorial and not a monument because monuments celebrate things. Here there is no celebration. Also, monuments tend to be too unified, too unitary, restricting different possibilities of readings and interpretations. So "memorial" seems to be better. But the site of this memorial is right at the nexus of those national monuments that stand for an optimistic view of all of the values that early America supposedly had, that America now tries to absorb [see p. 90]. This ad hoc site is, in fact, sandwiched between the Washington Monument and the Jefferson Memorial. This is not lost on official Washington.

Directly adjacent to the site, to the north, is the Victorian brick Auditors' Building, with its annex, a low brick addition, fronting on Fifteenth Street. To the south of the site is the neoclassical limestone Bureau of Printing and Engraving [see p. 91]. It seemed clear to me that any memorial ought to be on the open, park side, toward Fifteenth Street to the west, freed from the pressure of the urban fabric and allowed to exist somewhat isolated. But one of the major political issues had to do with keeping it within the wall line of the city. But there is really no wall line here, no coherent urban edge. Yet both adjacent buildings are very frontal and dominant, particularly the Bureau of Printing and Engraving owing to its phenomenal length. We started to worry that the project might be subsumed into that — which some people thought would be a good thing and which I thought would be terrible. At the same time, because of the buses that will bring children and other groups, Fourteenth Street, which

Hall of Remembrance, United States Holocaust Memorial Museum in Washington, D.C. Designed by James Ingo Freed, Design Partner/Pei Cobb Freed & Partners, the museum was opened in 1993.

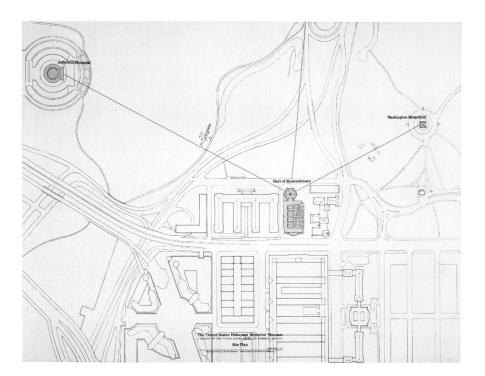

Site plan of the museum, symbolically located between the Jefferson Memorial and the Washington Monument.

may be one of the most unfortunate streets in the capital—a very unhappy, ugly street—had to be the most important point of access [see p. 97].

We decided that if we could make the building part brick and part limestone, it would make a bridge urbanistically. We felt that this contextual reading was important, that the building take the conditional circumstances of its location and weave them together with its content. What we were after from the very beginning was a reading of its relation to the Holocaust, but also a reading of an urban construct—two different levels. Bringing the brick in from one side and the limestone from the other reflects a condition of the Holocaust: on the one end you have the structure of the modern state—the monumental—and yet that structure embraces the most primitive kind of condition on the other end—the little village. This strategy accomplished several things. It tied us to Washington, and also made this building very particular to its site, while permitting us to do things with the form of the building that we could never have done otherwise. It allowed us to argue with the Fine Arts Commission for the need to deal differently with the scale of the forms. And it allowed me to form certain critiques of the monumental Washington front.

But, inevitably, right next to the center of monumental Washington, to bring in this little memorial that is not at all celebratory. . . . So they said, sandpaper it smooth, get rid of all those quirky things. The public process is one of sandpapering away irregularities, to the extent that the building loses some of its bite. That's why public projects tend very literally to be symmetrical objects, with very few extruded elements. I lost a number of battles. It's hard to try to keep the things that will tell you that this is not a typical "good times" building. There was always the conflict between the extrinsic and intrinsic character of the building and what the city would tolerate. In an earlier version, the Fifteenth Street entry had a large steel plate projecting above, creating a real sense of discomfort. This was another battle that I lost.

It was not only tension with the city that made it difficult to accomplish certain things, but tension with the client as well. There are several different groups of people involved. There are the survivors who never forget what their parents or brothers and sisters said to them as they moved into the gas chamber: "Remember us, remember us." To remember has become what they want to do. Others are not clear that they want to remember at all. They want to say that this building is to combat any sort of racism or intolerance. But to combat intolerance is missing the main issue because this is an intolerance that is absolute. So what you have are some who believe that their historic obligation is to memorialize and others who say that this building should deal not with lack of perception but with some more positive, upbeat thing that anyone can understand. There was always the unadmitted drive to neutralize, to make it less potent. They would like things to be more heroic, with more marble, more central spaces. I can't deal with this. I have to make a building that allows for horror, sadness. I don't know if you can make a building that does this, if you can make an architecture of sensibility. Because that is really what it is.

It is interesting to read the original document, the president's report, which Elie Wiesel wrote, about the building. Wiesel said that this is a building that should disturb. At the same time, it must not be a reconstruction because that would devalue the Holocaust; a reconstruction would be a Disneyland—clean, cute, no tension. There is a profound risk of aestheticization with this particular subject, of leaching out the raw power.

On the Process

View of the 15th Street façade. The museum, built of limestone and brick, harmonizes with the neighboring buildings on the Mall.

The first six months of the project essentially involved intuiting our way into the building. When we got the project, frankly, we were not really able to cope with the material because we didn't know enough. We went ahead and we read as much as we

View of the Hall of Witness.

Hall of Witness, interior of scale model.

could, and we looked at films until we were blurry eyed. One of the things that we looked at very early on was the buildings that the Jews had inhabited before the Holocaust. As a child, I lived in Essen. The Essen synagogue has been rebuilt and turned into a museum now, but it was in flames. I saw it burn. But the most important thing about it for us was that the imagery was not a unique imagery. It was vaguely oriental, vaguely romanesque. But it certainly was a part of the whole entourage of public buildings.

In Poland, on the other hand, there was Jewish architecture. It is important here to realize that while this building, the memorial, is not entirely about Jews in the Holocaust, it was stated to me that though it was about many groups, Jews were the central issue: as Elie Wiesel put it, very eloquently, "All victims were not Jews, but all Jews were victims." The Polish synagogue looks strange in our context, but in the context of the Polish wood structures, it's not so strange. It is very beautiful, very articulate. These structures were not like the cathedrals, but more like working spaces. These images and others that we saw had a residual, lingering presence in our minds, and that's partially what our building is about [see p. 99].

Then, of course, we began to think about images and conditions of the Holocaust. The survivors say you came to it first as alienation, separation from the body politic. Then there's transportation, then concentration. Then there is death.

I went to the death camps, to the concentration camps. All Holocaust people said that everything closed in on them. They felt themselves to be constantly closed in. The only thing they had left was the sky. The Germans could not remove the sky from them. Fences became an obsessive thing for me: the fencing in of a people.

The concentration camps all had gates, layers of lies, lies such as *Arbeit macht frei* (work makes free). The gate as lie, screen. The gate at Birkenau is an entrance to a one-way train station. I was asked if I did not know it was Birkenau, what would I say it was? My own feeling was that, in spite of its monumentality, it certainly was not a grand, celebratory entrance to a place. You have to step back about a hundred feet to where you see all the points converging toward the chimneys. Apparently, twenty minutes after you got in there, on an efficient day, you were smoke. When I walked into this, some archaic memories must have been stirred because emotionally this was

The enclosure and encirclement of victims in the death camps is evoked in the Hall of Witness.

a turning point for me. As we walked to the crematorium, there were scuffed-up little bones everywhere that had never turned to dust.

Bridges were another thing we looked at. The bridge was there to insulate people from the virus of Judaism. The issue was turned into a biological metaphor. The body politic was a real body, and the Jews were the infective agents.

As the Warsaw Ghetto began to be demolished, you had these towerlike objects. They demolished parts of the buildings and let the rest crumble. It's a way of undermining structures — not to go to the trouble of taking down the whole structure, only parts of it. Which is also a metaphor for the entire Holocaust. The Holocaust was not the gassing of 6 million Jews because at least 3 million died in the ghettos from a policy of overcrowding. After the Warsaw Ghetto was razed, everything was gone except the church and the grid of the streets. It was finally vacant, a void. This says as much to me about the Holocaust as anything else: that after you have exterminated a people, you have a void, silence.

When you walk into the courtyard at Block 10 at Auschwitz, you face a blank, black wall — the Killing Wall. To your left is the wall of what was Dr. Mengele's laboratory, where the windows were covered over to let light come in only from the top. Now, clearly, when you see this you wonder why it was done. Was it to keep people from looking in or from looking out? I'm perfectly convinced it was to keep people from looking into the buildings at all the things that were being done. The metaphor of the guard tower was the watching, the overview, the distancing of the persecutors from the prisoners. Everywhere you were being watched.

We have all seen pictures of the special troops. It is hard to put that into anything, except to say that if you lived in a town, and the Germans marched in, you could expect to be rounded up at night, moved, and shot. At Treblinka, the earth heaved for years. Blood seeped through the earth. You can do nothing with that. You can do absolutely nothing with that. You can know it.

Another image that remained in the memory was the triangle. Triangles were different colors. Jews were yellow, priests black, criminals green, homosexuals pink. If you were a Jew and a homosexual, you wore two triangles, one inverted to make the Star of David.

Structures—everything was structured in such a primary way. The aesthetic sensibility managed to inform even the objective of mass murder. Even the horse barns, which were used as barracks, were always built in particular ways with a certain attention to detail.

There are certain methodologies of construction, certain tectonics that begin to be very powerful in the memory of the place, if not of the event. The memory of the place has to stand in lieu of the event. The silence. Also, when you look at this con-

The meticulous construction is intended to reflect the perfectionism of the extermination machinery. Detail of the Hall of Witness.

struction, you see that the sort of modernist attitude toward the showing of structure and the perfection of things is a way of thinking that can also lead to the perfection of a process, but in this case the perfection of the death factory. It was always incomprehensible to me why the places where the most atrocious things happened were so often the most beautiful places. The Germans had a sort of purist aesthetic sensibility. Treblinka was carved out of the birch forest. People came to it thinking it was a transfer station. The only thing that happened at Treblinka was murder.

To me the mass burial was the most terrifying thing of all. Death was one thing. But the exact and precise disintegration of the memory of a people.... There would be no gravestone, no memory left. No memory — other than that the Germans once proposed a museum of artifacts of vanished races.

The showers also had a sort of rational look. They had duckboards. Who would think of putting duckboards into a shower that was really a gas chamber? Who would think of putting in windows? One of the gas chambers was a concrete building placed inside a Tyrolean château that had glass in the windows and lace curtains.

There were many forms of crematoria. If you look at the ovens at Auschwitz, you can see that they are strapped together with steel. Originally they were built out of brick, but the steel strapping was needed because the ovens were so overused that they tended to explode from internal gases. This became one of the more obvious elements that we begin to utilize. The way the memorial is built may never come across to anyone, and it doesn't have to because the whole entourage of the thing is what must come across. But the memory of the way the camps were built stayed with me. As I suppose a doctor would remember what the hospitals were like, so an architect remembers. The addition of heavy steel to a raw wall became for me a very important thing.

It's interesting to speculate on why the Holocaust seems to be the event that dominates the second half of the twentieth century. Hiroshima is one, the Holocaust the other. The twentieth century is supposed to be one of rationality, but here we find that reason doesn't take us very far. So memory is important, letting that memory be sufficiently ambiguous and open-ended so that others can inhabit the space, can imbue the forms with their own memories.

On the Design

To begin with, we were given carte blanche with one exception. The committee that interviewed me said, would you please see if the memorial itself, wherever you put it, could be a hexagonal shape. They clearly wanted it for the most symbolic of reasons. A hexagon is a terrible shape — long in one direction, short in another direction, and yet it doesn't have direction. As you move around it, the short dimension becomes the long dimension. It's rotational, it doesn't stop spatially, but keeps bouncing you. Still, I came to like the hexagonal precisely for its imbalance, for the fact that it could not tie in [see pp. 91, 98].

I am reluctant to talk about the imagery. The problem, of course, is that if you deal with the conceptualization of metaphors you run the risk of the metaphor not being understood in the same way by others. What we have tried to do is to construct symbolic forms that in some cases are very banal, ought to be banal, and in other cases are more abstract and open-ended. People read different things into these forms, but they are not empty. The idiosyncrasies create something to jog the memory. The multiple readings that occur are sometimes intentional, sometimes not. We consciously

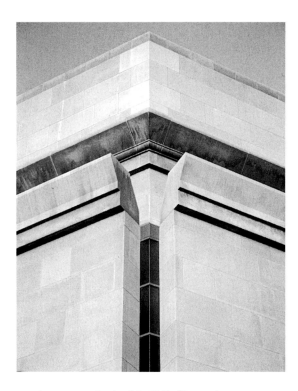

Detail on exterior façade of the Hall of Remembrance.

didn't want to force the one reading that we knew, and we had to have several reasons for doing each thing. Whenever the architecture became too concrete, whenever the metaphor became too insistent, we had to soften. We wanted an evocation of the incomplete. Irresolution, imbalances are built in. For instance, the screen in the front portal is not there to force a reading, but to make evident the need for interpretation [see p. 97]. Things call for interpretation but remain insufficient in themselves. The more you know, the greater the difficulty. This kind of distancing with ambiguity was also important because every survivor has his or her own story that is so personal, so stripping. It is essential that people are left with what separates them more than with what joins them together. We created differences, so that memory must play a part.

Perception, or memory, is the most important thing. Because memory is a charlatan. Everybody I talked to has reconstructed a different memory of the event. I as the architect reconstruct yet another memory that never was, but it can act as a resonator for the memories of others.

I was working with the idea of a visceral memory, visceral as well as visual. I would be very unhappy if it turned out to be entirely visual because then it would be scenographic, and then it would become a display. I came to believe that certain abstract monuments have the power to move us when we are very much immersed in an abstraction. For example, that remarkable museum, the Danteum, done in the thirties. The problem with that project is that unless you have very specialized knowledge, you don't understand it. It is very cerebral. And I don't believe that you could ever understand the Holocaust with the mind. You have to feel it. Feeling may be a better way of getting at it because horror is not an intellectual category as far as I can tell. But I did not want to make it a visual building. I wanted to make it abstractly symbolic. I was not interested in resuscitating the forms of the Holocaust.

I did want to use everything that was possible in the building, for instance, acoustics. When you walked out of Washington, I wanted to separate you from the city formally and spatially; but before you stepped into the Hall of Witness [see pp. 90-92], I also felt that you had to go through an acoustical change, a disturbance like a drumbeat. Something to tell you that you are coming to this place, to make you pay attention.

I believe that architecture can do a lot, particularly if you are not absolutely overwhelmed by the need to come to closure, if you start at the end, with irresolution as a positive thing. Now I gave up all hope of doing a modern building, something that would work in that context. First of all, I wouldn't have gotten it past the city. As a matter of fact, the Fine Arts Commission tried to get us to go in a far more neoclassical direction, which I did not want to do.

From the sky, or from the Washington Monument, the building begins to look like a ratchet, like teeth about to close on you [plate 27]. There is the brick, the large scale, and then the sort of more intimate gnashing teeth, and then the simple wall that edges the wall of the neoclassical building. Neoclassicism joined to Victorianism by a gnashing of teeth.

There was always the problem of the use of classical language, in relation to the Nazi appropriation of monumental classicism. I think that I've got a critique of neoclassicism in this building. Rather than appropriation, it is classicism used as a tool of critical dialogue, a tool for expressing duality. This building is decisively meant to put you in a deceptive frame of mind, to separate you from Washington. It does not synthesize. The Hall of Witness, the Hall of Remembrance, the theater—each is a deliberate injection of another attitude. There is no cohesive theory but instead a variety of spaces held together by a mucilage. The objective was to make it cohere without being explicit, without being one thing. I wanted accident to come in because accident is part of the Holocaust.

In front, on Fourteenth Street, there is a sort of neoclassical screen that is a pure façade, a pure fake, because it is open to the sky [see below]. We had to have a big plaza, an open space in the front where people would gather, schoolchildren would come. And it is such an awful street that setting the building back seemed the wrong idea, so we screened it. The screen is there as a façade like all the government buildings, but at the same time it's a lie. You pass through the limestone screen to enter a concrete world. We disorient you, shifting and recentering you three times, to separate you emotionally as well as visually from Washington.

The attempt was always to disengage from Washington. Yet the building had to be part of Washington urbanistically, otherwise we would never have gotten it approved. You could say it should have been a chasm in the earth, but that was not in the cards. It's a big building, 250,000 square feet, with two theaters, a library, an archive, a conference center, administrative offices, and a permanent exhibition space of about 40,000 square feet.

The beginning of the experience varies. On Fourteenth Street there are two main entries, separated by a kiosk. Busloads enter to the right, individuals to the left. We made the two entries different. Visitors will experience a selection, a segregation of movement, arbitrary if you will, not a life and death situation, but a selection. We always deal in dualities: dark and light, transparency and opacity. Everywhere there are two options: down or up, left or right.

If you enter to the left, you penetrate the screen to go in through a little pavilion that also has a screen in front of it, then through a door in to the Hall of Witness. You cross a canopied area and step out onto a hollow steel deck. You are now in a raw steel structure, without cover or enclosing planes, except that the walls have panels of glass. These panels are the Wall of Nations, where every nation that suffered deaths is identified by a panel of glass. The walls are transparent witnesses. This structure orients you to the elevators, or lets you go out to the temporary exhibits, or to the stairs. There is a slot in the floor where it is broken and the grid shifts. This is perhaps banal,

Main entrance on 14th Street.

A system of bridges connects the library and research institute on the upper floor. Here a view from below where visitors cross a bridge with the first names of victims etched into the glass windows.

Interior of the Hall of Remembrance, a place for silence and meditation. Large rectangular niches in its six walls hold candles lit by visitors.

but it is important for two reasons. One is that it allows light downstairs. The other is that it separates the experience of going into and out of museums from the experience of the content of the building.

The skylight over the Hall of Witness cuts diagonally across the hall because that is the path of travel. We did this to disengage you, to move you diagonally across the space. If you think of it, it becomes apparent that such a skylight would be twisted — twisted by the geometry, but also by the force of the logic that sends you diagonally across, the tension of the diagonal splitting the space in two.

At the fifth floor, open only to scholars, bridges cross the skylight to the library and the archive. The elevators take the public to the fourth level, to the entrance of the exhibits. Here you come across a bridge with a glass-block floor, a dangerous path. You are walking on air, while from below people see ghosts crossing overhead. There is an abort stair, so if it is too unpleasant kids can go out, to an area that is more pleasant. But if you continue, it becomes increasingly dense and constricted. Then you descend to the third floor, overlooking a high, two-story space. You go around again and cross another bridge that is opaque on the outside and translucent on the inside, except for special windows.

From the third floor you come down another way, under a slot of light. This is the "death march," where the experience becomes more brutal; the stairs are steel, the slot is very narrow, movement is very constricted. Then you enter a one-story space and pass through to the end of the exhibit where you see a high, lit space and an open door that takes you into the Hall of Remembrance. When you leave the hall, you enter a gallery and then descend the stairs out again. This gallery is important because it both connects and separates the Hall of Remembrance from the Hall of Learning.

The corners of the Hall of Remembrance are broken away so that the walls become freestanding plaques or tablets. It is never understood as a closed form. The cracks at the corners become skylights in the ambulatory. Here some of the memories of the synagogue in Poland came through. The ambulatory has niches in the walls where people may light memorial candles. When you turn around to face the center, you see broad steps for seating that go down to the empty central chamber. For the floor we used verde antica marble, a stone that is by nature cracked, disintegrating in

an unpredictable fashion. The roof is fragmented, skylit with a structure that diffuses light everywhere but at the flattened center, where it is left open; from here the sun sends a moving finger of light into the space, tracing the configuration of its rotational path. The perception of sky within the Hall of Remembrance differs greatly from that in the Hall of Witness. The Hall of Witness is like a camp; people are walking above you, you are always being observed, but you can't see who observes you because they are hidden behind screens. The Hall of Remembrance, by contrast, is a place for contemplation, a quiet place.

We had to give up the idea of bricked-in windows. We substituted a recess, a classical recess done in a classical manner, to clash with the coursing of the stone. It's as if you were trying to remember a window but you could not quite place it so you indented the stone, without any classical attention to detail, except to make sure that the joints conflicted at the indentation. What looks like a window is, in fact, not a window.

Section through the hexagonal Hall of Remembrance, reminiscent of Polish wooden synagogues.

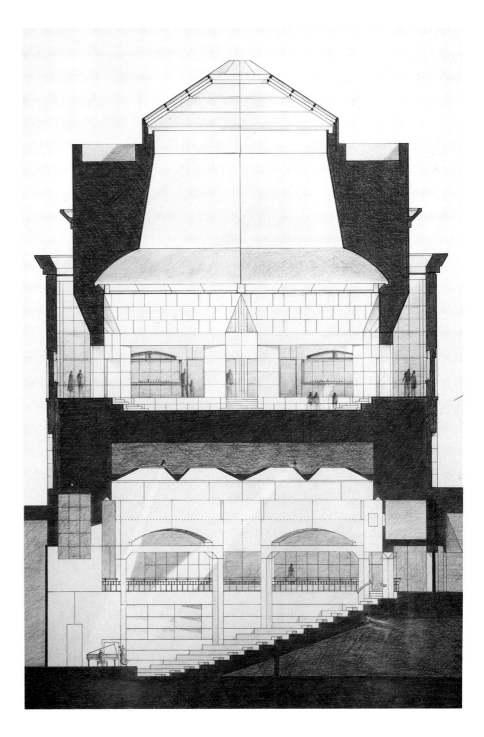

The crack in the granite wall is, again, a bit banal. I'm bothered by the literality, but I think we have to go through with it. We intend to take hammers and go at it with them. I don't want to make a drawing. I want to go ahead and smash it.

When you enter the temporary exhibits on the main level, you have to cross a little bridge. The doorways are gates: screens stand not in, but in front of, the doorway, so you have a chance to reconsider whether you want to enter the building. The freestanding gate, backlit, becomes a ghostly, shimmering object. The railing is detailed with strapping the same way that the gate is strapped, so that one flows into the other.

As to the language, we would always only use an angle: primary angle construction, where everything, bracing, bridges, trusswork is built up of double angles. We encountered a problem when people working on the project began to understand and use the language to make poetry of their own. They made things that were too pretty, too resolved.

As far as the actual form is concerned, nowhere in the imagery of the Holocaust is there crisscrossed strapping such as we have used. But it speaks of the Holocaust. I don't know why. Now, some things were deliberate appropriations, in thought, not in fact. For example, the logical angle construction with which the oven doors were attached was a kind of perversion of a Miesian idea. That struck me as one of the most obvious points of departure. Without copying, taking the rationalism of the modern movement, in a way that as you have steel inside, you still have to have steel outside, as a sort of symbolic cover. You've made a reading as it should be, not as it is. That is actually highly irrational.

I'm a very rational person. All my life I've done rational stuff. I've accepted that. But reason doesn't work here. For instance, at one point I was thinking of hats. The SS hat is soaring with power; it has a skull and crossbones, it has a visor that does not shade the eyes, but draws a line across the face. It is one of the most intimidating hats that I have ever seen. There is also the hat that the cantor wears, during the Days of Atonement, a hat that speaks volumes, a bulging thing, with the purity of nakedness. At one point, I realized that the entry on Fourteenth Street was really like an SS hat. We had not meant it to be, but it had a surging power as if the screen were breaking away, a kind of swelling. This was too much for the Fine Arts Commission. The top of the memorial was like a hat too, an open cantorial hat. I changed that also, but it's interesting to me what happens to you.

The danger always existed of making the images too heroic, too monumental, too beautiful. We've tried to level that tendency by not resolving things. But it's very hard not to do what architects always do: you start with a concept, you work your way into it, then you try to solve problems that should not be solved. I go around and take things away from people in the office who are trying to resolve them. I don't want this building to look too worked over. I want it to be a little raw still. Not just in the materials but in the conceptualization and even in the actualization.

You could make an argument that this is not the way to do a building like this. I've thought very hard about other ways. One is to use an existing building, a found building, which is the case with ninety-five percent of the museums like this. If it's a found building, the building itself resonates. Another way is a perfectly neutral building, so neutral that your teeth ache over it. Just nothing. If it could be done. The third way, which is what many people do, is to make a black box and let the exhibits carry all the weight. The fourth way, which I chose, is to see if you can do something that deals very directly with the emotions. Now, who's going to see this museum? People who don't even know what the Holocaust is.

Intrinsically, the intentions are all greater than the reality. It is not meant to be an architectural walk, or a walk through memory, or an exposition of emotion, but all of this. I want to leave it open as a resonator of emotions. Odd or quiet is not enough. It must be intestinal, visceral; it must take you in its grip. This is an indeterminate thing to do, and we are not saying that we are using architecture to do it.

Editor's note: This essay is based on a series of interviews with architect James Ingo Freed conducted by the editors of *Assemblage* during the winter of 1988-89. Since it first appeared (*Assemblage* 9 [1989]: 59-73), the concept and design of the U.S. Holocaust Memorial Museum, adjacent to the National Mall in Washington, D.C., continued to evolve until the Museum's dedication in April 1993. Reprinted by permission of MIT Press Journals.

Nathan Rapoport

Memoir of the
Warsaw Ghetto Monument

Nathan Rapoport's *Warsaw Ghetto Monument*, constructed in 1948 in commemoration of the Warsaw Ghetto Uprising in 1943. The bronze relief depicts the heroism of the resistance fighters.

September 7, 1939, was a turning point in our lives. On that day, the Polish Army was defeated, the soldiers fleeing before the Nazis, leaving the inhabitants defenseless. We, the Jewish people, were particularly filled with fear and terror. Hearing the announcement that the army was regrouping and reorganizing, I resolved to find them and to fight the Germans. I parted from my family and started to walk east expecting to find the army close to Warsaw, but I never found them. Instead, I found roads full of refugees fleeing in panic. My search took over one month. I walked almost 400 kilometers without success. By then my feet were bloody and sore, and I was tired and discouraged. That is how I arrived in Bialystock, which was already in the hands of the Russian Army.

The Russians treated me kindly when they learned I was a sculptor. I found myself in a group of 120 artists who had also made their way there from Warsaw. In this group were painters, writers, musicians, and sculptors, many of them old friends of mine. I was chosen to become one of their art executives. I also succeeded in sending a message to my wife telling her that I was alive and where I was. I received an answer, my clothes, and the most important thing, my portfolio with photos of my work, including the correspondence and prize I won in the competition sponsored by the newspaper *Humanité*. At that time, a government art delegation visited the city. I showed them my work. They were very impressed, and the director of the Tretiakowskia Museum in Moscow took my portfolio with him. A short time later, I was invited to Minsk, the capital of Belorussia, where I could have much better facilities as a sculptor. I went gladly, happy at the prospect of getting back to work.

Meanwhile, my wife joined me in Minsk after she had succeeded in crossing the border. Soon after we left Minsk, Bialystock fell to the Nazis. I never saw the 120 artists who remained there again. I was the only artist who survived.

In Minsk, the Russians treated me very well. They offered me a studio outside the city that I would share with another artist named Brezer who was well known but had the bad luck of being preoccupied for more than a year with a statue of Stalin, which the committee did not accept. As a result, his studio was almost empty.

Now I started to work again, but this time everything was different. The world I came from existed no more. Fear and insecurity based on dreadful rumors which arrived from conquered territories changed my whole attitude. I began to search for a new means of expression which would be strong enough to express the events. I understood that it would be almost impossible to create a form which would show the determination of human nature and its evil consequences. I had to find one, so I decided on a large group which might perhaps give a symbolic expression of a whole nation in chaos.

I had many problems to overcome, not only artistic; among them was how to make a living. We were almost starving, but in spite of everything, I finished the model and presented it to the art council which was preparing a show of ten years of art in White Russia to be shown in Moscow. It made an immense impact on them and was accepted unanimously. . . .

In June 1941 the war between Russia and Germany started. Minsk was attacked, and once more I had to run away, this time with my wife and our little daughter, Nina, who was only four months old. I also had my younger brother with me whom, after great effort and thanks to Kulagin's influence, I succeeded in having released from prison. At that time, Russia was in need of fighters and workers, and thousands of people were transported from one place to another by train, no matter how far the distance. Not only people were transported, but whole factories were reconstructed in open fields as far as possible from the frontier. The trains were overloaded and

103

The monument, shortly after its unveiling in 1948, on the site of the destroyed Warsaw Ghetto.

overcrowded. Our trip took us more than six weeks. We did not have food, and my wife, who was starving, could not nurse our baby. All we could get was boiling water at train stations, a custom in Russia. Finally, we arrived at our stop, a border city near Iran, Alma Ata. We thought that we might be able to cross the border and try to get to Israel. But, as it happened, Alma Ata became our home for nearly two years....

I was suddenly taken by the Russians to a military labor camp in Novosibirsk. The Russians, because of their great need for workers, took all the refugees. My wife and child remained in Alma Ata. The conditions in the labor camp were impossible. It was winter in Siberia. There were no warm clothes, very little food, and what little we had was bad. We lived in huge damp barracks frozen even on the inside. We worked for many hours, mostly at night, loading and unloading trains of supplies so they could depart the next day for the battlefields. We also built constructions for the army. We were treated as prisoners of war.

One day, when I was sent to work in town, I learned that Kulagin [one of the sculptor's sponsors in Minsk] was now the governor of Novosibirsk. I was miserable.

The monument as it appears today showing the former Ghetto redeveloped with apartment blocks.

Early clay model for the monument, 1945-46. Original lost.

The granite relief on the back of the memorial shows a procession of deportees, symbolizing the martyrs of the Uprising.

Earliest model for the monument with only two figures, a Moses-inspired prophet and a figure in the guise of Liberty, Novosibirsk, 1943. The sculptor later renounced the style of the model as "too romantic." Original lost.

I had to communicate with him. Perhaps he might help me. But how to get word to him. It was extremely difficult, as I was in the labor camp and had no papers, nor could I walk in the streets. But somehow I managed to call his secretary who was astonished when she heard my voice, recognized me, and was willing to help. I asked to see Kulagin. Because of my lack of papers, the meeting was arranged for late at night. I arrived at Kulagin's office at two o'clock, and I was brought right in to see him, passing his heavy bodyguards only by telling them my name. As he looked at me, I could tell that my appearance shocked him. Kulagin released me from the labor camp. He also gave me a room in a hotel and a studio in the opera house to work in. I was given permission to bring my wife and child, too. His intention was that around me he would organize groups of artists who would create art . . . .

The cultural life in Novosibirsk was very exciting. The people who had established the city were once publicly exiled and sent by the Czar to Siberia. Basically, they were the educated and cultured people of Russia, the intellectuals. As the Germans were advancing into the country, many artists from cultural centers were moved there. The newcomers were poets, writers, actors, and politicians, many of whose

busts I made, and I enjoyed doing it. Once I was asked by the government to make a head of the best coal miner. In no time, every worker in the mine was competing in his work for the privilege of having his bust sculpted. The busts were sent to museums in Russia.

In the year 1942, dreadful rumors began to reach us which were not formally announced or confirmed but were brought by refugees who had succeeded in escaping. Some news was also obtained through the Jewish Anti-Fascist Committee from Michaels and Feffer, both well-known writers who were later killed during Stalin's purge against Jewish writers and actors.

Restless, I started to work to express my feelings of pain, anger, and sorrow. In the beginning, while the whole tragedy was not yet known, the model had a vague romantic form. But the more I heard about the camps and the ghettos, the more I understood the terrible acts of the Nazis, the more I searched for a means adequate to commemorate the tragedy of my people. I had to change the aspect of my model until I could get the compactness and strength I was looking for. I changed the model, constantly influenced by every rumor, but I felt I had to learn the truth. That is why I decided to go to Moscow.

I arrived there carrying a small plaster model, the first form of the Warsaw monument to come (plate 3). My wife and child came later. In Moscow I met Ber Mark, the Jewish historian and journalist, also a refugee, who told me about the epic uprising of the Jewish people against the German army in the Warsaw Ghetto. I started, once again, a sculptor spurred on by this event. This model also changed continuously. Only when the terrible news arrived that the Nazis had finally burned the Ghetto did I complete the model, trying to describe the horrors and the resistance . . . .

One can imagine how difficult it was to plan a work of such emotional impact. The site in Warsaw was a wilderness; therefore, I decided to build a wall as a support and as a symbol of the vanished Ghetto. The front relief in bronze is dedicated to the Uprising; the rear in granite represents the deportation.

The artistic climate, at that time, was predominantly abstract. That was very strong and fashionable. In spite of this, I felt that I would not be true to myself if I went in that direction. We were for life. We hold the tree of life. My purpose was to

Jewish visitors in silent prayer at the monument.

give back, at least spiritually, what had been taken away by deadly destruction. My task was to recreate shadows of mothers and fathers, young and old; the epic and tragic end of their lives should be remembered for generations to come. Thirty years have passed, and the monument stands well in time.

The front wall piece was cast in bronze and shipped by boat from France to Poland, for the political climate was changing and we were afraid that the sculpture would be held in Berlin or even disappear there. The second wall piece had been prepared in granite by carvers in Warsaw. When I went there, I finished it within two weeks.

April 19, 1948, marked the day of the fifth anniversary of the Jewish Uprising in the Warsaw Ghetto, the first civilian armed resistance against the Nazis in Europe. On the very site of the headquarters where the Uprising by the Jewish fighters against their persecutors erupted, my monument was erected in commemoration of that historic, tragic event and of the deportation of the Jewish people to the death camps.

Official ceremony at the unveiling of the monument in 1948.

On that day in 1948 thousands of people were gathered for the unveiling of the monument. Among them were survivors of the Holocaust, Jewish delegations from all over the world, and representatives of the Polish government.

As we stood on the ashes of the Ghetto, fragments of burned pages of Jewish prayer books fluttered in the air around us; a profound silence prevailed. On a temporary altar, the Rabbi chanted mournful prayers for the martyrs. The *Menoroth* on the monument were aglow with flames. People were crying....

On the next day, I left Poland for France.

A wreath inscribed "We are your children" in Hebrew, Yiddish, and Polish is laid annually by young Polish Jews at the foot of the *Warsaw Ghetto Monument*.

Editor's note: Before his death in 1987, sculptor Nathan Rapoport had begun to write a memoir recording his own version of the events surrounding his many memorial commissions. This excerpt on his best-known memorial, the *Warsaw Ghetto Monument*, is taken from his memoir and appears here for the first time.

The Holocaust in
National Memorial Traditions

Claudia Koonz

Germany's Buchenwald
Whose Shrine? Whose Memory?

During my visit to Buchenwald in April 1991, as the city bus climbed the hill from Weimar to the camp, I prepared myself for the contradictions I had experienced at Auschwitz, a memorial to unspeakable cruelty, crowded with tourists, sausage stands, and ice cream vendors. When the bus driver called out "Buchenwald," I came upon a sight that in some ways was even more unnerving than the boisterous atmosphere at Auschwitz: a vast, deserted parking lot, empty buildings, overgrown lawns, and a "closed" sign on the canteen. I explored the grounds for the rest of the afternoon and encountered only one guide and a half dozen tourists. This memorial, built to accommodate hundreds of visitors per day, had fallen into disuse.

Between 1937 and 1945, the Nazis dispatched over 250,000 prisoners to Buchenwald. Over 60,000 victims perished in Buchenwald and its satellites, and untold thousands were transported from there to Auschwitz and the death camps in Poland. In the 1960s the Buchenwald central camp became the major East German memorial to the victims of Hitler's regime, and over 11 million people had visited the site. Normally, a staff of sixty-three managed the crowds of visitors, and a bookstore sold historical publications about the camp in all major European languages. Yet during my visit, the grounds were virtually empty. When I returned to the bus stop at sunset, the mystery deepened. The parking lot behind the Buchenwald Guest House was crammed with Volkswagens and Opels, a "no vacancy" sign hung on the door, and the bar was crowded. No one I spoke to displayed the slightest interest in the historical significance of the small hotel (a former SS officers' residence). The clientele, it turned out, were businessmen who appreciated the low prices, good food, convenient gas station, and clean air.

"What about the concentration camp memorial?" I asked at dinner.

A guest looked at me, amazed. "Who would ever go to such a gloomy place?"

Another chimed in, "This stuff is all bogus anyway."

"What do we care about the Poles and Ruskies who died here? As far as I am concerned," declared a traveling salesman, "a few more German Communists could have died and I wouldn't feel sorry either."

"What about the Jews who died here?" I inquired.

"Oh, you mean that talk about the Holocaust? All that is Wessi [slang for West German] history. It has nothing to do with us," answered a used-car dealer.

These casual remarks touched the surface of deep divisions that had not yet been bridged in the newly unified Germany. Civic identity in any nation emerges from a shared sense of purpose and a common heritage. In Germany, postwar national identity developed on a negation. Politicians in the East and West erected what Paul Connerton called a "memory wall" against Nazism and claimed that their nations started fresh, at "zero hour" *(Stunde Null)*.[1] The similarity stopped there, however. Not even a shared vocabulary emerged to describe the years between 1933 and 1945. In the Federal Republic (FRG, or West Germany), people used the words *Diktatur, Gewaltherrschaft*, or *Hitler-Staat*, while in the Democratic Republic (GDR, or East Germany), fascism became the standard term. Further complicating the process of identity formation in both Germanys was a second negation: the governments in each German state anchored the national purpose in opposition to that of the other. The General Secretary of the Communist party (SED) Walter Ulbricht railed against the "Fascist stooges" in Bonn, while Chancellor Konrad Adenauer denounced the "totalitarian Communists" in the GDR. Each side accused the other of having perpetuated the worst features of Nazism.

As Germans work to stitch together a common identity, deep conflicts about their history emerge. Nowhere are the difficulties more dramatic than at Buchen-

Fritz Cremer's bronze group *Revolt of the Prisoners* in front of the Buchenwald concentration camp clock tower, 1958.

Buchenwald concentration camp near Weimar, Germany. Signposts direct visitors to history and art exhibitions.

wald, where the Communist GDR government transformed the terrain of mass murder into a celebration of antifascism. For residents of the former GDR, therefore, the concentration camps appear as extensions of the Communist rhetoric that permeated textbooks, leaders' speeches, films, and novels. All the victims were celebrated as "anti-Fascist resistance fighters," which obliterated Jews, religious dissidents, and "unwanted" racial minorities from public memory. The government disavowed any connection with the Nazi past and never offered reparations to Jewish victims, at least not until the short-lived Modrow government in early 1990.[2]

Unlike the Communist leaders in the East, the conservative West German politicians forgot Nazi criminals and even welcomed many former Nazis into influential positions during the late 1940s and 1950s. But, at the same time, the Adenauer government accepted responsibility for Hitler's racial war and agreed in 1952 to pay reparations to Jews who suffered under Nazism. Despite the lack of public support (polls showed that only 11 percent of all West Germans approved the act), the legislature ratified the agreement. Their action transformed Germany from a "moral leper" into a responsible member of the Western military alliance.[3] Tolerating former Nazis in high office, while simultaneously compensating victims of Nazi racial policies, the Adenauer government put the past to rest.

But painful memories broke through public amnesia in the 1960s with the widespread popularity of Anne Frank's diary, the trials of Auschwitz guards in Frankfurt and Eichmann in Jerusalem, and the performance of controversial dramas by Rolf Hochhuth and Peter Weiss. Student protesters demanded that their elders admit their responsibility for Nazi crimes and that victims be commemorated. In 1972 Social Democratic Chancellor Willy Brandt knelt at the memorial to the Warsaw Ghetto Uprising and began a new era of official remembering. During the 1980s, President Richard von Weizsäcker called on all Germans to atone for Nazi racial crimes. Official mourning for Jewish victims of Nazism became so important that when the President of the Bundestag, Philipp Jenninger, delivered a speech many considered inappropriate for the fiftieth anniversary of the *Kristallnacht*, November 9-10, 1938, public outrage abruptly ended his career.[4]

Since the late 1970s and 1980s, a veritable culture of commemoration has inspired cities and towns to erect monuments, to invite former residents who fled Nazi persecution for goodwill visits, to maintain Jewish cemeteries, and to educate children

On the site of the ruins, bricks outline the locations of the long-destroyed camp barracks. Goethe's oak in the foreground.

1   Paul Connerton, *How Societies Remember* (Cambridge: Cambridge University Press, 1989), p. 7.

2   A few Jewish Socialists returned to live in the GDR and received public recognition as well as material aid in reestablishing themselves. John Borneman, Martin Patek, and Jeffrey Peck are currently making a film to document their experiences called *Dies ist auch mein Land*. The parallels between Austrian and GDR pasts are worth noting. Both states offered to pay reparations beginning only in early 1990. In Austria, the museum in Mauthausen virtually ignores genocide, and official literature describes Austrians as Hitler's first victims. Since the late 1980s, however, the guides and pamphlets have reflected a change.

3   Anson Rabinbach, "The Jewish Question in the German Question," *New German Critique* 44 (Spring-Summer 1988): 165-66. Lilly Gardner-Feldman, *The Special Relationship between West Germany and Israel* (Boston: Allen and Unwin, 1984).

4   Elisabeth Domansky, "'Kristallnacht', the Holocaust and German Unity: The Meaning of November 9 as an Anniversary in Germany," *History and Memory. Studies in Representation of the Past* 4 (Spring-Summer 1992): 60–87. In November 1992 a member of the city council of the former East German city of Rostock was forced to resign because of his tactless comments to a representative of the Jewish community.

5   Judith Miller, *One, by One, by One: Facing the Holocaust* (New York: Simon and Schuster, 1990), pp. 13–60.

about Judaism.[5] The Federal German Tourist Board published a brochure called *Germany for the Jewish Traveler*. The work of a Jewish-Christian friendship society *(Aktion Sühnezeichen)* is considered so important that conscientious objectors who refuse military service may fulfill their alternative service requirement by working for it. Leaders routinely have marked the fortieth and fiftieth anniversary dates of Nazi crimes, promising "Never Again."

In the GDR, by contrast, the anniversaries of so-called liberation by Soviet troops received great fanfare. Leaders presented themselves as the heirs to the anti-Fascist tradition that, in turn, became the raison d'être of the GDR. At Buchenwald itself, the monuments erected by the Communist party overwhelm the actual site of the concentration camp. Atop the wooded hill stands a veritable shrine to antifascism, including a bell tower, spacious processional aisles, quiet places for meditation, imposing sculpture, and commemorations of heroic martyrs. Beyond the massive entrance gate lies the majestic Stelae Way. Bas-reliefs on the front of the immense stelae depict the camp prisoners' suffering, and terse inspirational poems on the reverse sides pay homage to their courage. Visitors pass three circular mass graves as they walk along another wide avenue, the Street of all Nations, which is flanked by eighteen towering pylons capped by shallow bowls in which flames were lit during special celebrations. Passing the last of the circular grave memorials, visitors turn into the Street of Freedom. The rectangular 150-foot-high bell tower looms ahead and faces out over the peaceful fields far below. Its inscription reads: "The destruction of Nazism with its roots is our rallying cry. The building of a new world of peace and freedom is our goal." Just in front of the bell monument, there are eleven bronze statues of gaunt men in defiant postures. As I wandered alone through the deserted monuments, I felt the eerie affinity between the outsized scale embodied here and in Albert Speer's models for Nazi Berlin. What would become of the tons of concrete and granite in this shrine? Would it be bulldozed as inappropriate or preserved as a memory of GDR antifascism?

I continued on to the museum, where I learned the historical details of the "glorious struggle" against fascism. The carefully presented collection displayed prisoners' bunks, uniforms, eating utensils, and work tools juxtaposed with the instruments used by camp guards to torture, humiliate, and murder. Weapons of resistance, such as a secret radio transmitter, texts of forbidden songs, and handmade grenades,

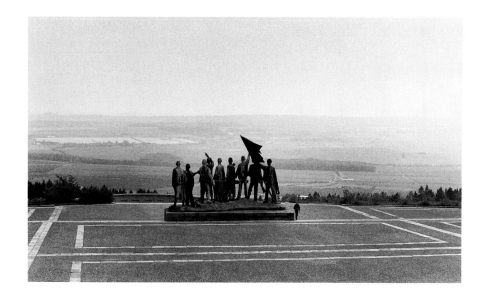

Fritz Cremer's *Revolt of the Prisoners*, 1958. The view into the distance shows the German countryside near Weimar.

attested to the prisoners' fighting spirit. Two separate buildings heightened the perpetrators' cruelty. The former "hospital" preserved the equipment used in medical experiments as well as the shrunken heads and lampshades made with tattooed human skin. A permanent exhibition of prisoners' art work deepened viewers' respect for the victims' humanity even in this wretched place.[6]

But empathy was interrupted, at least for me, by the texts which, at the time of my visit, still accompanied every segment of the camp museum.[7] In wooden, dogmatic language, a single message crowded out complexity. Capitalists and their Fascist henchmen waged a war of aggression against workers everywhere. In the museum texts, all victims, regardless of national origin, religion, or reason for deportation, became "anti-Fascist fighters." GDR Ministerpräsident Otto Grotewohl laid down the orthodoxy at the dedication of the camp in 1958, and it had not changed during the next three decades: "We bow in love and admiration before the dead heroes of the Anti-Fascist Resistance Struggle, before the millions of victims of Fascist barbarism. Their idea is alive; it is resurrected out of war, misery, and ruins. Like a seed which has fallen into fertile soil, it has sunk its roots deep into the hearts of the people." Grotewohl called on East Germans to continue the struggle against "the old Fascist system in West Germany which has been made acceptable again."[8]

A photomontage in the museum featured "Capitalists" (Thyssen and Krupp) pulling the strings of their puppets Hitler, Himmler, and the camp commandant. A wall-sized chart documented the profit motive that caused the mass murder by breaking down the surplus value produced by each prisoner: industrialists paid 6 marks per day to the SS per slave laborer; it cost 60 pfennigs to feed him, and each worker subsisted for an average of nine months before dying. "Yes," said the guide, "the same length of time as it takes to produce an infant." The money and valuables stolen upon arrival together with the corpse's dental gold, hair, and ashes completed the profit side of the ledger. "Rational utilization" netted 1,631 marks per head.[9] Graphics on the museum walls identified victims only by red triangles (the Nazis' symbol for political criminals) and national origin.[10] As visitors left the museum, they read the ex-prisoners' exhortation: "Remember that the German anti-Fascists were the first victims of the Nazi concentration camp, that they worked together with international anti-Fascists to liberate the camp and in so doing became the founders of a Nazi-free, democratic Germany."[11] Photo murals near the exit of the museum glorified the Soviet-led troops for liberating Buchenwald, without mentioning the role of the U.S. Third Army under General George Patton.

The narrative at Buchenwald, like those at Ravensbrück and Sachsenhausen, the other major camp memorials in the former GDR, was mandated by a government commission appointed in 1955. Their most urgent goal was to make the connection between "fascism and NATO capitalism."

Visitors to the museum could view a well-made film that concluded with the image of a mushroom-shaped cloud. "Capitalist warmongers" had used nuclear weapons before and might do so again. "Never Again!" admonished the solemn voice, while the Buchenwald bell tolled in the background. Before 1945, the Nazis destroyed world peace. Later, Adenauer's Germany, backed by "Western Imperialists" threatened war. Thus, the moral of Buchenwald was not "never again" to racism, genocide, and political terror as much as "never forget" the destructive power of "international Fascist capitalism."

There was no room for the Holocaust in this memory. Buchenwald, the shrine and museum, was built to anchor the GDR in the anti-Fascist heritage of the Communist resistance against National Socialism. Although thousands of women had to

The Buchenwald Museum, dedicated in 1958, was meant to extol Communist anti-Fascists. Here, the monumental Street of all Nations with eighteen pylons dedicated to Warsaw Pact states. The architects were Ludwig Deiters, Hans Grotewohl, Horst Kutzat, Karl Tausendschön, Hugo Namslauer, and Hubert Mathas.

work in the Buchenwald satellite slave-labor camps, the statues, photos, and memorials omitted any mention of female victims. Neither Jews, Gypsies, religious dissenters, nor the socially "unfit" figured in public memory.[12] Buchenwald commemorated only "anti-Fascists," i.e., the Communist men who founded the GDR.

Suddenly, in November 1989, the political wall separating Germans disappeared. Buchenwald, long perceived by non-Communists as the very "bastion *(Hochburg)* of communism," became the center of controversy. Residents used their new freedoms in their letters to the editor of local newspapers. Christel Holz, who lived nearby, vented the resentment she had felt for years every time she passed the Ernst Thälmann monument on her daily walk to work. "I don't think that all Buchenwald prisoners and victims agreed with Socialist views. They could not have approved of the acts praised by the SED Communist dictatorship." To commemorate the thousands who died with slogans that betrayed their beliefs mocked their suffering.[13]

Besides resentment engendered by specifically Communist forms of commemoration, people who live near the GDR camps could now, after German reunification, for the first time publicly oppose any monument in order to protect the region's

6 The exhibit will probably be redone in 1995, and eventually the entire memorial will be changed.
7 For a discussion of the exhibit, see also Christa Piotrowski, "Dem 'Schwur vom Buchenwald' verpflichtet. DDR Ausstellung in Gropius-Bau," *Der Tagesspiegel* [Berlin], April 12, 1990.
8 *Buchenwald mahnt. Rede des Ministerpräsidenten Otto Grotewohl zur Weihe der Nationalen Mahn- und Gedenkstätte Buchenwald am 14. September 1958* (Weimar: Volksverlag, 1961), pp. 7, 8, 13.
9 Text copied from the museum graph.
10 Later, new exhibits included yellow triangles (Jews), purple triangles (Jehovah's Witnesses), and even one small pink triangle (for homosexuals).
11 Nationale Mahn- und Gedenkstätte Buchenwald, ed., *Konzentrationslager Buchenwald*, catalogue for exhibition in the Gropius-Bau, Berlin, April-June 1990, p. 165.
12 A few historians, such as Kurt Pätzold, for example, had begun to inquire into genocide as a separate phenomenon from capitalism; see Pätzold und Runge, *Pogromnacht 1938*. A collection of essays published only weeks before the demise of Honecker's government, however, *Erbe und Tradition in der DDR. Die Diskussion der Historiker* (Cologne: Pahl-Rugenstein, 1989), illustrated just how unchanged official history had remained.
13 "Leserpost. Ärgernis," *Thüringer Landeszeitung* (hereafter *TLZ*), May 22, 1991.

reputation — concerns that had blocked the memorials at Dachau and other West German camps over twenty years earlier. Along the roads through the rolling fields and forests near Weimar, the former government erected large plaques with red triangles and black lettering to mark the routes of the death marches ordered by the Nazis in the very last months of the war. Because the former Soviet barracks just outside the Buchenwald grounds were about to be converted into housing for the elderly, Weimar residents demanded the removal of the signs, which, they said, would remind older people of death whenever they went for a walk.[14] But others are now demanding more than just the removal of Communist-inspired memories of Nazism.

From abroad come hopes that Jewish and other victims of racial hatred will be added to the commemorative markers and museum exhibits. On *Yom Hashoah* in 1991, survivors from Western Europe arranged a memorial ceremony at the small stone honoring the 600 Jewish men deported to Buchenwald after the *Kristallnacht*, November 9-10, 1938.[15] Just before noon, a few visitors gathered on the breezy hilltop at the entrance to Buchenwald. Passing through the cast-iron gate, we shuddered at its message, "To Each His Own" *(Jedem das Seine)*. One of the group was a former inmate who had come from Holland. Others were journalists and cameramen. Six were staff members of the museum. The assistant acting museum director, Berndt Gempe, delivered a eulogy for the Jews who had died there. A staff member read a poem by Gertrud Kolmar, a Jewish writer. We silently placed pebbles on the memorial stone and dispersed. This simple ceremony, I thought, might have represented a welcome departure from the skewed historical vision embodied in the Buchenwald camp. But no Weimar citizen cared enough to take the six-kilometer bus trip. Perhaps years of lavish commemoration ceremonies by Communist party leaders on Liberation Day, April 11, had now made them apathetic to all other events at the camp.[16]

Speaking to some Weimar residents in April 1991, I learned that, far from ignoring Buchenwald, a powerful civic action group wanted to commemorate the suffering of an entirely different group of martyrs. Between 1945 and 1950, apart from being a prison for members of the NSDAP or the SS, Buchenwald was used as a camp for the opponents of the Soviet Occupation Forces and for those who committed minor offenses as well. This lobby, led by the Reverend Erich Kranz, insisted on the dismissal of the entire Buchenwald staff for the crime of "falsifying history." Under pressure, the director resigned in early 1990. His West German replacement was terminated

An early memorial at Buchenwald honored Ernst Thälmann, German Communist leader, who was murdered by the Nazis and became an East German martyr. After German reunification, the memorial was dismantled.

Entrance to the Buchenwald Museum. A sign notes the internment of Soviet prisoners of war in concentration camps by the "Hitler Fascists" and identifies a reconstruction of a stable where 8,483 Soviet POWs were shot in the head.

after a few days because he had once belonged to the West German Communist party. The interim acting director, Irmgard Seidel, who had accepted a post at Buchenwald just before the collapse of the Honecker government, denied any complicity with historical crimes. "For those of us born in 1940," she told me, "it seemed natural to see the Soviet soldiers as our liberators. When I wrote my dissertation, I used the accepted scholarly references and misattributed the guilt for the Katyn Forest Massacre. Was that a crime? Will I lose my job because of a footnote? Can citizens be punished for 'thought crimes' in a democracy [*Rechtsstaat*]?" But if Kranz and the citizens' initiative have their way, Buchenwald will commemorate the thousands of Germans who suffered in Buchenwald *after* April 1945 at the hands of the "Soviet oppressors." In fact, a provisional exhibition has now been set up there which memorializes this group.

No one alleges that Soviets tortured these prisoners or even forced them to work. No documents testify to execution orders from Moscow. No artifacts of cruelty are on view. The exhibit cases feature letters from loved ones and hand-knit underwear sent to prisoners by their wives and mothers. No text describes the desperate conditions everywhere in Germany in the years after the war. Nor does one learn that because the Soviets, unlike the Western Allies, took de-Nazification seriously and investigated each prisoner on a case-by-case basis, some prisoners were held for years before being released. Many, perhaps 10,000 of the 50,000 prisoners, died of disease or the cold before they came to trial. These Germans, in the minds of many East Germans, represent their own martyrdom under Soviet rule.[17]

Paradoxically, the memory of Communist rule in the East and West has reversed itself since 1989. In post-cold-war West Germany, one rarely hears denunciations of Nazism and communism as twin "totalitarian" threats. Far from seeing East Germans as victims, West Germans often perceive them as collaborators in the *Stasi*-driven police state. Citizens of the former GDR often depict themselves as the victims of first Nazi and then Communist oppression. They want this distinct heritage commemorated.

The urgency of their desire became clear to me when I visited Buchenwald in June 1991. Swarms of politicians, Weimar citizens, newsmen, and tourists joined

14 "Gedenkstein paßt nicht mehr!," *TLZ*, May 22, 1991.
15 The memorial also honors the 100,000 Jews who arrived in Buchenwald, many of whom were transported to other camps. In 1993 a formal competition was held for the first Jewish memorial at Buchenwald to be constructed on the former site of Block 22 of the prisoner's barracks.
16 "Commemorative Ceremony at Buchenwald," British Broadcasting Corporation, World Service, April 20, 1989.
17 Francine S. Kiefer, "East Germans Learn of Nazi Camps Used by Communists until 1950," *Christian Science Monitor*, April 5, 1990. Ernst Jäckel, "Demands for a More 'Inclusive' Monument," German Information Center, *This Week in Germany*, September 27, 1991.

The clock above the main gate is stopped at the hour of liberation on April 11, 1945.

Chancellor Helmut Kohl as he dedicated six large wooden crosses to commemorate the victims "of the Communist terror dictatorship" *(der kommunistischen Schreckensherrschaft)* and as he placed identical yellow and white wreaths at the graves of victims of Nazi and Soviet crimes.[18] Major newspapers and television channels carried the story.

Since then, many families have erected small wooden crosses in memory of relatives thought to have died in the post-1945 Buchenwald camp. At Buchenwald, as elsewhere in Central Europe, these wooden crosses for Christian victims implicitly express a populist resentment against the massive marble and granite monuments erected by Soviet-sponsored governments.

The International Committee of Buchenwald Survivors immediately registered a strong protest against memorializing men who died in Buchenwald because they were suspected of being Nazis or war criminals. According to them, this terrain is property of the European Community and cannot be structured by Germans alone.[19]

Since 1989, as before, the memory of Jewish victims in the former GDR has been actively and passively pushed into oblivion. Right-wing groups attacked a new educational exhibit designed to educate people against anti-Semitism at the Sachsenhausen concentration camp, and the town of Ravensbrück issued building permits for a shopping mall virtually on the site of the women's concentration camp memorial. Desecration of graves and memorials has increased in tandem with attacks against non-Germans throughout unified Germany. A liberal Berlin daily connected the fires set at refugee shelters and at concentration camps. "The flames were meant for the stranger and for a memory.... Once the memory and the stranger have been burned, no *political* subject remains, but rather an enormous... privatized subject, ...*one* people [*Volk*], one 'family'."[20]

A unified Germany gropes for a shared identity on which to anchor civil society just when tens of thousands of refugees have been seeking asylum from "ethnic cleansing" in Central Europe. Gradually, West Germans are casting off the mantle of mourning for the victims of Nazi crimes.[21] While politicians continue to commemorate victims and extend reparations to those who were previously ineligible, other signs suggest the normalization of memory in the West as well. A recent film, *Restless Conscience* (1992), enshrined the noble German resisters as if they typified all Ger-

18 Yellow and white are the traditional Catholic colors. See "Die CDU will ihre Leistungen und Erfolge stärker betonen," *Frankfurter Allgemeine Zeitung*, June 11, 1991.

19 German Information Center, "Buchenwald Observance: Appeals to Preserve Holocaust Memorials," *The Week in Germany*, April 17, 1992. Three thousand people gathered on Liberation Day, April 11, 1992, to honor the victims of Nazism and communism.

20 *Die Tageszeitung* [Berlin], November 6, 1992.

21 Ferdinand Protzman, "German Attacks Rise as Foreigners Become Scapegoat," *The New York Times*, November 2, 1992.

22 Stephen Kinzer, "Germans Plan Celebration of Nazi Rocket, Then Cancel It as Protests Grow," *The New York Times*, September 29, 1992.

23 See the preface in Johannes Steinhoff, Peter Pechel, and Dennis Showalter, eds., *Voices from the Third Reich: An Oral History* (Washington, D.C.: Regnery Gateway, 1989), p. xvi.

mans. In September 1992 the Bonn government prepared a celebration of the fiftieth anniversary of the launching of the V-2 rocket, hailing it as a major step in the conquest of outer space and forgetting about the 26,000 slave laborers who died during its construction. Only vehement protest halted the celebration at the last minute.[22]

West Germans have felt entitled to describe their own victimization under Hitler.[23] The myth of German victimization, so widely denounced after Ronald Reagan's Bitburg remarks, became commonplace in unified Germany.

Still, the landscapes of Nazi brutality retain their power to horrify. Their emotional impact cannot be erased. But the interpretation of the history they represent is in flux. Who were the criminals? What were the crimes? Which racial, ethnic, political, cultural, or religious identity led to the victims' arrests and death? To whom does the terrain of terror belong? In the post-postwar world, the enduring legacy of the camps must be to serve as warnings *(Mahnmale)* against all forms of political terror and racial hatred.

Konstanty Gebert

The Dialectics of Memory in Poland
Holocaust Memorials in Warsaw

At a press conference during a visit to Belgium in the mid-1980s, Polish Primate Cardinal Glemp was asked why he kept referring to the "6 million Polish dead" during World War II, when everybody knew that half of these dead were Jewish. The church dignitary replied that this fact was unimportant, since the 6 million died "because they were Polish citizens." Though Glemp's words provoked a minor outcry in Warsaw, they were never retracted—and thus came to illustrate, all too well, the contested and paradoxical memory of the *Shoah* in Polish historical consciousness.

On the one hand, a great commitment has been made in Poland to preserve both the memory of genocide and the material remains that now embody such memory. A visit to the rebuilt and preserved concentration camp complex at Auschwitz-Birkenau, now a memorial and museum, is an obligatory element of the high-school curriculum. This curriculum is replete with references to Nazi genocide, not only in history courses, but also in literature and even geography. There is no threat of the denial of the Holocaust in Poland: the gruesome evidence is here for all to see.

At the same time, the museum in Auschwitz-Birkenau was, until recently, called the Museum of Martyrology of the Polish and Other Nations. A long alphabetical list of these "other nations"—from Bulgaria, through France, to the Ukraine—was displayed, but no reason was given for the Nazis' deporting their citizens thousands of kilometers away to send them to gas chambers in Poland. The Jewish dimension was concealed, if not outright denied. In 1968, during Poland's anti-Semitic purges, the staff of the main Polish encyclopedia was fired for writing that in "Nazi concentration camps over 90 percent of the victims were Jewish."

Though these distortions and falsehoods, part and parcel of Communist propaganda, are now being corrected, a more subtle issue remains. Not only their past Communist rulers, but the Poles themselves, are often reluctant to recognize the immensity of Jewish suffering in the *Shoah*. Why? Of the many possible reasons, one seems to be particularly striking. For both Polish and Jewish nations, their very real suffering plays a major role in their self-images—in the very way they define themselves—and this influences the way they now see each other. If 3 out of the 6 million of Poland's war dead were Jewish, the other 3 million were ethnically Polish. It is hard for the Poles to see a substantial difference between these two fates.

At the same time, both nations feel it is important to establish a difference between their respective suffering during World War II. For both Poles and Jews base much of their present-day claims to existence on past suffering (another shared national trait: what other nations are compelled to justify their very existence so often?). Indeed, it would be difficult to find two nations for whom remembered martyrdom plays a more central role than it does for Poles and Jews. Whether consciously or not, the Poles have thus conflated the suffering of Poles and Jews, claiming the Holocaust as part of Polish heritage.

This two-sided nature of Holocaust memory in Poland is reflected in most of its monuments, dozens of which have sprung up over the years, though, in numbers, hardly adequate considering the immensity of the event which occurred within its borders. These memorials—until recently constructed solely by the state—reflect the changing official version of how the Holocaust will be remembered in Poland. Just as significant is the absence of memorials in places which would have been commemorated had historical criteria alone been taken into account, sites which were considered uninteresting or problematic by government authorities. In recent years, however, a number of memorials have been built by organizations and private individuals, both in hitherto uncommemorated sites or alongside already-existing official monuments. State control over the past in Poland has finally begun to relax.

Memorial Route of Jewish Martyrdom and Struggle, Warsaw, 1988, between the *Warsaw Ghetto Monument* and the *Umschlagplatz* memorial. Nineteen granite blocks on the trail bear black syenite tablets, three feet high, inscribed in Polish and Hebrew. Architect: Hanna Szmalenberg. Sculptor: Wladyslaw Klamerus.

Leon Marek Suzin's *Memorial to the Warsaw Ghetto Uprising*, 1946. A red sandstone plate marks the spot where armed confrontation began.

Warsaw, Poland's capital and the site of Nazi-occupied Europe's largest Ghetto, is particularly interesting from this standpoint. Because of the city's political importance, the government's control of the way the past has been commemorated has been particularly strict. On the other hand, the significance of the Warsaw Ghetto Uprising, and of the destruction of the half-million-strong Ghetto population, has generated an especially strong demand for a different kind of commemoration. Since state control of physical monuments was virtually absolute, this alternative memory expressed itself through ceremonies held at various memorial sites, infusing them with new, and sometimes unexpected, meanings.

The first World War II–related memorial was built in Warsaw in 1946 to mark the third anniversary of the Ghetto Uprising. Designed by the architect L. M. Suzin, this red sandstone disk, tilted toward the Ghetto gate, marks the site of the first armed clash on April 19, 1943, and bears the following inscription in Polish, Yiddish, and Hebrew: "To the memory of those who died in unparalleled and heroic struggle for the dignity and freedom of the Jewish nation, for free Poland, and for the liberation

Detail of the plate inscription in Polish, Hebrew, and Yiddish.

of mankind—the Jews of Poland." A plaque with the Hebrew letter *beth*—for *Bereshit*—accompanies the inscription. The monument faces the now nonexistent gate through which German tanks attempted to enter the Ghetto.[1]

Subsequent urban renewal has deprived the monument of its specific point of reference, however; the Ghetto gate no longer exists, and the former meaning of the site has been lost. Thus, contemporary sources, probably on the basis of the monument's circular form, erroneously interpret it as being a sewer entrance, like those used by fighters to leave the Ghetto.

Shortly after the monument's unveiling in 1946, Suzin also designed a memorial plaque for the wall of the *Umschlagplatz* (loading dock), the railroad platform from which some 350,000 of the Ghetto's Jews were deported to Treblinka. The text, again in Polish, Yiddish, and Hebrew reads: "This was the gate through which hundreds of thousands of Warsaw Jews, victims of Nazi genocide from 1942 to 1943, went to martyrs' deaths in extermination camps."

It is interesting to compare these first two memorials. Both commemorate the victims as a group: neither mentions any individual name or fate. But while the fighters' monument contains an appreciation of their heroism and an interpretation of the meaning of their struggle, the *Umschlagplatz* plaque seems—with the exception of the expression "martyrs' deaths"—exclusively informative. It is also unsigned and functions as a historical marker for visitors, rather than as an attempt to enshrine the memory of those it speaks about. This disparity in memorial approaches to the victims and to those who resisted was to remain a feature of Warsaw memorials until the late 1980s.

Leon Marek Suzin's *Umschlagplatz* memorial in Warsaw with Polish, Hebrew, and Yiddish inscriptions, 1946.

1 Henryk Kroszczor, ed., *Kartki z historii Żydów w Warszawie,* vols. 19-20 (Warsaw: Jewish Historical Institute, 1979), p. 329.
2 For a full history of the *Warsaw Ghetto Monument,* see James E. Young, "The Biography of a Memorial Icon," in *The Texture of Memory: Holocaust Memorials and Meaning* (New Haven and London: Yale University Press, 1993), pp. 155-84.

Another important element of early Polish memorials was the unambiguous identification of both the victims and the commemorators as Jews. In time, however, such explicit references gave way to more convoluted expressions, such as "victims of Nazi genocide" for the martyrs and organizations' names for the fighters. As official emphasis shifted from remembering the dead to accusing the perpetrators, expressions of Jewish national identity became increasingly problematic. Finally, the choice of languages for the plaques reflects the languages spoken by Polish Jews at the time, but this can also be seen as a conscious attempt to communicate with the Gentile majority. The use of Hebrew was dropped because of politically unacceptable associations with Israel and resumed again only in the late 1980s, while Yiddish was replaced with English, in order to accommodate the increasing numbers of American Jewish visitors.

The *Umschlagplatz* plaque was to remain the only memorial there for over forty years, but Suzin's small monument was dwarfed two years later by sculptor Nathan Rapoport's huge *Warsaw Ghetto Monument,* which soon became the standard icon of the Uprising (plate 3). Built on a square especially cleared for the occasion, amid piles of rubble five meters high, this monument was to immortalize the Ghetto's heroic story.[2]

The main body of the monument, a rectangle which narrows slightly toward the top, is set on a pedestal several steps high. Two stone menorahs, each guarded by two lions, stand at the front corners of the pedestal and can be lighted for ceremonies. A larger-than-life group sculpture emerges from the front of the monument, each figure representing a typical Ghetto fighter. The central figure is of an adult man, gaze uplifted, holding a grenade in his left hand. A muscular, bearded prophet figure crouches by him in a gesture of defiance, while a fallen body lies at his feet. A boy and a girl clutching a gun stand by the sides of the central figure, while a woman holding a baby emerges from behind. The background suggests flames and billows of smoke. The overall impression is one of heroic resistance and courage, of victory even in defeat. The trilingual inscription reads: "The Jewish nation — to its fighters and martyrs."

This main, front side of the monument commemorates the fighters but not the victims. It is dedicated to the memory of those who took up arms, not those who went to their deaths in cattle cars. This is the image presented to participants in mass rallies held annually at the monument to commemorate the Uprising. The other side of the monument tells a different story. It is adorned with a simple bas-relief depicting an exilic procession of Jews being taken to their deaths, heads covered and bowed. The central figure is that of a rabbi holding a Torah scroll. There are no inscriptions, no lion-guarded menorahs. One has to walk around to the back of the monument to see this story.

The message — which echoes Suzin's similarly counterposed monument and plaque — is clear. Resistance and struggle are what one should remember from the story of the Ghetto, not the mass destruction of hundreds of thousands. On this point, both the Socialist and Zionist Jewish organizations and the Polish authorities agreed. The entire monument is filled with this kind of symbolism — from the labradorite stone used for the monument's body, originally selected by the Nazis for a victory monument, to the sand from *Eretz Israel* laid at the monument's foundation.

Thus, the main elements for commemorating the Holocaust in Poland emerged: the emphasis on resistance and the relegation of mass murder to a secondary role. A third element, that of "noncommemoration," was soon to join these two.

At the time of the construction of the monument, the entire Ghetto area, as well as most of Warsaw itself, was in ruins. Gradually, however, the rebuilding of the city began. Streets, often with new names, were mapped out, and did not necessarily correspond to the prewar grid. Old landmarks disappeared or were not rebuilt. The entire Ghetto area was to be turned into a downtown residential district; thus the original Nazi effort to destroy Warsaw was defeated. But reconstruction was also renovation — not only the Ghetto, but the very fabric of prewar Warsaw, with its division into rich and poor districts, was to be made a thing of the past. "In no way," said Poland's Communist President Boleslaw Bierut in 1949, "will the district be reminiscent of the crowded, crammed mass of tenement houses of the past. Detached buildings, separated by greenery, will ensure calm and hygienic conditions for their inhabitants."[3] In the process of rebuilding, what was left of prewar Jewish Warsaw, or of sites connected with the Holocaust period, was leveled or transformed. The *Umschlagplatz* itself, which had survived the war, was transformed into a truck depot using the existing infrastructure. The adjoining Jewish hospital became a high school, and the former SS headquarters eventually housed one of the departments at Warsaw University. No effort was made to commemorate, or even indicate, their wartime functions.

Only the new street names suggested the area's link to its past, commemorating Ghetto commander Mordechai Anielewicz, or the Ghetto's Communist organizers Edward Fundaminski and Jozef Lewartowski. A plaque in honor of the latter was unveiled on the spot where his house had stood; for a long time he remained the only individual acknowledged in what had been an essentially collective historical vision. Curiously enough, the street named after Janusz Korczak (Henryk Goldszmit), the Ghetto teacher who refused to abandon his pupils and went with them to Treblinka, is located outside the Ghetto area.

The residents of the new buildings on these streets were, of course, not Jewish, nor did they have a special relationship to the Jewish monument standing at the edge of the huge square. Apart from the anniversary ceremonies, the monument was dead, its meaning lost on the new inhabitants of the district. As a Polish book published on the twentieth anniversary of the Uprising described it, "Month after month, year after year, the ruins give way to new streets and new houses. The Polish nation was

A stone memorial inscribed in Polish, Hebrew, and Yiddish marks the ruins of Mordechai Anielewicz's Ghetto bunker at Mila 18, Warsaw.

3   Boleslaw Bierut, *Szescioletni plan odbudowy Warszawy* (Warsaw: Ksiaka i Wiedza, 1949), p. 201 (my translation).

Commemorative ceremony at Mila 18, April 18, 1986.

giving life back to its heroic capital."⁴ The square became a favorite place for strolling and, in the summer, for sunbathing.

Nearby, at Mila 18, approximately at the site where Mordechai Anielewicz and the Jewish Fighting Organization's command committed mass suicide in a bunker discovered by the Nazis, a memorial mound was built (see p. 125). The trilingual, unsigned inscription explains the nature of the site but does not contain any particular commemorative elements. The mound rises to the level of the wartime rubble in the Ghetto and is a favorite spot for local children, who use it for sledding in winter.⁵

The attitude of local inhabitants to the Jewish monuments was not merely neutral, however. These Jewish memorials reminded many of the Poles of the monument to the Warsaw Uprising of 1944, one year after the Ghetto Uprising, which had *not* been built. The 1944 struggle, led by the non-Communist underground army (the *Armia Krajowa*), had become almost a nonevent in Polish Communist historiography. The speedy commemoration of the Jewish Uprising, coupled with the official nonrecognition of the Polish one, provided grounds for years of bitter feelings.⁶

Meanwhile, the official anniversary ceremonies held at the monument were becoming more and more Polish in spirit, due both to the dwindling of Poland's remaining Jewish community and to the regime's more and more hostile attitude to things Jewish. Officially, the Ghetto Uprising was considered part of the history of Polish resistance to the Nazis. In 1970 German Chancellor Willy Brandt, during his trail-blazing initial visit to Warsaw, spontaneously knelt at the monument; this was interpreted as a gesture of contrition toward Poland, not necessarily as a gesture to the Jews. Similarly, a monument to victims of concentration camps built in Warsaw's Powazki cemetery also included a reference to Jewish extermination camps such as Treblinka in an inscription that reads, "The ashes of murdered Poles call out for peace in the world."

The messages of such monuments still reflected the basic duality of Poland's official memory of the Holocaust. A symbolic grave for the Ghetto fighters was dedicated at the Jewish cemetery on Okopowa Street, complete with the realistic sculpture of a fighter, arms in hand, emerging from the flames, despite the religious ban on representative art. In this same cemetery, mass graves of Ghetto victims remain uncommemorated and—until recently—unmarked.

Other remains of the Ghetto gradually disappeared, since the process of urban renewal did not take into account the need to preserve monuments that were not officially sanctioned. A piece of the original Ghetto wall at 3 Leszno Street[7] was preserved because it had been the site of a mass execution of Poles by the Germans on October 26, 1943. No plaque informs passersby of the history of this wall, which incongruously juts out from the middle of the sidewalk.

Another piece of the Ghetto wall is preserved in a courtyard between Zlota and Sienna Streets. Since the late 1970s, a local resident and *Armia Krajowa* veteran, Mieczyslaw Jedruszczak, has fought to preserve this historical site. "History is an exact science," says Jedruszczak, whose main concern is to prevent the reality of the event he is trying to commemorate from fading into vague generalizations. This puts him at odds with both the official institutions set up to preserve historical monuments, which still have not officially registered the site, and the local inhabitants, who find that Jedruszczak's memorial is obstructing their projected construction of a new parking lot. With painstaking care, Jedruszczak has prevented a building contractor from covering up a corner of the Ghetto wall with a fence, and has re-created, on the ground level, the foundations of a now nonexistent wall section. He has set up plaques on the remaining fragments and has had the satisfaction of hosting at his wall the Israeli President Haim Herzog, who set up a plaque of his own. Its wording, in Hebrew and English, is an exact translation of Jedruszczak's informative plaque.

Jedruszczak's initiative is characteristic of a new climate surrounding Poland's Holocaust memorials over the last few years. As the government's control of the past has started to loosen, private individuals and organizations have stepped in to fill in the gaps left by the official version of history. Since the late 1970s, a group of dissident intellectuals, Gentile and Jewish, has held its own unofficial ceremonies at the major memorials: the Ghetto monument and the *Umschlagplatz*. In the early 1980s, when the city was under martial law, there were clashes with the authorities, who then monopolized commemorations of the Ghetto dead.

A granite block on the *Memorial Route of Jewish Martyrdom and Struggle* dedicated to Józef Lewartowski, a leading figure in the Ghetto.

4   Stanislaw Poznanski, *Le combat, la mort, le souvenir* (Warsaw: Conseil de Sauvegarde des Monuments de la Lutte et du Martyre, 1963), p. [158].

5   The banalization of the Ghetto area was compounded by uncaring urban development. For example, a gas station was built next to the *Umschlagplatz* wall, and while the gruesome irony does not come across in Polish, it made many foreign visitors reel. The station was removed when a new memorial was built at the site.

6   A monument commemorating the Uprising of 1944 was finally built in 1989.

7   From 1947 to 1983, it was known as Swierczewski Street and from 1983 to 1991, as Solidarnosci Avenue.

For the fortieth anniversary of the Uprising, in 1983, the Polish government, in an unprecedented gesture, invited Jewish organizations from all over the world to participate. Just as unprecedented was the call of Marek Edelman, the last surviving member of the Jewish Fighting Organization's command and activist of the then-banned Solidarity Trade Union, for a boycott of the official ceremonies. Edelman's call went largely unheeded, while Solidarity endorsed the unofficial ceremony. Police forcibly prevented trade union participants from laying wreaths at the memorials, outraging local inhabitants, who then joined in the ceremony-turned-demonstration. Thereafter, until the end of martial law, unofficial ceremonies at the memorials became important Polish patriotic events with the mass participation of the Gentile population.

An offshoot of the activities of the dissident group was the creation of a Civic Committee for the Preservation of Jewish Monuments. Having gained official recognition, the Committee decided to build a new Holocaust memorial, breaking with the traditional emphasis on both the Uprising and the de-individualized approach to the Jewish victims who were being commemorated. The project, called the *Memorial Route of Jewish Martyrdom and Struggle,* designed by architect Hanna Szmalenberg and sculptor Wladyslaw Klamerus, received official approval and was unveiled in 1988, on the forty-fifth anniversary of the Ghetto Uprising.

Its basic idea, based on the format adopted by participants in unofficial ceremonies, consists of nineteen one-meter high, black syenite blocks spread out between the monument and the *Umschlagplatz,* two commemorative plaques on the buildings that housed the SS headquarters and the Jewish hospital, and a new *Umschlagplatz* memorial. Each block commemorates an individual connected with the Ghetto, such

The new *Umschlagplatz* memorial constructed in 1988 by Hanna Szmalenberg, architect, and Wladyslaw Klamerus, sculptor.

Detail of names incised into the internal wall of the memorial.

as the poet Itzhak Katzenelson, Ghetto fighter Frumka Plotnicka, or religious leader Itzhak Nyssenbaum. Walking along this route, which is a kind of "memory lane," passersby can acquaint themselves with the fates of these leaders and thus gain insight into the personal fates of some of the half million Ghetto victims.

This route leads visitors to the new *Umschlagplatz* memorial, an enclosure in white marble, with a narrow entrance capped by a black bas-relief representing a forest of felled trees. Facing that entrance is a gap in the opposite wall through which a living tree can be seen. On the inner walls of the memorial, several hundred names are engraved — the first names of the Ghetto victims who were deported to Treblinka. The languages used are Polish, Hebrew, and English, but the list of names is only in Polish, for lack of space.

This new memorial merges with the community's real-life, urban surroundings. Its physically and metaphorically human scale, and the shift in emphasis from the heroic resistance of the few to the tragic fate of the hundreds of thousands, enables passersby to experience a personal relationship with those who lived there. Thus, the history of the Warsaw Ghetto has again become connected with the lives of its latter-day inhabitants, re-creating a bond which the former official version of events had all but broken.

James E. Young

The Anne Frank House
Holland's Memorial
"Shrine of the Book"

The Anne Frank House in Amsterdam is a museum that appeals especially to the young.

Given the innumerable Anne Frank streets, squares, and schools spread throughout Dutch land- and cityscapes, many have suggested that the young diarist may well be the patron saint of Holland.[1] But this is not the mere appropriation of a Jewish life by a country in search of a national martyr or the simple self-aggrandizement of Anne Frank's adopted motherland. Rather, the memorial canonization of Anne Frank in Holland has much more to do with the deeply mixed Dutch self-perception as traditional refuge, on the one hand, and as a nation of passive bystanders, on the other.

As a young girl, Anne Frank exemplifies the blamelessness of Jews killed for no reason other than for being Jews. By extension, she represents for the Dutch their own, uninvited violation by the Nazis; at the same time, she reminds the Dutch that even though they harbored her, they also betrayed her in the end, as well as 100,000 Dutch Jews. By reflecting back to the Dutch their own mixed record of resistance and neutrality, victimization and passive complicity, Anne Frank has effectively become an archetypal figure for all of Holland's war memory.

In addition, since going into hiding is officially recognized in Holland as a form of wartime resistance, Otto Frank and his family have come to represent all who hid, turning all into heroes, Jews and non-Jews, even those who took refuge only during roundups. According to the Museum of Dutch Resistance, over 300,000 Dutch were in hiding by 1944, including about 25,000 Jews.[2] Thus, depending on how one looks at these numbers, either the Jews in Holland are to be regarded as a mainstay of Dutch resistance, or vast numbers of non-Jews in Holland can be seen as having shared part of their Jewish neighbors' experiences under the Nazis. In both cases, Holland's national memory of resistance is linked specifically to the memory of the Dutch Jews' fate during the war, the memory a distillation of pride, shame, and ambivalence.

That the Anne Frank House at Prinsengracht 263 has become the preeminent Dutch war shrine cannot be surprising in this context. After the Rijksmuseum and Van Gogh Museum, it is the most popular tourist site in Amsterdam for foreign tourists, practically a place of pilgrimage for student backpackers in Europe. In fact, the Anne Frank house tends to perform on at least two different, if parallel, memorial tracks, one each for foreign and domestic tourists. Before Eastern Europe opened up, the Anne Frank House was the most likely introduction to the Holocaust for young Americans traveling abroad. By the early 1960s, most American tourists were at least nominally familiar with the diary and play, which constituted much of their knowledge of the Jews' plight during World War II. It was an easy, accessible window to this period, for like the version of the diary they found in the play, the Anne Frank House represented an open, universal, even optimistic understanding of events.

Domestic tourists from Holland, however, especially from the city of Amsterdam itself, find a subtly different memorial on the canal at Prinsengracht 263. As surely as its place on the canal links the building to the rest of Amsterdam, this house is also part of a neighborhood that was already legendary in Dutch tradition for its hospitality to political refugees, the Dutch equivalent of a "freedom trail." For the Dutch know, if no one else does, that a year after finding refuge in Amsterdam at Westermarkt 6 in 1634, exiled French philosopher René Descartes probably watched construction of the house and annex at Prinsengracht 263, which were visible from his back window. Though the original annex was torn down and replaced by a larger one in 1739, the front part of the house stood intact over the years, remodeled on occasion to accommodate stables, offices, a merchant warehouse, and, for ten years, until 1939, a factory for player-piano roll music. To the Dutch mind, it seems only fitting that the radically enlightened Descartes, a refugee from seventeenth-century France,

Statue of Anne Frank by Mari Andriessen at the Westermarkt in Amsterdam.

should have gazed at what would become the national shrine to persecution and refuge of the twentieth century. Both sites are now linked spatially and metaphysically, reinforcing each other as shrines to Dutch enlightenment and tolerance.

Like Descartes's, the Frank family's own trail to Amsterdam started in another place, this time in Frankfurt am Main. Here, at Marbachweg 30, Annelies Marie, the second daughter of Otto and Edith Frank, was born on June 12, 1929. Both this house and the house where she lived as a small child, at Ganghoferstrasse 24, still stand in Frankfurt, the latter marked by a memorial plaque.[3] Partly because the nursery school Anne was supposed to enter in September 1933 was already closed to Jews, Otto Frank decided to leave Germany for Holland that fall. After ensuring that his new pectin manufacturing firm, Opekta, was viable, he found a flat on the Merwedeplein in Amsterdam's southern river district, a neighborhood that would become crowded with other German-Jewish refugees during the next few years, and sent for his family. Anne and her sister, Margot, grew up in this neighborhood, happy and well protected from both the twists and turns of Otto's business and from signs of the approaching calamity.

When the Germans invaded Holland on May 10, 1940, Otto Frank's first impulse was to take his family to England on an illegal ship. Unable to secure passage, however, he began making other plans. First, he transferred his business to his office manager, Koophuis, so that the Germans could not confiscate it as a Jewish enterprise. Then, in November 1940, he moved Opekta into Prinsengracht 263, one of several rundown buildings on the canal. A month later, he added another franchise specializing in sausage herbs and spices and turned the management of the new company, Pectacon, over to his other associate, Kraler. Not long after that, without his daughters' knowledge, he began to convert the unused *achterhuis* (rear house) into a hiding place for his family.

During the first months of 1942, Otto Frank, his coworkers, and their two typists, Miep Gies and Elli Vossen, moved furniture into the annex, which had by then been cleared of laboratory equipment. He had planned to move his family in on July 16, 1942, but on Sunday, July 5, a registered letter from General Rauter of the SD arrived for Anne's sixteen-year-old sister Margot: she was to report to a "work camp" transport the next day. That night Otto and Edith decided to take the family into hiding immediately, bundling them off at 7:30 the next morning in a warm rain, each girl wearing several layers of clothes and carrying school satchels instead of suitcases. They walked the entire way, their "gaudy yellow stars" (Anne's words) warding off all potential lifts.[4]

What happened between July 6, 1942, and August 4, 1944, can be found in the pages of Anne's diary, which she received on her thirteenth birthday in 1942, three weeks before moving into the annex. What it all means depends on how we read her diary—and on how the diary itself is remembered by the building and museum exhibitions now housing it. On August 4, 1944, a German policeman, accompanied by four Dutch accomplices, marched into Prinsengracht 263, up the stairs straight to the second floor, and demanded that Kraler open the entrance to the annex, hidden behind a movable bookcase. While the family was being arrested and an armored car called for, the policeman and his helpers ransacked the entire annex looking for money, jewelry, and documents. The four Dutch accomplices received cash rewards for each prisoner and a share of the household valuables, it seems. Their arms overloaded with loot, they emptied the contents of Otto Frank's briefcase onto the floor and stashed most of it with their booty. Among the papers that came spilling out were Anne's diary and notebooks, which were left on the floor with other jumbled papers

Exterior view of the rear of the Anne Frank House, taken just after the war.

1 See, for example, Judith Miller, *One, by One, by One: Facing the Holocaust* (New York: Simon and Schuster, 1990), pp. 95-96.

2 Karel Magry, "Texts of Permanent Exhibition," *Museum of the Dutch Resistance* (Amsterdam: Heiermann & Co., n.d.), pp. 4-5.

3 The spring of 1990 saw a readoption of Anne by the city of Frankfurt in an exhibition at the Jewish Museum there called "Anne Frank in Frankfurt." Without explicitly reclaiming the lost daughter of their city, Frankfurt has, through this show, begun to re-Germanize her by establishing her family's German roots. By extension, the show creates a new German martyr by which to remember other Germans put to death by the Nazi Reich.

4 See Anne Frank, *The Diary of a Young Girl,* trans. B. M. Mooyaart-Doubleday (Garden City, New York: Doubleday & Company, 1952), p. 26.

and photographs until Miep Gies gathered them up five hours later. With a duplicate key, the assistant had let herself, her husband, Elli Vossen (whose father had built the false bookshelf on hinges), and a warehouse assistant back into the office to salvage whatever personal belongings they could before the Germans returned with trucks to ship the remaining furniture back to bombed-out German cities. Miep kept the diary and notebooks, unread, in a dresser drawer until Otto Frank returned to Amsterdam in June 1945, the only one of the hidden household to survive.

For the first five years after the war, the houses between the corner at Westermarkt and Prinsengracht 263 stood empty and delapidated. Between 1950 and 1953, a large textile firm, Berghaus, bought up the entire block with a plan to demolish the old buildings and erect modern offices. Published in America in 1952, the diary had already become an international best-seller; it was adapted for the stage and became a prize-winning Broadway play in 1955. Thus, when Berghaus announced plans to raze the block and begin building new offices, a great hue and cry rose up across the country. The house had already become a tourist attraction, open, by appointment only, to visitors who could wend their way through the maze of abandoned rooms to the creaking hinged bookcase and annex behind. Concerned citizens throughout the city joined with the historical society Amstelodamum to block demolition. At one point, an Amsterdam artist, Anton Witsel, and several of his friends posted a day and night vigil in front of the house to protect it from demolition teams. As protests grew, Berghaus ran into further difficulties securing approval from the city architectural commission, which declared their planned buildings "out of harmony" with their surroundings. Finally, in January 1956, Berghaus announced that other property was being sought for the office buildings. A city-wide campaign led by Mayor Gijs van Hall and Otto Frank was then launched to save the Anne Frank House.

Fund-raising was unexpectedly, extraordinarily successful, presaging the power of the Holocaust to raise money for all kinds of causes. Major contributions poured in from West Germany, Otto Frank, and hundreds of private donors. On May 3, 1957, the eve of Dutch National Memorial Day, the Anne Frank Foundation was established. A further outpouring of support followed, including donations from Berg-haus itself, which gave the house and annex to the foundation on the condition that they be used as a cultural center. Otto Frank put up funds to buy the house next door and stipulated that it be used as a center for education. Exactly three years later, May 3, 1960, again on the eve of Dutch National Memorial Day, the doors opened to the Anne Frank House and Museum.

Between 1957 and 1960, the Anne Frank House was open two hours a day, and about 10,000 visitors a year were guided through the annex by student volunteers. When it opened officially as a museum in 1960, Otto Frank convened the first public meeting of the International Youth Center next door. In Frank's words, it would "create a dynamic meeting-place for young people from all over the world,... propagate and help realize the ideals bequeathed by Anne Frank in her diary.... At the same time, an attempt [would] be made through international youth congresses and conferences to stimulate young people to discuss international cooperation, mutual understanding, tolerance, a confrontation of life-philosophies, world peace, modern upbringing, youth problems, modern art, the questions of race and the fight against illiteracy."[5]

Such an ambitious agenda could not be completely realized, of course, but it reflected all those issues Otto believed Anne would have honored and pursued. For both Otto Frank and the foundation had set out to fulfill the ideals that Anne had entrusted to her diary. Given Anne's famous July 15, 1944 entry that begins, "It's really a wonder I haven't dropped all my ideals" and ends, "In the meantime, I must uphold my ideals, for perhaps the time will come when I shall be able to carry them out," the foundation clearly sees itself as carrying out Anne's ideals as if they were a kind of last will and testament. The Anne Frank House is thus very much a Dutch "shrine of the book," a place where the nearly holy testament of her diary is to be taught and studied. But if the aim is to impart the lessons of Anne's diary, these lessons depend wholly on who draws them. Since the foundation is in Holland, Anne's experiences have been regarded as part of the Dutch experience as a whole.

The mixing of national and Jewish ideals at the Anne Frank House may be due as much to the redactor of Anne's diary, her father, as they are to the Dutch caretakers of the foundation. While Otto Frank would never have denied his daughter's Jewishness, he felt from the outset that her diary, her story, and now the house would serve humanity best through their universal implications. Accordingly, he wrote that "the Jewish origins of the diary will not be specifically emphasized, but nevertheless, the insights it provides as a Jewish testament may not be forgotten. The diary is a human document of the foundation, whose aim is to keep the annex in its original state as a symbol of the past and as a warning for the future.... In this place, one can see the diary in its authentic perspective..., the best place to discuss the possibilities of a great future."[6] Whether it was because of the universal success of the diary and the play it spawned or Otto's own universalist reading of the diary itself, Anne's father set a clear precedent for the widest possible application of Anne's beliefs against discrimination and racism of all kinds.

The universalist message of the Anne Frank House has been tapped often and widely. In 1961, for example, John F. Kennedy had his secretary of labor, Arthur Goldberg, lay a wreath at the Anne Frank House, a gesture which he described as "an expression of the American people's enduring sympathy and support for all those who seek freedom.... [Anne's] words, written as they were in the face of a monstrous tyranny, have significant meaning today as millions who read them live in the shadow of fear of another such tyranny."[7] Nearing the height of the cold war, and just after

Bookcase hiding the entrance to the Frank family's hiding place.

the Berlin Blockade, Kennedy's implied reference to the Soviet Union was unmistakable. Since then, dozens of other visiting statesmen and -women have cast their messages in Anne Frank's memorial form. In its universal raison d'être, the house invites all the oppressed into its memorial sanctuary.

On any given day, the area in front of the museum and the steps leading into the museum are swarming with teenagers waiting to enter or meditating about what they have just seen. Their bicycles chained to rails on the canal, Dutch families mingle with Americans, Germans, Italians, and tourists from other European countries; to each, it seems Anne Frank is one of their own. Every year nearly 600,000 people wend their way up the creaking staircase to the annex, where Anne's family lived and where Anne recorded their refuge. Today we are among them: on the third floor, we watch a brief film of Anne Frank's life and her diary, a short history of World War II through Anne's eyes, ending with brutal images of bulldozed bodies at Bergen-Belsen, where Anne died. We then crowd through the false wall behind the bookshelf into the annex proper: the expectation here is slightly magical, as if through this invisible door we were able to go back to both the place and the time of the events. Instead, we find an empty room, where Otto and Edith Frank once slept with Anne's sister, Margot. The next room is Anne's, which she shared with Mr. Dussel, a Jewish dentist who sought refuge with the family later on. As we enter, we note that the wall to the left is covered with Anne's childhood photograph and picture collection,

A wall in Anne's room.

carefully clipped from magazines, which she taped and pasted above her bed. Photographs of Greta Garbo; Deanna Durbin in the film *First Love;* Rudy Vallee; the Dutch royal family; Queen Elizabeth, then a young princess of twelve; and romantic drawings of the outside world, of farms and hills, are now sealed behind a pane of glass. Pictures of the Dutch royal family suggest Anne's strong feelings for her Dutch refuge — and no doubt endear her further to Dutch visitors, in whose eyes every celebration of the royal family was an act of resistance during the war. As we are compelled by the intimacy of her diary, we are similarly drawn to her decorative handiwork: touched by that which Anne has touched, traces of her being, the images she may have fallen asleep with at night, the same sense of intimacy she has unknowingly shared with us in her diary.

5   Anne Frank Foundation, *Concerning the Diary of Anne Frank, the House, and the Foundation from the Beginning up until the Present* (Catalogue for the Anne Frank House) (Amsterdam, 1978), p. 45.
6   From an internal bulletin of the Anne Frank Centre, courtesy of the Anne Frank Stichting.
7   From *The New York Times,* September 20, 1961.

Exhibition at the Anne Frank House.

Next to her room, we see the family's sink and floral-patterned, porcelain toilet. For a moment, visitors are apt to submit to the reverie created by these remnants of Anne's daily life, forgetting that this setting is not exactly as it was. The contact paper that covered the windows, first to protect Opekta's spices from light and then to protect the refugees from prying eyes, is gone. Light floods into the annex now, children lean out of the great windows, and the scent of trees and sounds of birds wash over us. Anne's only exposure to the outside world during her years in hiding was through a small square window in the attic, from which she and her companion Peter would follow the seasons by the quality of light on the Westerkerk bell tower or catch a glimpse of a blue, black, or cloudy sky. The attic, Anne's inner sanctum, where she wrote most of her diary, is now completely closed to visitors; it remains a space unknown to the masses, unreachable.

As we descend to the exhibition hall, we carry with us such imagined memory, an emotional sense of having "been there," without a corresponding notion of what it means. The permanent exhibition offers the images and information to frame all significance here. First, the diary as holy text is displayed in both facsimile (the original is in the Dutch War Documentation Center) and in over fifty languages. The diary functions as the heart around which the rest of the installation is given meaning: images depicting the rise of Nazism and massacre of European Jewry. A temporary exhibition called "2,000 Years of Anti-Semitism," inaugurated by Elie Wiesel, was one of dozens of revolving exhibitions documenting current examples of racism and other forms of discrimination in Europe, Africa, and America: the resurgence of neo-Nazis, the oppression of foreign immigrants in Europe, the Palestinians' plight in the West Bank.[8] The thrust here is as universal as Anne seems to have been. Though persecuted and put to death because she was a Jew, she perceived her suffering in terms of both Jew and adopted daughter of the Dutch.

The Anne Frank House functions on at least two planes: for adults, it remains a shrine to innocence, a museum representing what they already know. Anne Frank epitomizes the blameless victim, a child whose life, but not hope, was extinguished by the Nazis. Teenagers and children visit the house under slightly different circumstances. For them, Anne's experiences and observations provide perhaps the only somewhat direct access they can have to this period: the keenly observed minutiae of

8 For an unsympathetic response to the content of these exhibitions, see Mark Segal, "The Second Agony of Anne Frank," *The Jerusalem Post*, June 17, 1977, magazine section.

daily life in hiding. The child's view of the war, however precocious and sophisticated, is to some extent also the adolescent visitor's view of the war: changes in daily habits; squabbles with friends and family; young love; limited food, space, and room for playing. Unlike adults, children do not come with a memory of the time to be sparked, but come, instead, to learn what it is the space would have them remember. As such, it is the only truly youthful memorial to the *Shoah* period, not a children's memorial so much as a memorial for children to visit, conceived and executed with the child's view in mind. Anne and her youthfulness remain forever alive in this way. Her devotion to reading and writing, her curiosity about love, and her insights into a family's suffering are all motifs through which another, younger generation comes to know — and then to remember — war and Holocaust.

Zvi Gitelman

The Soviet Politics of the Holocaust

For Communists, the arts have always been weapons in the political struggle. The idea of art for art's sake is anathema. As Leon Trotsky declared: "If the Revolution has the right to destroy bridges and art monuments whenever necessary, it will stop still less from laying its hand on any tendency in art which, no matter how great its achievement in form, threatens the... proletariat.... Our standard is, clearly, political, imperative, and intolerant."[1] Similarly, in Soviet practice, history has been "politics projected into the past." As a Soviet joke used to go, "the most difficult thing to predict in our country is history."

Thus, it is not surprising that so enormous and traumatic an event as the Holocaust was treated in the Soviet period in a highly politicized manner designed to serve state interests. The presentation and interpretation of the Holocaust remain a contentious and troublesome issue in several post-Soviet republics, notably the Baltic states, the Ukraine, and, to a lesser extent, Belorussia and Russia. A powerful state may be able to control history, but memory is harder to shape. As long as there are still people with living memories of the Holocaust, the struggle between individual memories and official histories goes on.

The Holocaust in the U.S.S.R.

In 1939, there were about 3 million Jews in the U.S.S.R. When the Soviets annexed Eastern Poland, the Baltic states, and Bessarabia, between 1939 and 1941, about 2 million more Jews came under their control. Thus, on the eve of the Nazi invasion (June 22, 1941), there were about 5 million Jews in Soviet territory. Most estimates, based necessarily on fragmentary information, are that about 1.5 million Soviet Jews who lived in the pre-1939 borders were murdered by the Nazis and their local collaborators and that 200,000 more died in combat or as prisoners of war. Perhaps as many as 1 million Jews from the annexed territories were also murdered. Thus, the total number of Jews killed was, at the very least, over 2 million and possibly over 3 million.[2] About 250,000 Jews from the annexed territories fled to the interior or were inadvertently saved from annihilation because Soviet authorities considered them "unreliable" elements and so deported them to Siberia and Central Asia.

Soviet occupation of the western territories created a tragic and fateful divergence in the perceptions and interests of Jews and non-Jews. These continue to influence relations between Jews and Ukrainians, Balts, and others to this day. In the interwar Baltic states, Poland, and Romania, Jews had lived under increasingly anti-Semitic regimes and in ever more straitened economic circumstances. In the Soviet Ukraine, there were tensions between Jews and Ukrainians over such issues as Jewish settlement on land; the tendency of Jews to choose Russian, rather than Ukrainian, culture; and the Ukrainian hostility toward communism, especially in the West Ukraine (annexed from Poland in 1939). Many West Ukrainians identified Jews with the despised ideology of communism. The occupation of all of these areas by the Red Army, with its Jewish officers and soldiers, and its promises of national equality and social justice, gave hope to some Jews, especially to the young, that the days of discrimination and oppression were over. Despite misgivings about the Communists' militant atheism, nationalization of private property, and hostility to Zionism, some Jews welcomed the Soviet Army as a liberator.

At the same time, Poles, Lithuanians, Latvians, Romanians, and West Ukrainians saw the Red Army as an invader who was depriving them of independence, which, in the case of Poland and the Baltic states, had been achieved only two short decades be-

Memorial in Velizh, Ukraine.

fore.[3] The myth of *Zhido-Kommuna,* "the Jewish-Bolshevik conspiracy," was thus reinforced and was then given greater weight by intense Nazi propaganda which "explained" that people were suffering only because of the need to eliminate the "Jewish-Bolshevist system," which, they said, had taken land from the peasants, stolen property, impoverished large numbers of people, and persecuted so many. Thousands of Ukrainians, Lithuanians, and Latvians joined "police" battalions, SS units, and other armed formations under German command. It seems that their motivations included the desire to fight the Communists, illusions about gaining national independence under German sponsorship, anti-Semitism, and a desire to profit from the spoils of war. In addition, individuals cooperated with the occupiers by, for example, pointing out Jews attempting to hide and sometimes even attacking their former Jewish neighbors and acquaintances. They did this either in order to protect themselves, take over Jewish property, or settle old scores, real and imagined. The result was that Jews felt betrayed, suspicious, and bitter. Many concluded that their non-Jewish compatriots could never be trusted again and that, when attacked, the Jews had no friends.

Following the Nazi-Soviet pact in August 1939, the Soviet media had remained silent about Nazi atrocities in Germany and occupied Poland. From the time of World War I, older Soviet Jews remembered the Germans as "decent people." Many Soviet Jews were thus left unprepared for the war that would be waged against them by the special mobile killing squads, the *Einsatzgruppen,* who liquidated much of Soviet Jewry by machine-gunning them down near or in their hometowns, sometimes with the help of *Wehrmacht* units and "police" drawn from the local population.[4] Within five months, about half a million Jewish civilians had been killed.

The Soviet Interpretation of the Holocaust

The Soviet media, and many of their post-Soviet successors, have assigned the Holocaust far less significance than it has been given in the West. This disinclination to distinguish Jewish from non-Jewish suffering during what came to be known as the Great Patriotic War can be traced to several sources. First, unlike their brethren in the West, the Jewish population of the U.S.S.R. was unable to press for broader and deeper treatment of the Holocaust. In addition, because no Western country lost as many non-Jewish citizens as did the Soviets, in the West the fate of Jews stands in sharper contrast to that of their conationals or coreligionists than it does in the U.S.S.R. Finally, the Soviet authorities had explicitly political reasons for playing down the Holocaust. In any case, in striking contrast to the way it has been presented in most other countries, in the Soviet Union the Holocaust was not portrayed as a unique, separate phenomenon, though in the post-Soviet period slightly more attention is being paid to its unique characteristics.

In the official Soviet view, the Holocaust was an integral part of a larger phenomenon — the deliberate murder of civilians — which was said to be a natural consequence of racist fascism, which is, in turn, the logical culmination of capitalism. Thus, the roots of the Holocaust lay in capitalism, expressed in its most degenerate form. For the Soviets, as a result, there was no mystery about the Holocaust; the cultural, sociological, psychological, historical, and even theological explorations which have typified Western writings on the Holocaust were not a Soviet concern. In fact, I am not aware of a single book published in the U.S.S.R. which seeks to explain the Holocaust as sui generis.

The word *holocaust* does not even appear in Soviet literature; only in recent years have words such as "catastrophe," "annihilation" (*unichtozhenie*), or "kholokaust" (transliterated from English) been used. *The Black Book,* a book about Soviet Jewry containing documentation gathered by the writers Ilya Ehrenburg and Vassily Grossman was 1,200 typescript pages long by 1944 and was printed in 1946. But nearly every single copy was sent to storage warehouses where they were destroyed in 1948. Only one or two copies survived abroad. Later, Hebrew, English, and Russian (published in Jerusalem) editions appeared, but the book has not yet been published in any of the Soviet successor states.[5] The Holocaust was not mentioned in Soviet textbooks, and, needless to say, no courses on the Holocaust were offered in schools and universities.

Nevertheless, in contrast to what some Western observers have claimed, there was no uniform Communist party line on the Holocaust, and thus significant variations in the way the Holocaust was presented can be seen. For example, a large history of the Ukraine, published in 1982, does not mention Jews even once, not even in connection with the Holocaust, despite the fact that on the eve of the war, over 1.5 million Jews lived there, descendants of people who had lived there for centuries. By contrast, a study of World War II in Estonia, where only 5,000 Jews lived, sympathetically portrays Jewish suffering and openly discusses Estonian collaboration with the Nazis.[6] A documentary collection on Belorussia contains considerable material on Nazi persecution of Jews and the ghettos. A Lithuanian pamphlet, describing the Ninth Fort in Kaunas, where thousands of Jews were killed, nevertheless attempts to obscure the specifically Jewish tragedy. The pamphlet reproduces a German document which reports on the "special handling" of 4,000 Jews in the death camp at Ponary; the caption reads, "the Hitlerite security police report: another 4,000 people have been killed."[7]

One of the more curious treatments is by S. S. Smirnov, a popular writer on World War II. In three volumes on the war, he refers to the Jews' suffering several times but goes out of his way to avoid portraying Jews as fighters and resisters. He does talk about the genocide of the Jews, however, "Millions of people of Jewish nationality or with a tinge of Jewish blood became victims of mass shootings, were burned in crematoria, or were asphyxiated in the gas chambers and trucks." But when Smirnov describes the heroic defense of the Brest fortress, he mentions only "the Russians Anatoly Vinogradov and Raisa Abakumova, the Armenian Samvel Matevosian, the Ukrainian Aleksandr Semenenko, the Belorussian Aleksandr Makhnach . . . the Tatar Petr Gavrilov" and even "the German Viacheslav Meyer." The one hero whose nationality is never mentioned is Efim Moisevich Fomin. Lest there be any doubt about his nationality, Fomin is described as "short . . . dark-haired with intelligent and mournful eyes, a political commissar from a small town near Vitebsk, the son of a smith and a seamstress."[8] All these are, for Soviet readers, clear identifying marks of a Jew. Why Smirnov freely described Jewish martyrdom but assiduously avoided any hint of Jewish heroism is difficult to explain.

The only Soviet publication that paid considerable attention to the Holocaust was the Yiddish language monthly, *Sovetish haimland,* whose circulation was down to about 5,000 at the end of the Soviet period. In any case, it was accessible only to a dwindling group of Yiddish readers, most of whom probably knew the events of the Holocaust firsthand. In almost every issue, there is material on the Holocaust — stories, poems, memoirs, and factual information. Even here, however, certain themes appear consistently and serve a didactic and propagandistic purpose. Thus, for example, Gentiles frequently saved Jews in occupied territories; the only collaborators

1   Leon Trotsky, "Communist Policy toward Art," in *Literature and Revolution* (New York: Russell and Russell, n. d.), pp. 220-21.

2   Mordechai Altshuler points out that the estimates range from 2.5 million to 3.3 million. See his *Soviet Jewry since the Second World War* (New York: Greenwood Press, 1987), p. 4.

3   A fairly balanced treatment of these complicated and painful episodes can be found in Norman Davies and Antony Polonsky, eds., *Jews in Eastern Poland and the U.S.S.R., 1939-46* (New York: St. Martin's, 1991), pp. 1-76.

4   See Heinz-Heinrich Wilhelm, *Rassenpolitik und Kriegsführung* (Passau: Wissenschaftsverlag Richard Rothe, 1991), and Yitzhak Arad, Shmuel Krakowski, and Shmuel Spector, eds., *The* Einsatzgruppen *Reports* (New York: Holocaust Library, 1989).

5   See Ilya Ehrenburg and Vassily Grossman, *The Black Book* (New York: Holocaust Library, 1981).

6   The Ukranian history is Yu. Yu. Kondufor et al., *Istoriia Ukrainskoi S.S.R.* (Kiev: Naukova dumka, 1982). The Estonian book is L. N. Lentzmann et al., *Estonskii narod v velikoi otechestvennoi voine Sovetskogo Soiuza, 1941-45* (Tallinn: Eesti Raamat, 1973). Ironically, Kondufor, director of the Institute of History of the Ukrainian Academy of Sciences, made the opening remarks at the scholarly conference in Kiev in 1991 marking the fiftieth anniversary of Babi Yar.

7   O. Kaplanas, *Deviatyi fort obvinaet* (Vilnius: Mintis, 1964), pp. 37-38, 40.

8   S. S. Smirnov, *Sobranie sochinenii: tom pervyi, Brestkaia krepost', krepost' nad Bugiem* (Moscow: Moladaia gvardiia, 1973), pp. 331-32 (translations mine).

were from among the bourgeoisie, and they are all living now in the West; there was cooperation among all Soviet nationalities in the struggle against the Fascists; the Jews who resisted did so for universalist, not parochial, reasons.[9]

Thus, while the general tendency in the Soviet Union was to gloss over the Holocaust, though never to deny it, treatment of the subject was not uniform. It is not clear, however, whether the differences in treatment are due to local or republic-level policies, the vagaries of censorship, the predilections of individual authors, or some other reasons. Overall, the Holocaust was submerged in the greater tragedy of the 27 million Soviet people, including the Jews, who died during the war.

The most likely explanation for this version of events is that in the 1940s and 1950s Stalin and his followers had become committed to explicitly anti-Semitic policies and thus could not brook expressions of sympathy for Jews. After de-Stalinization, and especially in the 1960s and 1970s, there is a different explanation for Soviet behavior. At this point, the legitimating myth of the Soviet system had ceased to be the Revolution, which fewer and fewer people remembered. Judging by the enormous number of books, films, plays, and radio and television programs devoted to the Great Patriotic War, the Soviet struggle and victory in that war had replaced the Revolution as the justification for the system and the deprivations it had brought to its citizenry. To draw attention to the special suffering of the Jews would diminish the suffering and heroism of all the others, it might have been reasoned, and would give the war the same Jewish cast which the Revolution had acquired in many circles, thus weakening its appeal as a heroic and truly Soviet historic episode. Moreover, playing up the Holocaust would undoubtedly fan Jewish national consciousness, raise uncomfortable questions about attitudes toward Jews and collaboration during the war, and possibly lead Jews to Zionist conclusions.

Monuments and Memory

The policy of burying the Jewish tragedy under general Soviet suffering was even more clear and consistent in visual commemorations of the war. Publications are more numerous and difficult to control than monuments, which are, in any case, more visible. It is well known that monuments at the sites of mass slaughter of Jews did not mention Jews specifically. The best-known instance is Babi Yar, a ravine then on the outskirts of Kiev where, at the end of September 1941, in the course of two days, about 35,000 Jews were shot. For years, there was no monument at the site. In 1959 the Russian writer Viktor Nekrasov protested plans to build a park and soccer stadium there. The poet Yevgenyi Yevtushenko made one of the first public protests against anti-Semitism in a poem entitled "Babi Yar," which begins with the line, "Over Babi Yar there are no monuments." Typically, a conservative criticism of Yevtushenko charged that "the anti-Semitism of the Fascists is only part of their misanthropic policy of genocide . . . the destruction of the 'lower races', including the Slavs."[10]

Public pressure eventually resulted in the construction of a typically Soviet monument on a heroic scale. But the inscription read, "Here between 1941 and 1943, the German Fascist invaders executed more than 100,000 citizens of Kiev and prisoners of war." There was no mention of the Jews. True, for two years after the great massacre of the Jews, the Nazis killed others at the site. But Babi Yar was originally the site of the destruction of the third largest Jewish population of the U.S.S.R., that of the Ukrainian capital. The monuments at Ponary (Paneriai, Ponar), where the majority of the Jews of Vilnius (Vilna) were shot, and at Rumbuli, where thousands of Latvian Jews were murdered, also make no reference to the Jews. There, however, the inscriptions are in three languages, including Yiddish. The one at Rumbuli simply reads, "To the victims of fascism."

At Ponary, shortly after the war, as seems to have happened elsewhere, Jews erected a modest monument to their martyrs. Sometime in the late 1940s the authorities took it down, replaced it with an obelisk crowned by a Soviet star, and closed the small museum to Jewish martyrdom which had been erected nearby. In the late 1980s the museum was reopened, after a good deal of political struggle, and Israeli flags began to appear on the monument, only to be taken down daily by an unidentified group and restored daily also by persons unknown.

In 1991, after a good deal of negotiation, an Israeli former resident of Lithuania, Yeshayahu Epstein, persuaded the Lithuanian authorities to erect a new monument at Ponary, which he and other non-Lithuanians financed. Lithuanian authorities re-

Public pressure led to the construction of the memorial at Babi Yar, a ravine near Kiev, where the Germans murdered 34,000 Jews in 1941. The inscription to the "Citizens of Kiev" bears no mention of the Jews.

9 See, for example, Henrikh Koffman, "Dos is geshen in Taganrog," *Sovetish haimland* 2 (1966): 119-24; Hirsh Dobin, "Der koiech fun lebn," *Sovetish haimland* 3 (1966): 44-68; Yechiel Falikman, "Der shvartser vint," *Sovetish haimland* 8 (1967): 39-87. Further discussion is found in my article, "History, Memory and Politics: The Holocaust in the Soviet Union," *Holocaust and Genocide Studies* 5 (1990): 23-37.

10 Quoted in William Korey, "No Monument over Babi Yar," in *The Soviet Cage* (New York: Viking, 1973), p. 109.

Jewish victims were mentioned on only one monument in one major city in the former Soviet Union: here in Minsk, the capital of Belorussia.

jected the proposal that the inscription read, "Here in the Ponary forest, from July 1941 to July 1944, the Hitlerite occupiers and their local assistants murdered 100,000 people, of whom 70,000 were Jews—men, women, and children." The authorities objected to the phrase "their local assistants," arguing that this besmirched the Lithuanian people. Besides, they asserted, there had been collaborators from among the Jews as well. The inscription was to be in Yiddish, Hebrew, Lithuanian, and Russian. After much debate, prior to a visit by an Israeli delegation, it was agreed to keep the text but to inscribe the monument only in Hebrew and Yiddish, so that the local population would not be able to read the "offensive" phrase.[11]

It appears that the only monument in a major city which specifically mentions Jews is the one in Minsk, capital of Belorussia, the inscription of which is in both Russian and Yiddish. In the city's Museum of the Great Patriotic War, however, photographs of the heroine, Masha Bruskina, who was killed by the Germans at the age of seventeen when it was discovered that she was aiding Soviet prisoners, do not

A simple gravestone in memory of the Holocaust victims in Seta, Lithuania.

Mass grave in Dobele, Latvia.

A family at the site of a mass grave in Zidikai in Lithuania where 3,000 were killed. Since such sites remained unofficial in the former USSR and memorials were often destroyed, snapshots from family albums serve as their only documentation.

11   Tom Segev, "Sippurah shel Matsevah," *Ha'aretz,* June 14, 1991.
12   An interesting discussion of the case is in Judith Miller, *One, by One, by One: Facing the Holocaust* (New York: Simon and Schuster, 1990), pp. 174-85.
13   "'Chernaia Kniga' sushchesvuet," *Vechernii Kiev,* September 29, 1989.

identify her as Jewish, nor do they even mention her name (she is labeled "unknown," even though her surviving relatives and acquaintances identified her). Despite repeated protests, officials have refused to identify her.[12]

In many small towns, immediately after the war, apparently, Jews erected modest monuments to the victims of Nazism. These were often artistically crude, some of the inscriptions containing mistakes in the spelling of Yiddish and Hebrew words. They were genuine folk creations, coming from the broken hearts of survivors rather than from the studios of regime-approved artists. Beginning in 1948, however, when Stalin launched the "anti-cosmopolitan" campaign, arrested the leading Jewish cultural figures of the U.S.S.R.—some of whom he executed in 1952—and signaled a mass campaign against Jews, these monuments were taken away. Some were replaced with "sanitized" and Sovietized versions, others were not.[13]

Spontaneous expressions of sorrow were replaced by manipulated memorialization. Nevertheless, when the terror of Stalinism receded, Jews began to gather at the sites of mass murder to commemorate their dead and insist on the history which officials wanted to take away from them. Before such gatherings became possible, younger Jews learned about the Holocaust at home. There were few European Jews who had not lost a family member, so that knowledge of the Holocaust came not from books or films but from parents and grandparents, siblings and cousins. Of 358 recent Soviet immigrants I interviewed in Detroit, 69 percent said they first learned of the Holocaust from family conversations, 27 percent from reading, and only 10 percent at school.

Toward the end of the Communist era, as part of *glasnost* and the attempt to fill in "blank spots" in Soviet historiography, some more candid discussions of the Holocaust began to appear. By 1990 *Yom Hashoah* ceremonies in St. Petersburg, which had earlier been broken up by the police, proceeded unimpeded. A Kiev newspaper devoted an entire page to an excerpt from Ehrenburg and Grossman's *Black Book,* referring to an earlier article in a Moscow evening newspaper which had revealed the fate

Residents of Rovno, Ukraine, gather at a memorial for their townspeople who died in 1941-42.

of that documentary compilation.[14] In September 1988, a large gathering in Moscow commemorated Babi Yar. By the fall of 1991, just before the breakup of the Soviet Union, Ukrainian officials decided to commemorate the fiftieth anniversary of the massacre in dramatic fashion. Many visitors, including former residents of Kiev, traveled to the Ukraine for a week of meetings and ceremonies. Banners were strung across main boulevards of the city announcing the commemoration. An international scholarly conference was held, and several ceremonies, some at the controversial monument, were staged. Commemorative pins, postcards, and medallions were distributed. A memorial book, listing many of the victims, was published with a print run of 75,000 copies,[15] and several boulevards were lined with photographs of the victims. In the newly independent Ukraine, however, the sensitive subject of Ukrainian collaboration has so far been handled very cautiously. In 1991 in independent Lithuania, after the government announced an indiscriminate wholesale pardon of thousands convicted by the Soviets of collaboration or war crimes, foreign protests forced an examination of some of the cases. While thousands were pardoned, about 500 cases were held back for further investigation. In Minsk, Lvov, and Vilnius, memorial sculptures commemorating the Holocaust have been commissioned or planned.[16]

Memorial service at a mass grave in Belogorye, Ukraine, for Jews from Yampol, Kornizi, and Belogorye who were murdered on June 27, 1942.

14   See the photographs of the unofficial monuments in Utian (Lithuania) and Glubokoye (Belorussia) in my *A Century of Ambivalence: The Jews of Russia and the Soviet Union, 1881 to the Present* (New York: Schocken, 1988), pp. 185-89. Another unofficial monument, unusual for its Hebrew inscription, can be seen in the photograph section in B. F. Sabrin, *Alliance for Murder* (New York: Sarpedon, 1991), pp. 160-80. The monument was erected in Trembowla, Ukraine.

15   *Kniga pamyatii* (Kiev: MIP-Oberg, 1991).

16   See Mordechai Altshuler, "Changes in Soviet Jewry," *Jews and Jewish Topics in the Soviet Union and Eastern Europe* 2 (Summer 1989): 28.

The uniqueness of the Holocaust is finally being acknowledged in some of the Soviet successor states. Israeli and American researchers have been given access to Soviet archives with materials on the Holocaust, and officials from the archives of Yad Vashem in Jerusalem have microfilmed a large amount of material. Soviet researchers of the Holocaust have begun to go to Israel for training and guidance, and several people from the former Soviet states have launched projects involving the interviewing of survivors. Still, the subject is treated cautiously because it inevitably raises the question of collaborators and their fate. The atmosphere is tense; the air has not been cleared. A major chapter in contemporary Jewish history is slowly being restored from memory to history, but until the newly independent peoples of the former U.S.S.R. summon up the courage to confront their own pasts, "blank spots" will remain.

Saul Friedländer
in collaboration
with Adam Seligman

Memory of the *Shoah* in Israel
Symbols, Rituals, and Ideological Polarization

The trauma of the Holocaust leaves an indelible mark on [Israel's] national psychology, the tenor and content of public life, the conduct of public affairs, on politics, education, literature and the arts.... All over the country, countless private and public monuments to the grimmest phase of European history perpetuate a memory which lies in all morbidity at the center of Israel's historic self-image. If, in Israeli eyes, the world at large has tended to forget too soon, Israelis hardly give themselves a chance. The traumatic memory is part of the rhythm and ritual of public life.[1]

If anything, this impact grew during the 1970s and 1980s, sometimes, as will be seen, in paradoxical ways. Indeed, the lasting impact of this past on the hundreds of thousands of survivors who reached the country—often on their children as well—the establishment of national rituals of commemoration, the development of specific school curricula, a fast-growing historiography, the ongoing use of media dramatizations, as well as artistic and literary reelaborations of the events, have created a vast domain of public reference to this past. Its effects can be diversely evaluated but in no way dismissed. In this chapter, I will consider a very limited aspect of this representation: its congruence with religious tradition, a few of its symbolic expressions in Israeli public life, and, in passing, the growing ideological instrumentalization of this ritualized memory.[2]

The Mold of Tradition

Jewish tradition is often characterized by its attempts to define collective identity in time through the elaboration of a meaningful history. Collective existence within historical time was understood in terms of a theodicy of history. Consequently, there developed within Judaism a continual and salient tension between historical existence and redemption. The short period of time that elapsed between the catastrophe of European Jewry and the creation of the Jewish state presented the official discourse with a framework both natural and deeply embedded in Jewish tradition, that of "catastrophe and redemption." The basic elements of this framework are essential for understanding the place of the Holocaust in Israel's memorial tradition.

On the one hand, redemption, as conceived in the Bible and by the apocalyptic writers, bore no relation to historical processes. Redemption broke with ordinary history, or in Gershom Scholem's words, it is "transcendence breaking in on history."[3] Indeed, during the centuries of Jewish dispersion, exile had no meaning in its relation to redemption and was mostly considered a cathartic preparation for it. As divine punishment, only God could terminate the exile, and so, for the majority of Jews, messianism had to be of a passive nature. The very dichotomy of historical delay and anticipated redemption resulted in strict warnings against any attempt to "hasten the End."

On the other hand, the very constitution of the Jewish people was posited in history. Both the archetypical images of society's emergence into history and redemption from history were of this world and were played out in the arena of history. The covenant of Abraham and the Laws of Moses, both historical events marking the birth of the nation, were perceived as taking place within the course of historical time. Similarly, the images of redemption, the resurgence of the rule of the House of David, the building of the Temple, and the ingathering of the exiles, were treated as events taking place within the orders of the world and so within history proper. Consequently, and in marked contradiction to the above tradition, a concept of an active messianism emerged which entailed the Jews' active participation in furthering the process of salvation.[4]

The conflation of these traditions — the devalorization of the Exile, on the one hand, and the historical nature of collective identity on the other — was of great consequence for the patterning of Jewish memory over the ages. In a condition where "the biblical past was known, the messianic future assured [and] the in-between-time obscure," historical events were interpreted according to a particular mythic and biblical pattern.[5]

Traditional memory that was organized religiously according to Jewish law, however, could not, by definition, include a realized time of redemption, except in its ritualized form during Passover and Yom Kippur — the two holy days which celebrate the collective and individual moments of redemption respectively. With the restructuring of Jewish history in the twentieth century, however, the ritual definition of redemption was transformed and the perception of current events as well.

For ultra-Orthodox Jews, the *Haredim,* who rejected any idea of redemption as a process actively fostered within historical time, the very essence of Zionism was, therefore, unacceptable and could not but have led to punishment and catastrophe. For other Orthodox Jews, who accommodated Zionism to Judaism, and for secular Jews as well, with the creation of the State of Israel, historical events leading to national rebirth were viewed as part of a process of redemption. As we shall see, however, this view was itself variable and complex, running from an allegorical interpretation by most, to a literal interpretation by those proponents of the active messianism which emerged in Israel in the 1970s and 1980s. In both cases, however, past models of structuring historical memory around exile and exodus were consummated, not in religious rituals, but in a vision of national-religious or secular redemption. Within these frameworks, the *Shoah* seemed to find its deeply significant place.

Commemorative Dates, Rituals, and Sites

For some ultra-Orthodox Jews, such as the Satmar Rebbe Yoel Teitelbaum, the extermination of the Jews of Europe was divine punishment for attempting to hasten the End, i. e., for Zionism. Usually, however, such extreme positions have not been commonly expressed, even in the ultra-Orthodox community. Though the commemoration of the *Shoah* was linked to the framework of catastrophe and redemption, redemption still remained outside historical time.

More significant within Israeli society is the interpretation of the *Shoah* as adopted by religious Zionism. In December 1949 the ashes of Jews exterminated in the concentration camp at Flossenbürg were transferred to Israel. The director of a department in the Ministry of Religious Affairs, Rabbi S. Z. Kahana, made the decision to have these ashes buried in Jerusalem on Mount Zion, on the 10th of Teveth, the day in Jewish tradition for reciting the prayer for all the departed. He suggested that this should become the fixed date for the commemoration of the *Shoah.*[6] The Chief Rabbinate accepted Kahana's proposal, and a symbolic pattern emerged, firmly structuring commemoration of the *Shoah* among religious Zionists.

The 10th of Teveth is the date on which the first siege of Jerusalem by the Babylonian king Nebuchadnezzar began, the beginning of the traditional Jewish sequence of catastrophes shaped by repeated destruction and exile. According to religious tradition, Mount Zion is the burial place of King David. Since the Messiah is related to King David (Ben David), Mount Zion is fundamentally a site and symbol of redemption. Thus, in the decision made by the Rabbinate, we see the reflection of an

Courtyard in the "Chamber of the Holocaust" at the memorial site on Mount Zion, Jerusalem. Memorial plaques, inscribed to religious Jewish individuals, families, and communities who perished in Europe, cover the walls.

1   Amos Elon, *The Israelis: Founders and Sons* (New York: Holt, Rinehart and Winston, 1971), p. 199.

2   For very perceptive references to this issue, see Charles S. Liebman and Eliezar Don-Yehiya, *Civil Religion in Israel: Traditional Judaism and Political Culture in the Jewish State* (Berkeley: University of California Press, 1983).

3   Gershom Scholem, "Towards an Understanding of the Messianic Idea in Judaism," *The Messianic Idea in Judaism* (New York: Allen and Unwin, 1971), p. 10.

4   For an elaboration on this theme, see Amos Funkenstein, *Maimonide: Nature, histoire, et messianisme* (Paris: Les Editions du Cerf, 1988), pp. 97, 103.

5   Yosef Yerushalmi, *Zakhor: Jewish History and Jewish Memory* (Seattle: University of Washington Press, 1982), p. 24.

6   Letter from S. Z. Kahana to the Chief Rabbinate, Jerusalem, December 25, 1949, Archive of the Chief Rabbinate, Jerusalem.

7   S. Z. Kahana, "Hamashmaut Haleumit Simlit shel Martef Hashoah be Har Zion," *Hatzofeh*, December 16, 1956.

8   Liebman and Don-Yehiya, *Civil Religion in Israel*, p. 23.

9   One tends to forget that two major debates of the early and mid-1950s dealt indirectly with the *Shoah:* the German reparations debate and the Kasztner trial. One may argue, however, that, in both cases, the immediate internal political issues linked to the debates drew most of the attention. Thus, the importance of the Eichmann trial in this process remains central: "The trial," in Alan Mintz's words "had the force of an electrifying discovery.... The trial resembled nothing so much as, *mutatis mutandis,* a massive Passion play, in which the members of an entire community play parts"; see Alan Mintz, *Hurban: Responses to Catastrophe in Hebrew Literature* (New York: Columbia University Press, 1984), pp. 239-40.

10 It was initially called The Holocaust and Ghetto Uprising Memorial Day—A Day of Perpetual Remembrance for the House of Israel. From 1953 on, it became known as Holocaust and Heroism Remembrance Day. Only in 1959 did another law impose public observance; an amendment to the law, passed in 1961, required that places of entertainment be closed on the eve of that day. See Nathan Eck, "Holocaust Remembrance Day," *Encyclopaedia Judaica,* vol. 8 (Jerusalem, 1971), pp. 916-17 and James E. Young, "When a Day Remembers: A Performative History of Yom Hashoah Vehagvurah," *History and Memory* 2 (Winter 1990): 54-75.

ever-recurring symbolic pattern, a link between destruction and redemption: "At the Holocaust memorial site on Mount Zion," said Rabbi Pinchas from Karlitz, "we mourn and grieve, bow and sit in ashes, and at the same time we are resurrected and lift our heads."[7] By uniting both temporal and spatial metaphors, a unitary symbol congruent with tradition was being established. In what is now called "the chamber of the Holocaust," administered by the Diaspora Yeshiva, the catastrophe of European Jews is thus likened to the redemption of Israel and the beginning of the messianic process.

In *Civil Religion in Israel,* Charles Liebmann and Eliezer Don-Yehiya make the distinction between two main periods in the process of symbol formation of the new Jewish state. During the first period, until the late 1950s, which they call the "statist" era, they perceive mixed strategies of confrontation with the traditional symbolic world of Judaism and of dissolution, aiming at a limited instrumental choice of some traditional symbolic elements; in both cases, traditional symbols and values are reinterpreted and reappropriated according to the needs of the state. The second period witnesses the stage-by-stage creation of a civil religion, with its myths and rituals, increasingly dominated by the strategy of reinterpretation.[8] According to this analysis, the *Shoah* was of minor significance during the statist period, as the values of the *Yishuv,* "the settlement," and the new state seemed drastically discordant with the so-called passivity of European Jewry which led to their extermination "like sheep to slaughter." During the early statist period, a commemoration day and commemoration sites were established, but it was only during the later phase that the *Shoah* became a central component of Israel's civil religion.

That the evolution took place according to these general lines of development is unquestionable, but it may also be correct to describe it as a continuous process in which the *Shoah* took on increasing centrality in public life from the Eichmann trial onwards.[9] Moreover, from the outset, whatever the "strategy" leading from religious tradition to civil religion, it nonetheless seems to have maintained the traditional mythic patterns of historical memory.

On April 12, 1951, a law was passed establishing a formal Holocaust commemoration day: *Yom Hashoah* (Holocaust Day).[10] The Warsaw Ghetto Uprising had started on the eve of Passover, the 15th of Nissan (April 19) in 1943. The commemoration day was set on the 27th of Nissan, as close to the 15th of Nissan as religious laws

Commemoration of *Yom Hashoah*, Holocaust Remembrance Day, 27th day of Nissan, Jerusalem. Pedestrians and traffic halt as a siren is sounded and a two-minute silence is observed.

prohibiting mourning during the days of Passover would allow. According to Rabbi Mordechai Nurock, who headed the Knesset Committee that chose the 27th of Nissan: "We had to choose a date that also fits most massacres of European Jewry and the ghetto revolt that took place in Nissan. The Knesset committee therefore chose the end of Nissan, when so many sacred communities were killed by the Crusaders, forefathers of the Nazis."[11] During the Knesset debate, Rabbi Nurock also clearly linked the destruction of European Jewry to the creation of the state. "Honorable members of the Knesset," he declared, "we have seen a graveyard in front of us, a graveyard for six million of our brothers and sisters, and maybe because of their blood, shed like water, have we been privileged to have our state."[12] Thus the link between destruction and heroism was consecrated.

Moreover, within the same global framework of interpretation, the date chosen starts a series of three closely related commemorations: *Yom Hashoah* is followed by the commemoration day for soldiers fallen during Israel's wars, and at sunset Independence Day celebrations begin. Together, the choice of date and Nurock's statements work to reinsert the Holocaust into an historical series of Jewish catastrophes and to suggest a mythic link between the destruction of European Jewry and the birth of Israel — i. e., catastrophe and redemption — which, in turn, give a new dignity to the Jews of the Diaspora, as victims or survivors. By repeating the fundamentally religious sequence of catastrophe and redemption in a secular, civic context, these elements lose their explicitly religious charge but remain no less mythic and metahistorical. The traditional patterns are implicitly maintained.

The shifting emphasis from the catastrophe and destruction to the centrality of armed revolt, which seemed to have been the main reason for the choice of the date of the commemoration in Nissan, has, in itself, a redemptive aspect: from passive catastrophe to a redemptive struggle, linking the fighting Zionist youth of the ghettos to the armed struggle for the state. In this sense, *Shoah Vegvurah* (catastrophe and heroism) is actually just another formula for *Shoah Vetekumah* (catastrophe and rebirth), that is, for *Shoah Vegeulah* (catastrophe and redemption).

Indeed, the shift from "catastrophe" to "catastrophe and heroism" has become the focal point of the representation of the destruction of European Jewry in Israel's official memory. It is aimed not only at commemorative affirmation, but at "saving the honor" of Diaspora Jewry by countering the prevalent contempt for the so-called passivity of the victims.[13] The simplistic symmetry of catastrophe and heroism has been criticized by nonreligious survivors, for whom armed revolt was not the only form of heroism, and by religious circles, which considered martyrdom itself as the supreme value and not heroism or armed revolt. This basic structure nonetheless remained at center stage of official memory, at least until the mid- or late 1960s. The mobilizing and integrative function of this symbolic structure was too essential during the early years of the new state to be easily discarded. Moreover, one should remember in this regard, the substantial influence of the various organizations of Ghetto fighters and partisans. The "shame" of the mere survivor was being mythically erased.[14]

The official attempts to mold and remold this mythic pattern continued well into the 1970s. In 1977, when the Likkud came to power, Prime Minister Menachem Begin suggested that the *Shoah* as such be commemorated on the 9th of Av, a traditional fast day commemorating the Temples' destruction. At the same time, Begin proposed moving commemorations of Holocaust resistance to *Yom Hazikkaron*, the day before Independence Day, already set aside to recall Israel's fallen soldiers.[15] We do not know why he tried to separate the commemoration of the "catastrophe" from that of "heroism." In any event, his rhetoric of commemoration, as far as the *Shoah* itself was concerned, was consonant with the religious pathos which permeated his political rhetoric and vision. By linking the *Shoah* to the main religious commemoration of destruction in Jewish tradition, he made of the *Shoah* itself a symbol of the *Galut* (exile), itself resonant with all its historical and theological meanings. In so doing, however, he divorced it from the redemptive context of *Gevurah* (heroism), and, by implication, the establishment of the state, unless he remembered the old folk tradition which placed the birth of the Messiah on the very day the Temple was destroyed. He thus reinserted the *Shoah* into the traditional pattern of Jewish history, dissociating it from the vision of historical fulfillment embodied in the state. It is perhaps for this very reason that Begin's proposal was rejected by the Knesset.

Inside the museum at Kibbutz Yad Mordechai.

11   *The Knesset Record,* Third Session, First Knesset, April 12, 1951, p. 1656.

12   Ibid., p. 1657.

13   For a particularly crass expression of this kind of contempt within Socialist-Zionist lore, see, for example, the following *Kibbutz Haggada* (Passover saga) excerpt: "Hitler alone is not responsible for the death of six million—but all of us, and above all, the six million. If they had known that the Jew has power, they would not have all been butchered.... This lack of faith, the ghettoish-exilic self-denigration...contributed its share to this great butchery"; quoted in Liebman and Don-Yehiya, *Civil Religion in Israel,* p. 102.

14   Another function of this emphasis put on the heroism of the Jews in Europe may well have been that of assuaging an underlying sense of guilt. An ongoing debate about the role of the *Yishuv* in potential efforts to save some of the European Jews from the *Shoah* has brought forth contending positions about what was done or could have been done. The facts are open to interpretation. What is certain, however, is that on the symbolic level, at least, the *Yishuv* did not offer convincing proof of its total commitment to help. As Antek Zuckerman, one of the leaders of the Warsaw Ghetto Uprising, expressed in a conversation with the writer Haim Gouri: "Why did not one come? Not a single one!" See Dina Porat, *The Blue and the Yellow Stars of David: The Zionist Leadership in Palestine and the Holocaust, 1939-1945* (Cambridge, Mass. and London: Harvard University Press, 1990).

15   *The Knesset Record,* First Session, Ninth Knesset, August 2, 1977, p. 567.

16   Mircea Eliade, *The Sacred and the Profane* (New York: Harcourt Brace and Company, 1956), pp. 20-67, esp. 17, 20-21; Jonathan Smith, *Map Is Not Territory* (Leiden: E. J. Brill, 1978), pp. 88-146.

17   Michael Fishbane, "The Sacred Center: The Symbolic Structure of the Bible," in Michael Fishbane and Paul Mendes-Flohr, eds. *Texts and Responses* (Leiden: E. J. Brill, 1975), p. 21.

18   Ibid.

19   Ibid.

Sites of Memory

One of the most explicit arenas where the mythic pattern of cosmic evil and redemption, of death and rebirth, is enacted is in the construction of sites dedicated to the memory of the *Shoah*. At ritual sites, the organization of space is often used as a metaphor for the ordering of human existence and as a symbolic referent for the ultimate values of a culture.[16] Judaism's sacred space, moreover, has a specific geopolitical locus—the land of Israel and, more specifically, Jerusalem. In Michael Fishbane's words: "God's shrine [in Jerusalem] is a confirmation of social and religious order, it is an *imago mundi* giving the land cosmic significance."[17] In modern Israeli society, however, the ethical valorization of sacred time and space and the social order is no longer expressed in strictly religious terms but in the secular idiom of modern Jewish national identity. It is therefore not surprising that the very archetypical structure of the locations commemorating the *Shoah* link the catastrophe of the *Shoah* and the redemptive aspects of the State of Israel. In this reenactment, the sacred center, the *axis mundi* of Zion as the "foundation stone of origins, the center point from which the cosmic spring swells"[18] is secularized in terms of the State of Israel. In the traditional view, by a return to Zion, "to the sacred center" where "time and space are redeemed,"[19] the chaos of exile is refuted.

A similar structuring of sacred space can be observed in the manner in which the *Shoah,* as epitome of evil and chaos, is located with respect to the modern symbol of order and integrated existence, the State of Israel. At Kibbutz Yad Mordechai's mu-

A tree planted along the Avenue of the Righteous Gentiles at Yad Vashem to honor non-Jews who helped Jewish victims during the Holocaust.

seum, for instance, we move from the dimly lit basement of the *Shoah,* up a few steps to the better-lit space commemorating the Ghetto fighters, and up again to the clear light of Israel's rebirth in the main hall. This sequence is expressed ever more starkly in the internal layout and function of Yad Vashem, Israel's official Martyrs' and Heroes' Remembrance Authority, established in August 1953 (plates 5-7).

In the museum's historical narrative at Yad Vashem, the first section describes the preextermination persecutions which took place between 1933 and 1939. The second section seems to stand by itself and is devoted to the annihilation process between 1941 and 1945. This annihilation cannot be linked to the traditional sequences of persecution, known throughout Jewish history and repeated during the first phase of the Nazi era. In the third section, liberation comes. But this is not the end of the museum's narrative, which necessarily leads to the shores of *Eretz Israel,* the ultimate redemption.[20] The coherence of the symbolic expression of this memory of the *Shoah* seems unquestionable. A closer look at both the message and the functions of the symbolic expressions of this memory, however, show fundamental paradoxes and, ultimately, a disturbing undertone.

Let us consider the site of Yad Vashem, that is, the area where it was built. A considerable number of possible places were suggested by various organizations when the law for the establishment of a Commemoration Authority was passed in 1953. In August of that year, the Minister of Education and Culture, Ben-Zion Dinur, decided that Yad Vashem would be built on Remembrance Hill, on the outskirts of Jerusalem. Theodor Herzl had been buried there in August 1949, and a military cemetery had been established on the same site soon after the end of the fighting around the city.

The Mount of Remembrance was, in a sense, divided into two very distinct areas: the part of the hill facing the city of Jerusalem is the military cemetery and the burial place for the founder of Zionism and some of its main leaders. The part facing the hills, with its back to the city, became the commemoration center for the destruction of European Jewry. This setting seems to establish a hierarchy within the symbolic reference points of the new society. On a manifest level, the symbols of the new state take precedence over those of destruction.

This last point is more ambiguous than it seems. In Israel, there is no equivalent of the Tomb of the Unknown Soldier. In some countries, this kind of tomb is replaced as a central symbol of national identity by the tomb of the founder of the state (the Tomb of the *Libertador* in Latin American countries — that of San Martín, for instance, in Argentina). Whatever the mode of commemoration used, such monuments are the hallowed places where foreign dignitaries express their respect for the country they visit and where the group ritually reaffirms its own identity. But in Israel, foreign dignitaries visit neither the military cemetery on Remembrance Hill nor the tomb of Herzl. It is Yad Vashem which fulfills this symbolic function.

One could argue that there is an element of psychological conditioning in this choice. I believe, however, that this ritual has a latent significance of much wider importance. In a strangely contradictory way, the Remembrance Authority, which does not face the city of Jerusalem but rather the hills — which, at first glance, is not the dominant symbol in the hierarchy of symbols — has become nonetheless the central hallowed place presented to the attention of the world, a place where the visitor identifies with what appears to be the raison d'être of the Jewish state. The message may be that here, at Yad Vashem, the central place of commemoration of the *Shoah,* is the very basis of the legitimacy of the State of Israel.

The hierarchic unity of the symbol — the Mount of Remembrance — thus betrays a continual tension. The metahistorical meaning of the *Shoah* is not only realized in the redemptive moment of the state, but the state itself is valorized in terms of the *Shoah*. This implicit mode of legitimation of the state entails, in fact, a link between the religious view of the uniqueness of Israel and its secular vision constantly present in Zionism—and always in contradiction with its manifest aim of normalizing Jewish fate.[21]

The Ideological Polarization

The Six-Day War, in June 1967, opened a new phase in the perception of the *Shoah*, as it opened a new phase in the very evolution of Israeli society.[22] The *Shoah*, after having a national significance, both formalized and ritualized, with an unperceived message and function, became increasingly part and parcel of the new ideological confrontations within Israeli society. As political polarization grew, it became instrumentalized at the partisan level.[23] In the national-messianic context, for example, this has shown itself in three principal ways: (1) in a tendency to equate the hostility of Arabs with Nazi attitudes toward the Jews; (2) in a willingness to use symbols of the *Shoah* for self-identification and self-justification in the context of the internal political fight; and (3) in an emphasis on the isolation of Israel, the rhetoric of destruction, the uniqueness of the Jewish fate, all leading to a vision of redemption.

These elements are well known, with Menachem Begin's rhetoric during the Lebanon War serving as a good illustration of the first.[24] The use of the yellow star by the settlers at Yamit—who forcibly resisted Israeli efforts to move them from their coastal community as part of the Camp David Agreement settlement with Egypt—is an example of the second point. Finally, by adopting the last point as one of the central tenets of Zionist ideology, the new messianic nationalism has begun to take over all the symbols elaborated within a framework of traditional Zionism and, by pushing them to the extreme, has appropriated their core content.

The significance of this move is obvious. The mythic memory of the *Shoah*, which emerged so clearly during the 1950s and 1960s, became an integral part of the mythology of the messianic Zionism of the 1970s and 1980s, due, in part, to the inherent logic of its message. The uniqueness of Jewish fate and the link between catastrophe and redemption have become the essential belief of an extremely vocal, if limited, sector of Israeli society. What had been an essentially symbolic pattern of commemoration of the past for a society achieving independence became a potent guiding myth for one of the extreme segments of this same society. The latent content of the message has become the explicit program of a political faith.

In contrast to these uses of Holocaust memory stands the discourse of the more liberal and left-wing elements of the population. Though much more diverse and less cohesive, the memorial interpretations of the left tend to integrate the memory of the *Shoah* with a more universalistic and rational discourse. Its major points can be summed up as follows: (1) a tendency to compare some Jewish behavior in the occupied territories or in relation to the Palestinians in general with some aspects of Nazi behavior toward the Jews or with fascism in more general terms; (2) the rejection of any form of mythical structuring of the memory of the *Shoah* and an emphasis on its overall human and more banal aspects; and (3) the belief in the comparability and universalization of the phenomenon as suggested in the first two points.

The identification of some Jewish behavior with that of the Nazis has found its expression in a new form of subversive literary use of symbols, in a kind of reversal of the accepted vision, in some sort of literary defiance and breaking of taboos, which

20 For elaboration, see James E. Young, *Writing and Rewriting the Holocaust: Narrative and the Consequences of Interpretation* (Bloomington and Indianapolis: Indiana University Press, 1988), pp. 186-87, and idem, "Yad Vashem: Israel's Memorial Authority," in *The Texture of Memory: Holocaust Memorials and Meaning* (New Haven and London: Yale University Press, 1993), pp. 243-61.

21 For more on the site's meaning, see Don Handelman, *Models and Minors: Towards an Anthropology of Public Events* (Cambridge and New York: Cambridge University Press, 1990), p. 201.

22 For Israeli society, this change is obviously linked to the effects of the occupation of the West Bank and Gaza and the political evolution that ensued. It may well be, moreover, that the perception of the possible destruction, during the weeks preceding the Six-Day War, reinforced the identification with the fate of European Jews within wide strata of the population. The 1973 Yom Kippur War was another stage in this process, as was the Lebanon War of 1983. The impact of the 1967 and 1973 wars in terms of awareness of the *Shoah* have been measured in various polls, as well as in terms of increased attention to the *Shoah* in school curricula and educational material. See Simon N. Herman, "In the Shadow of the Holocaust," *The Jerusalem Quarterly* 3 (Spring 1977): 85-97; Haim Schatzer, "The Holocaust in Israeli Education," *International Journal of Political Education* 5 (1982): 77. As for the Lebanon War, it was accompanied and followed by a considerable growth of literary responses to the war in the light of the *Shoah*, many of them regarded as subversive in their repudiation of the *Shoah* as a symbol for Jewish suffering only. See, in this context, James E. Young, "Anti-War Poetry in Israel: When Soldier-Poets Remember the Holocaust," *Partisan Review* (October 1987): 594-602.

23 For illustrations of some aspects of this instrumentalization, see Gerald Cromer, "Negotiating the Meaning of the Holocaust: An Observation on the Debate about Kahanism in Israeli Society," *Holocaust and Genocide Studies* 2 (1987): 289 ff.

24 See, for instance, the following excerpt of a letter Prime Minister Menachem Begin wrote to President Ronald Reagan in the midst of the war: "May I tell you, Mr. President, how I feel these days when I turn to the Creator of my soul in deep gratitude: I feel as a Prime Minister empowered to instruct a valiant army facing Berlin, where amongst innocent civilians, Hitler and his henchmen hide in a bunker deep beneath the surface," *Jerusalem Post* 3 (August 1982).

Military officers in training are led through the historical museum at Yad Vashem, where the lessons of history reinforce an understanding of their role in Israel's defense forces.

became particularly clear during the Lebanon War. In the words of one interpreter: "The images themselves, the emblems of Nazism, now seem to have been released from social taboo by acts of literary defiance against the very rhetoric which proclaims, officially, that Jews are constitutionally *incapable* of oppressive behavior and attitudes."[25]

The subversive use of symbols is but one expression among others of ideological defiance. The comparability and universalization of the *Shoah* it implies also lead to a number of contradictions. In the opening article of a 1986 issue of the left-wing periodical *Politika* devoted to the *Shoah*, Adi Ophir stressed the need for comparability and universalization, an imperative the ideological reasons for which were obvious. In stating his own position, however, the author introduced words which, in effect, may have canceled his own premises. "In no case do I wish to say," he wrote, "that the *Shoah* was less than absolute evil [*ro'ah muhlat*]."[26] "Absolute evil" makes comparability and universalization very difficult.

In a way, the political heirs of the left-wing organizations which thirty years before had more or less created the myth of catastrophe and rebirth were now those who, because of the evolution of Israeli society, were attempting to do away with this mythical memory of the past. At the same time, the political opposition of the 1950s and 1960s was appropriating, for its own cause, the core of that mythical memory, turning its latent content into a manifest message. In other words, with the establishment of the State of Israel, both the preceding destruction of European Jewry as well as the very creation of the state were formulated in collective memory in traditional religious patterns of catastrophe and redemption. Once the redemptive movement in history became identified with the state, however, its particular articulation became the province of competing political visions pursuing their own, mutually exclusive, interpretations of the state and of the fulfillment of redemption. It can perhaps be added that the conflicting ideologies of the present represent two poles of a dichotomy which has always existed within Jewish historical consciousness. For the redemptive vision in Judaism has always contained both particularistic elements focused on the national, ethnic, and ascriptive definitions of the messianic community, as well as a more universalistic vision of the end of days and freedom from the thralldom of history.

In *Zakhor*, Yosef Yerushalmi states that the image of the *Shoah* "is being shaped, not at the historian's anvil, but in the novelist's crucible"[27] and that the Jews are await-

Hall of Remembrance at Yad Vashem, dedicated in 1961.

25 Sidra Dekoven Ezrahi, "Revisioning the Past: The Changing Legacy of the Holocaust in Hebrew Literature," *Salmagundi* 68–69 (Fall 1985): 270.

26 Adi Ophir, "Al Chidush Hashem," *Politika* 8 (June-July 1986): 2–5.

27 Yerulshalmi, *Zakhor*, pp. 99–100.

28 Ezrahi, "Revisioning the Past," p. 270. The allusion here is probably to the work of writers such as Aharon Appelfeld and Dan Pagis.

In the Hall of Remembrance an eternal flame remains lit in memory of those who perished in the Holocaust. The names of the major extermination camps are inscribed on the floor.

ing the creation of some new metahistorical myth which, like the mystical world of the Kabbalah and after the expulsion from Spain, will give new meaning to the cataclysmic past. But, in fact, the evolution seems far more complex. In Israel, beyond the trends I alluded to, a new sensitivity, possibly a new authenticity regarding the *Shoah,* seems to be appearing, particularly on the literary scene. "The individual sensibilities," writes Sidra Ezrahi, "which had been rendered historically insignificant when juxtaposed with the socially ritualized codes, are now harnessed to an equally public enterprise of denationalizing memory and challenging exclusive claims to the inheritance...."[28]

On the other hand, it is also true that the hard-core mythification of the *Shoah* within a given sector of Israeli society still finds a significant echo. Conflicting tendencies in the representation and interpretation of the extermination of the Jews of Europe appear not only in international debates concerning the place and significance of these events in history. Within the Jewish world as well, we will probably be faced for a long time to come with an ongoing and conflicting process of shaping and reshaping, writing and rewriting the story of what, presently, appears to be an indelible but essentially opaque past.

Editor's note: Some of the issues addressed in this essay were first presented by Saul Friedländer on December 31, 1986, at the "Hanukkah Lecture" at the Jerusalem Van Leer Foundation, and published under the title, "Die Shoah als Element in der Konstruktion israelischer Erinnerung," in *Babylon* 2 (1987): 10-22.

Peter Novick

Holocaust Memory in America

In recent decades, to an extent unimaginable a generation ago, the United States has become Holocaust conscious. The Holocaust has been the subject of a flood of books, films, university courses, and docudramas; it is invoked as reference point in discussions of everything from AIDS to abortion. Every major American city has a substantial Holocaust memorial in place, under construction, or on the drawing board.

All of this raises two puzzling questions. The first is why here? Unlike Germany (the homeland of the perpetrators); unlike Israel (with a special relationship to the victims); unlike Poland (the site of the murder factories); unlike all European countries occupied by the Nazis, which experienced the Holocaust directly, the United States has no special relationship to the Holocaust. Why should the Holocaust have become so resonant in *America* — a country 97 percent non-Jewish, separated from the scene of the crime by a vast ocean? In truth, it is misleading to speak of wide or deep American interest in the Holocaust. Rather, what we have is, for the most part, American *Jewish* concern, which, because of the extraordinarily important role of American Jews in American society, particularly in the media, has reverberated throughout the culture at large. A good deal of American Gentile involvement in Holocaust commemoration is little more than polite deference to American Jewish sensibilities. Sometimes it is based on the kind of political calculation which leads candidates for election routinely to seek photo opportunities at Holocaust monuments or Jimmy Carter to establish the Presidential Commission on the Holocaust to mend fences with Jewish voters who thought him insufficiently supportive of Israel. To be sure, there are many American Gentiles for whom the Holocaust has become important, but the apparent resonance of the Holocaust in American culture should not be taken as an index of depth or breadth of that importance.

The second question is why now? During the first postwar decades, the Holocaust was quite marginal in American consciousness, even in the consciousness of most Jews. Then, between the late 1960s and the late 1970s, it moved to a central position. The slope of the curve of memory may vary but is just about always steadily downward: most vivid in the immediate aftermath of the events in question, declining with the passage of time. It has been quite otherwise with the Holocaust: virtual silence, apparent social amnesia, for a full generation, then, between the late 1960s and the late 1970s, a Rostovian "takeoff into self-sustained growth" — and growing ever since. The fact that the Holocaust was largely ignored for over twenty years after World War II is nowadays often explained in the language of repression. Jewish agony and Gentile guilt were too great to confront: the very silence is said to be testimony to the depth of feeling that was being repressed. Like all such dialectical, double-whammy psychoanalytic explanations, this is a hard argument to refute, nor should it be rejected out of hand. Certainly, in the case of immigrant survivors, there *was* often repression of memories too painful to bear. No doubt this was also true of some American Jews who experienced the Holocaust vicariously — particularly those who had active family connections with victims. But the notion of American Jewry, as a whole, having been traumatized by the Holocaust does not square with what we know of the rather thin wartime response, and of evidence for American Gentile guilt there is scarcely a trace. If we want to understand the evolution of Holocaust consciousness in America, we should look at conscious choices as well as subterranean forces; we should consider the changing circumstances, changing perceptions, changing communal needs, and changing American-Jewish self-understanding which led first to the marginalizing, then to the centering of the Holocaust.

During the war, and in the first postwar decades, there was no generally accepted term for the frightful events which we now call "the Holocaust" — emblematic of the

Nathan Rapoport's *Liberation*, a bronze memorial, showing an American soldier with a rescued concentration camp victim, stands in Liberty State Park, New Jersey, within sight of Ellis Island and the Statue of Liberty.

fact that for most Gentiles, and a great many Jews as well, it was seen as simply one among many dimensions of the horrors of Nazism. Looking at World War II retrospectively, we are inclined to stress what was distinctive in the murderous zeal with which European Jewry was destroyed. Things often appeared differently to contemporaries. Those whose adult memories reached back to 1933 were certainly well aware of Nazi anti-Semitism, but Jews did not stand out as the Nazis' prime victims until near the end of the Third Reich. Until 1938 there were hardly any Jews, qua Jews, in concentration camps, which were populated largely by Socialists, Communists, trade unionists, dissident intellectuals, and the like. Even when news of mass killings of Jews during the war reached the West, their murder was framed as one atrocity, albeit the largest, in a long list of crimes, such as the massacre of Czechs at Lidice, the French at Oradour, and American prisoners of war at Malmedy. American newspapers reported the liberation of camps such as Dachau and Buchenwald, where the overwhelming majority of the prisoners were Gentiles, but no coverage was given to the camps in Eastern Europe devoted to the murder of Jews. At the Nuremberg trials, in part because of the absence of those most directly involved in the Holocaust (Hitler, Himmler, Heydrich, Eichmann), the murder of European Jews did not figure prominently.

After the War, American Jewry turned — with great energy and generosity — to liquidating the legacy of the Holocaust by caring for the survivors. American Jews were not "converted to Zionism" by the Holocaust; they were dedicated to finding a safe refuge for those who had emerged from Hitler's inferno, be it in a new Jewish state, or in the United States. In both cases, survivors were urged to put the ghastly past behind them, to build new lives in their adopted homes. Though virtually all American Jews were acutely aware that but for their parents' or grandparents' immigration they would have shared the fate of European Jews, this tended to deepen *American* loyalty and *American* identity, promoting an integrationist rather than a particularist consciousness. Anti-Semitic barriers to full Jewish participation in American society were rapidly tumbling, and Jewish organizations sought to stress what united Jews with other Americans, not what separated them. When a proposal for a Holocaust memorial in New York City came before representatives of the leading Jewish organizations in the late 1940s, they unanimously rejected the idea: it would, they said, give currency to the image of Jews as "helpless victims," an idea they wished to repudiate.

Certainly the most important instrumental reason for downplaying the Holocaust, and probably a subconscious reason as well, was the rapid reversal of wartime alignments after 1945 — dramatically symbolized by the 1948 Berlin Blockade and followed shortly thereafter by preliminary moves for German rearmament. This made the moral relegitimation of Germany an urgent ideological task for American foreign policy. With this overriding agenda, to dwell on German crimes was, if not actively disloyal, at least unhelpful. Complaining to a colleague in 1950 that Jewish organizations were not as zealously anti-Soviet as they had been anti-Nazi, G. George Freedman, an official of the Jewish War Veterans, said: "I know, they'll bring up the question of two world wars, and 6,000,000 Jews exterminated. But that is past, and we must deal with the facts to-day."[1] On a more abstract level, the new alignments were justified by theorists of totalitarianism who emphasized what they saw as the striking, indeed uncanny, parallelism between the Nazi and Soviet regimes. To dwell on the singularity of the Nazi Holocaust would be subtly to undermine the equation. In these years, those who sought American ratification of the Genocide Convention spoke of Soviet genocide and downplayed the Holocaust.

1 Freedman to S. Andhil Fineberg, February 16, 1950, American Jewish Committee Papers, General Series 12, Box 3.

Heightened anti-communism raised fears that, as so often in the past, it would be accompanied by anti-Semitism. In the event, this did not happen; nonetheless, Jewish agencies were wary of taking a line which suggested less than total enthusiasm for new cold war alignments. On the whole, it was those marginalized sections of American Jewry which were nostalgic for the Popular Front, or actively pro-Soviet, that talked most about Nazism and the Holocaust. Holocaust imagery figured prominently, for example, in demonstrations against the execution of convicted Soviet spies Julius and Ethel Rosenberg. Distancing the Jewish community from its leftist fringe was a top priority item for communal leaders in this period, and insofar as Holocaust discourse was often pro-Soviet in origin and in thrust, it too was distanced.

By the early 1960s, however, things were beginning to change. The capture and trial of Eichmann and, in the following years, the controversies surrounding Hannah Arendt's *Eichmann in Jerusalem* were something of a curtain raiser to the era of transition. For the mass public this was the first time the Holocaust was framed as a distinct and separate process, separate from Nazi criminality in general. But Jewish organizations approached the trial with some nervousness: they were wary about charges — which appeared with some frequency in the press — that the whole episode illustrated the contrast between Jewish, Old Testament "vengefulness" and Christian forgiveness. At any event, whatever role the Eichmann trial played as a catalyst of later Holocaust consciousness, it seemed, at the time, a discrete event, over and done with by the mid-1960s.

There is no difficulty in specifying the proximate, and most important, catalyst of Holocaust consciousness: the fears of a renewed Holocaust in the weeks immediately preceding the Six-Day War of June 1967. There was a widespread perception, no less genuine for being mistaken, that the combined Arab armies would drive the Jews of Israel — or perhaps a remnant of surviving Jews — into the sea. All at once, the image of the mass slaughter of Jews was transformed from mere, albeit tragic, history into imminent present prospect. It is possible that this renewed salience of the idea of Holocaust would have proved ephemeral, particularly in the wake of Israel's stunning victory in 1967, had it not been for the reprise of fears for Israel's survival following early Israeli reversals in the 1973 Yom Kippur War — fears continually reinforced by Israel's diplomatic isolation in subsequent years.

Insofar as the Middle East conflict was seen as a potential reenactment of the Holocaust, it was invested with the moral clarity of the original. This, in turn, generated a sense of outraged betrayal when non-Jews were less than fully supportive of the Israeli cause. It was perceived as the world's indifference (or worse) to Jewish destruction all over again. Holocaust imagery had previously played a very subordinate role in mobilizing support for Israel — which, in any case, had not been a major problem before 1967. Such imagery henceforth became dominant and came to play a decisive role in Jewish framing of Middle Eastern issues.

Another contemporaneous, but quite separate, issue served to stimulate Holocaust consciousness. Conflicts between African Americans and Jews in the mid-to-late 1960s and particularly demands by some blacks for "reparations" to compensate for past oppression, set in motion a discourse of competitive claims to victimization. In this sordid competition, the Holocaust became a trump card, repeatedly slammed down on the table. This sometimes evoked provocative black responses and a spiral of escalating, unedifying exchanges.

Connected with all of this was the emergence of Meir Kahane and the Jewish Defense League, whose slogan "Never Again" — invoked in support of Israel and in confrontations with African Americans — became a central theme of Holocaust discourse. Mainstream Jewish organizations sometimes hastened to associate themselves with the Holocaust out of fear that Kahane would come to gain hegemony over it. Kahane represented — in grotesque caricature — a generational shift in Jewish leadership: the replacement of those committed to an earlier, low-profile, "don't-make-waves" posture, to a more assertive, younger generation which more often included — and the cultural difference is not insignificant — Jews of Eastern European rather than of German origin. Not yet in leadership positions, but not without influence either, were young Jews influenced by the moralistic and confrontational style of the New Left and a politics of catharsis — all of which became associated with Holocaust consciousness. (There is an almost straight line between Sproul Plaza in Berkeley in 1964 and Rabbi Avi Weiss and his followers at the Auschwitz Carmelite Convent in 1989.) If the style of emerging Holocaust discourse owed something to the radicals of the 1960s, its content was often philosophically conservative, meshing with the rightward turn of many leading American Jews. Discussion of the Holocaust has often treated it as a startling revelation of the existence of depravity in mankind, exposing the callow naïveté of those with utopian, or even meliorative, social aspirations. During these years, the quality, as well as the quantity, of Holocaust discourse changed. An apt symbol is the shift in the popular archetype of the Holocaust victim: from Anne Frank (assimilated, universalist in orientation, sheltered by Gentiles) to Elie Wiesel (of Hasidic background, Zionist and particularist in orientation, abandoned by Gentiles).

By the late 1970s, the Holocaust had fully "arrived" on the American scene, with tens of millions of Americans watching Gerald Green's Holocaust soap opera and the establishment of the Presidential Commission on the Holocaust. It has retained high visibility ever since, in part through a succession of events such as the ceremony at Bitburg, the trials of Klaus Barbie and John Demjanjuk, the Waldheim affair, and the imbroglio over the Carmelite convent at Auschwitz. But the centrality of the Holocaust has been chosen, not imposed: hundreds of millions of dollars have been raised for the U.S. Holocaust Memorial Museum, Washington, D.C., the Museum of Jewish Heritage, New York, and the Simon Wiesenthal Center's *Beit HaShoah*-Museum of Tolerance, Los Angeles, and countless other museums and memorial projects across the country. Such projects guarantee that the centrality of the Holocaust will be set in stone — and in organizational investment — for the indefinite future: with what consequences?

The Holocaust has become central to the self-understanding of American Jews. More than any set of religious beliefs (most American Jews do not have much in the way of religious beliefs), more than any set of distinctive ethnic characteristics (most American Jews do not have these either), a sense of connectedness to the Holocaust (and to Israel) has increasingly come to define Jewishness in America. Beleaguered Israel as the symbol of the eternal "Jewish condition" is complemented by the Holocaust as the archetype of Gentile-Jewish relations. The connection between the Holocaust and Israel — "from destruction to redemption," Israel as "the answer" to the Holocaust — is carefully nurtured. United Jewish Appeal tours for contributors and potential contributors, which once went directly to Israel, now include stopovers at Auschwitz and Treblinka. Since, in recent years, a growing minority of American Jews reluctantly have come to conclude that the rights and wrongs of the Israeli-Palestinian confrontation are not clear-cut, the Holocaust as the paradigm of the Jewish experience offers reassurance to some that Israel's cause must be supported whatever the ambiguities. To others it offers, in place of Israel, another, more morally impeccable, basis for grounding Jewish identity.

All American Jews are committed to some form of communal remembrance of the Holocaust—though many are dismayed by the glib and glitzy form of so many existing commemorations and memorials. But there has been increasing protest at the centrality of the Holocaust in grounding Jewish identity—its tendency to crowd out other foundations. The protests come, in the main, from the most religiously committed and the most Jewishly literate: that minority for whom the Torah and the covenant retain meaning, who are knowledgeable about how Jews have lived, not just about how they died. In large part, the concern is moral: the conviction that Jewish identity grounded in the Holocaust is perverse and pathological. But, in part, it is prudential: with the rate of intermarriage exceeding 50 percent and the long-range survival of the community in question, is a Holocaust-centered identity, they ask, an effective response to centrifugal forces?

Beyond its communal functions, the Holocaust is said to carry with it urgently important *lessons,* to which everyone should attend. This is the rationale for Holocaust curricula in the public schools; for Holocaust museums, which, even when housed within Jewish facilities, have a primarily Gentile audience, and for all general discourse about the Holocaust. But the lessons of the Holocaust are problematic— and made much more problematic by the axiom of its uniqueness, on which the great majority of Jewish spokesmen insist. (Indeed, those who question the Holocaust's uniqueness are frequently charged with anti-Semitism.) Uniqueness is, in fact, a term of art without any substantive content. Everything in the world is like some other

Crowds gather at the dedication ceremonies of the United States Holocaust Memorial Museum, Washington, D.C., April 1993. President Clinton and other dignitaries on the rostrum.

Model of the *Beit HaShoah*-Museum of Tolerance at the Simon Wiesenthal Center in Los Angeles.

things in some respects, unlike them in others. At best, to call something unique is to assert that for one's immediate purposes it is useful to stress what distinguishes the object under discussion from other things it might be compared with, rather than to stress similarities. In serious discussion, the word is worse than useless, and we would be well rid of it. But if the Holocaust *were* unique, it could not possibly carry with it any lessons, since any such lessons could only be applied in situations which are in some way analogous. (Of course, many who insist on the uniqueness of the Holocaust really mean something rather different: that it is, so to speak, horizontally unique, but not vertically unique, that it is inappropriate, indeed indecent, to compare the suffering of Jews during the Holocaust to the suffering of any other people, but at the same time the Holocaust is simply the latest and most ghastly instance of ubiquitous, permanent, murderous Gentile hostility toward Jews — it is, in fact, the apotheosis of the Jewish experience.)

What lessons can be drawn from the Holocaust? That it was a monstrous crime is true and important, but this hardly constitutes an interesting lesson. Those who encounter vivid testimony or representations of the Holocaust are — as they should be — overcome with awe and pain, but it is not at all clear where this *leads*, what the lesson is. If there are, in fact, lessons to be drawn from history, the Holocaust would seem singularly lacking in them, not because of its putative uniqueness, but because of its *extremity*. Lessons for dealing with the sort of issues that confront us in ordinary life, public or private, are not likely to be found in the most extraordinary of circumstances. There are more important lessons to be learned about how easily we become victimizers to be drawn from Stanley Milgram's experiments with ordinary citizens of New Haven than from the behavior of the criminally socialized SS in wartime. The case of the thirty-eight New Yorkers who in 1964 saw from their apartment windows Kitty Genovese being stabbed to death, heard her cries for help, and who could have easily called the police without putting themselves at risk, but did not, has more to teach us about "bystander" behavior than the case of Polish peasants who did not risk their lives to save Jews. The Holocaust, it is said, sensitizes us to oppression and atrocity. In principle it may; no doubt it sometimes does. Making it the touchstone of oppression and atrocity can as easily trivialize crimes of lesser magnitude.

Fifty years after the Holocaust, we are finally leaving the postwar/cold-war era, with all that it implies for a reorientation of consciousness. There is at least a glimmer of hope that, after almost as many years, the Israeli-Palestinian agon may be on the way to resolution, which would have major consequences for the role of the Holocaust in public discourse. In the United States, issues of pluralism and multiculturalism — of the negotiation of particular and common identity, very much including Jewish identity — are at the top of the agenda. The survivors of the Holocaust in the United States — no more than 2 or 3 percent of American Jewry but enormously influential in promoting Holocaust consciousness — will soon be leaving the scene. The future role of the "second generation," some of whom embrace and others of whom repudiate that designation, remains to be seen; certainly, they will not have the irresistible moral authority of their parents. No doubt many other changes, as yet dimly or not at all perceived, are taking place which are relevant to the future of the memory of the Holocaust.

None of this should be taken to mean that the future of the memory of the Holocaust is a matter of the confluence of contingent circumstances totally beyond our control. Such circumstances will surely influence the future of the memory of the Holocaust as they have its past. But the responsibility for giving form and content to that memory — for deciding how and to what ends it is used — remains ours. The injunctions "Remember!" and "Never Forget!" are completely appropriate. But if they lead, as they too often have, to unreflective and uncritical repetition of received shibboleths, they do as great a disservice to the memory of the dead as to the needs of the living.

Return to Memory

Jochen Spielmann

Auschwitz Is Debated in Oświęcim
The Topography of Remembrance

Railroad track to the gate of the extermination center in Birkenau.

---

1   It is published by Polskie Przedsiebiorstwo Wydawnictw Kartograficznych, Warsaw.

2   On the functions of the Monument with the triangle of memory, culture, and society, see my articles "Gedenken und Denkmal," in *Gedenken und Denkmal: Entwürfe zur Erinnerung an die Deportation und Vernichtung der jüdischen Bevölkerung Berlins*, exhibition catalogue of the Berlinische-Galerie and the Senator für Bau- und Wohnungswesen im Martin-Gropius-Bau (Berlin: Berlinische Galerie, 1988), pp. 7-46, and "Steine des Anstoßes: Denkmale in Erinnerung an den Nationalsozialismus in der Bundesrepublik Deutschland," in *Kritische Berichte* 3 (Gießen: Anabas-Verlag, 1988), pp. 5-16.

3   On the history and organization of the museum, see Jean-Charles Szurek, "Le musée de la camp de Auschwitz," in Alain Brossat et al., eds., *A l'Est mémoire retrouvée* (Paris: Editions la Découverte, 1990).

4   On the back of the map discussed here—alongside the floorplans for both museums, with recommendations for paths to follow indicated—it states that the concentration camp Auschwitz "was originally established for prisoners of various nations, and beginning in 1942, it was also the site of the mass extermination of European Jews.... Approximately one-and-a-half million people lost their lives there."

5   Kosciol Milosierdzia Bozego.

The map of the Polish city of Oświęcim, which was called Auschwitz from 1940 to 1945, is no different from those of other cities: city limits, railway and bus lines, hotels, cafés, and museums are shown along with parking lots, taxi stands, churches, and monuments. A look at the map that was first published in 1978 and updated in October 1991[1] reveals three different symbols which can be read in the context of coming to terms with National Socialism: "museums," "churches," and "monuments." Hidden behind these symbols are several very different systems of remembrance, which are both complementary to and in competition with one another.[2] In Oświęcim, the questions which arise are: who wants to remember, with what interests, and by what means? To whom does Auschwitz "belong"? Or, more precisely, who is attempting to legitimize current political interests by referring to historical events, and what means are being used to that end? This instrumentalist view of history seems to increase with the passing of time. The historical events and the sites of the former camps form the foil to the memories and involvement of the survivors and their descendants. This can be fairly clearly determined from a close look at the map.

The symbol for museums appears twice on the map. The first occurrence identifies the site of the former Auschwitz main camp as the "Panstowowe Muzeum w Oświęcimu" or the "State Museum of Auschwitz-Birkenau" in the official translation. Other symbols are used to represent two churches, a monument, parking lots, hotels, the post office, the tourist information center, as well as restaurants and bars. The State Museum today is a site of mass tourism, with more than a half million visitors per year. The official exhibition, which was established in the late 1950s, is considered outdated. It is supposed to be replaced by a completely new version within the next few years.[3] Over the years, specific texts and museum labels for the exhibition have been reformulated. Until 1989, for example, it remained virtually unmentioned that the majority of the camp victims were Jews. This fact has since been clearly stated.[4]

The second museum symbol marks the grounds of Brzezinka (Birkenau); other symbols are missing. This museum is outside the Oświęcim city limits and is depicted only partially on the map—it is cut off by the edge. Markedly fewer visitors travel to the extermination camp in Birkenau than to the museum of the Auschwitz main camp. It is currently being discussed whether, and if so how, to preserve or reconstruct what is left of the remains of the barracks, crematoria, fences, ramps, etc. In the summer of 1993, the "selection" ramp was extensively renovated, new ballast was placed between the rails, and gravel was added. The ramp is no longer "preserved as original" but is now more clearly visible. The museum administration has decided, moreover, to put up some forty signs on the grounds in order to provide more information to visitors.

At least four Catholic churches in the city are involved in coming to terms with National Socialism as well. For several years now, a church dedicated to God's mercy[5] has stood on the grounds of the extension to the camp for so-called protective custody. There have been many discussions in past years about a second church in the immediate vicinity of the main camp: the Carmelite convent housed in the so-called theater building. This building—which on the map of 1991 is designated as a church in a historical building, with the caption "Convent of the Carmelite Nuns" (*Klasztor Karmelitek*)—belongs to the grounds of the memorial and borders almost directly on the block in which the Catholic priest Maksymilian Kolbe, who was canonized in 1983, was murdered. Much less attention has been paid to a third church, however, which was built in the Birkenau camp commandant's office, a building which is not

Following the 1959 competition for a monument at Auschwitz-Birkenau the three finalist teams collaborated on this model combining the main components of their original entries. It was never built. On the left, a diagonal path is visible that cuts through the camp, ending at the destroyed gas chambers and crematoria. The railway cars joined together in the middle are dedicated to the victims' home countries. The former gas chambers and crematoria are surrounded by a large square.

part of the memorial. The cross on its roof can be seen from many points on the grounds of the former camp. After the pope's visit to Oświęcim in 1979, permission was granted to build a large church there to be dedicated to the martyred Saint Maksymilian (Kolbe).[6]

The symbol for monuments appears several times on the map: in the center of the city, there is a monument—which is still indicated on the map—built as an expression of gratitude for the liberation by the Red Army. In the fall of 1991, after a resolution by the city council, however, this monument was torn down, since—as the argument went—no one wished any longer to thank the Red Army as an institution, but, at most, only individual soldiers.[7] Thus, in 1945, in the immediate vicinity of the main camp, a monument was built in memory of the soldiers of the Red Army who liberated the camp. Due to the distinction made in its inscription, this monument has remained to the present day.

In the city, on Kosciuszko Square, there has been a monument to the Unknown Soldier since about 1967. It shows the figure of a charging soldier, whose weapon could be taken for a Kalashnikov. The possibility of this clearly political statement led to the redesigning of the monument in 1992. The double-sword symbol of the Grunwald Order, which is one of the highest decorations one can receive in Poland, was then introduced in the form of a medallion. Thus, the Unknown Soldier was changed from a Soviet to a Polish soldier.

In 1966 in Monowice, on the twenty-first anniversary of the liberation, a monument was dedicated on the grounds of the former concentration camp Auschwitz-Monowitz. Four pillars connected by barbed wire rise above a triangular base.[8] In close proximity to the main camp, there is a mass grave with plaques inscribed with the names of the prisoners who died immediately after the liberation.

On the left edge of the map an arrow and the words "To the International Monument to the Victims of Fascism" indicates the Monument constructed in 1967 between the two gas chambers and crematoria II and III.[9] In 1957 the International Auschwitz Committee, an association of survivors, announced an international competition for a monument. Four hundred twenty-six entries were evaluated by a jury chaired by the sculptor Henry Moore. Seven groups of artists were selected to participate in a second round of the competition and invited to come to Oświęcim to rework and concretize their designs. The design that won the prize in 1959, and which was intended to be realized, was a cooperative work of three of these seven groups of artists, but it was never built. Instead, this design was greatly altered several times for financial, but also political, reasons. The structure that was dedicated in 1967 has little in common with the prizewinning design. If the monument was originally intended to be a reminder of *all* the victims and to make clear their various religious, political, and geographical origins, the structure, as it was dedicated, limits the scope of the commemoration mainly to that of the political prisoners. A plaque added shortly before the opening ceremony displays the triangular symbol of the prisoners and was originally intended to be painted red. The letterhead of the museum is decorated with a red triangle even today.[10] At the monument's dedication ceremony, the

Model from the installation phase of the memorial complex, 1963-66. At the end of the tracks, between the ruins of the crematoria and the gas chambers, there is an arrangement of blocklike sarcophagi. The towerlike group of figures on the right was not built. Instead, during the installation, the abstract figures on the pedestal were replaced by a black marble slab with a triangle representing political prisoners.

6   Like other churches in Poland, this church was, both because of a shortage of materials and the difficulty involved in mobilizing the people, largely constructed as a "recreational center." Other churches dedicated to Maksymilian Kolbe are found in, among other places, Kraków and Kolnica, see Konrad Kucza-Kuczyński, *Nowy koscioly w Polsce* (Warsaw: Instytut Wydawniczy Pax, 1991). For more on the link between the anti-Semitic Kolbe and the controversy surrounding the Carmelite convent, see James E. Young, *The Texture of Memory: Holocaust Memorials and Meaning* (New Haven and London: Yale University Press, 1993), pp. 144-50.

7   For this and other suggestions in connection with the history of Oświęcim, I am grateful to Knut Dethlefsen. See also his essay, "Gesichter einer Stadt — Auschwitz — Oświęcim," in Till Bastian and Karl Bonhoeffer, eds., *Erinnern: Medizin und Massenvernichtung* (Stuttgart, 1992).

8   The triangle was the symbol used by the Nazis to identify prisoners. They were color-coded: yellow for Jews, red for Communists and Socialists, pink for homosexuals, purple for Jehovah's Witnesses, and so on.

9   See my "Entwürfe zur Sinngebung des Sinnlosen: Zu einer Theorie des Denkmals als Manifestation des 'kulturellen Gedächtnisses' — Der Wettbewerb für ein Denkmal für Auschwitz," Ph. D. diss., Freie Universität, Berlin, 1990 (microfiche).

10 See n. 8 above; thus the red used in this memorial was intended to remind one of the Communist and Socialist political prisoners.

Grunwald Order was awarded to the victims posthumously. Until 1990, the plaques in front of the monument inaccurately referred to more than 4 million rather than 1.5 million victims. They were removed and left empty, and, after much discussion, the plan now is to add a line from the book of Job in several languages.

This competition raised fundamental questions about the process of commemorating the victims of National Socialism. Why construct a monument at a former extermination camp? Is not the historical site itself a monument? What messages can be communicated by a monument on this site? Whose memory does the monument serve? What aesthetic statements are being made? Many of these questions were raised, not answered, by this competition.

Those who commissioned the monument, the International Auschwitz Council, clearly did not believe in the symbolic power of the concentration camp itself. Rather, during their lifetime, they wanted to establish a memory that would survive them. In the 1950s, it could not have been clear to them that some five decades after the historical event a new, enduring interpretation of the site — such as, perhaps, that represented by the forty signs mentioned above — would become necessary.

At that time, they felt the only form for establishing memory was the monument, which not only functioned as an aid to memory, but also as "proof" to the public that the crimes actually took place. When one examines the scholarly literature of the 1950s, it is obvious in retrospect how much the authors must have felt pressured to "prove" these crimes. This, too, was one of the reasons for announcing an international competition.

The monument that was constructed displays a series of gravestones and sarcophagi having very diverse forms. This multiformity refers to the various religious, political, and geographical origins of the victims and symbolically gives them a common grave.

The competition, which provoked an intense discussion, contributed much more to the memory of the Holocaust itself. Thus, in this case, it is clear that the process was more important than the result.

In addition to the monuments included on the map of the city, there are a number of other monuments, including the memorial to the victims of the Gypsy groups of Sinti and Rom that were constructed in the 1970s by private sponsors in the former extermination camp.

The inscriptions on the stone tablets in front of the memorial at Auschwitz-Birkenau were removed in 1990 because the information on the number of people murdered here was incorrect. They have not yet been replaced.

There are, of course, many places of remembrance in the town of Oświęcim that are not indicated by a symbol. In the small former synagogue, which still stands, a carpet wholesaler has set up shop. As in other cities, certain open spaces — in this case, for example, a parking lot — have been left at the site of former synagogues. Next to it, there is a replica of Philadelphia's Liberty Bell, which has been there since 1990. Also part of the unmarked topography of remembrance are the structural remains of the camp's compound, which were once scattered throughout the city, such as concrete pillars and entire industrial buildings. On the basis of individual buildings, it is also possible to conclude that the quarter identified on the map as a "osiedle chemików" (chemical site) goes back to the city planning of the National Socialists, in which a large section of the Jewish cemetery was destroyed in order to construct a road connecting to the Auschwitz-Monowitz Concentration Camp.

This brief inventory shows that very different systems of remembrance and their associated political interests exist side by side here. "Museums," "churches," and "monuments" — if they are to function as memorials — require institutional safeguards. Without visitors, believers, wreath layers, and ceremonies, these places would themselves become mere historical sites and works of art. Only in their connection to visits, excursions, guided tours, observances, worship, recitations, and rituals can memories

11   Jan Assmann has pointed out in his publications that it is only through "kultureller Formung" (cultural formation) and "institutionalisierter Kommunikation" (institutionalized communication) that "kulturelles Gedächtnis" (cultural memory) can be maintained over longer periods of time. See Jan Assmann, "Kollektives Gedächtnis und kulturelle Identität" in Jan Assmann and Tonio Hölscher, eds., *Kultur und Gedächtnis* (Frankfurt am Main: Suhrkamp, 1988), pp. 9-19.

be passed on over time and become part of society's understanding of itself.[11] Monuments without visitors have lost their function. Which groups feel a responsibility to keep the memory alive by means of laying wreaths, which groups by placing stones? Without institutionalizing memory, it cannot be passed on and endure.

To this day, Auschwitz is being debated in Oświęcim. It is not yet clear how the debate will turn out.

Jack Kugelmass

Why We Go to Poland
Holocaust Tourism as Secular Ritual

In an editorial written shortly after visiting Auschwitz, the publisher of *Moment* writes:

> People ask me, "How was it? What was it like?" All the words are wrong.
> So when I have to react in a word or two to casual, friendly inquiries, this is
> what I say: "Strangely enriching. You must go."[1]

For Jews, visiting Poland and the death camps has become obligatory. Indeed, it is the very seriousness of such visits that may ultimately distinguish Jewish travel to Poland from ordinary tourism. Those who go, particularly those who travel in tour groups — the majority of Jewish travelers to Poland — do so to participate in a secular ritual, one that confirms who they are as Jews, and perhaps, even more so, as North American Jews. I use the term "secular ritual" here for several reasons.

First, I want to distinguish it clearly from the traditional ritual of pilgrimage which has a long-standing place within East European and North African Jewish culture and which includes appropriate prayers and prescribed modes of behavior. For even though these secular rituals do not comply with traditional forms, they do appropriate them and, in part, invent whole new meanings. Participants in a United Synagogue youth tour to Treblinka, for example, were handed small index cards, told to disperse throughout the site, and to write a note to someone who died in the camp — an act clearly copied from the Hasidic custom of writing *kvitlekh*. At Treblinka, however, it was done to express solidarity between the living and the dead rather than to ask for divine intervention.

Second, we might consider the relative shallowness of these visits when compared to more traditional pilgrimages. Ritual's sense of efficacy derives from an elaborate cosmology. Secular ritual is much narrower in scope, and among contemporary Jews, reflects a movement which departs from a traditional Jewish worldview.

Finally, we also need to recognize that such tours are not totally idiosyncratic and that the concept of secular ritual allows us to distinguish the strictly personal from the collective. In fact, most visitors follow a well-trod route, and if they do not recite exactly the same prayers or read the same poems and narrative accounts, the texts are largely interchangeable.[2]

Participants of memorial tours are required to engage in activities that they often avoid in their everyday lives, for example, attending religious services three times daily, eating strictly kosher food prepackaged in Western Europe, attending lectures and evening discussions, and enduring sometimes arduous travel schedules. Such activities contribute to the "time out of time" quality of these visits. Their very liminality suggests to participants that what they are experiencing is marked in a special way. Indeed, the journeys themselves are often called "missions" by both the organizers and the participants. At the same time, the shared nature of the experience has tremendous potential for generating catharsis. Participants are encouraged to talk about their feelings and to discuss what they have seen either during the travel time between the site and the hotel or later in the evening during group discussions.

In fact, almost immediately, the involvement in these activities encourages participants away from disengagement and pulls them toward experiencing themselves as Holocaust victims. At Auschwitz-Birkenau, for example, a member of a Montreal synagogue group watched her fellow participants march towards the destroyed crematoria. As they walked, she could see the men at some distance. Crossing her vision was a barbed wire fence, and she commented to others near her that for a moment she imagined the men actually imprisoned in the camp. One traveler on a different journey, reflecting on the previous day's tour of Kraków and Kazimierz, wrote:

A Montreal synagogue group photographing the entrance of Birkenau, the extermination center at Auschwitz.

A Montreal synagogue group videotaping themselves as they enter Birkenau.

Last night I was transported from 1987 to earlier times: before the war and even back to the eighteenth and nineteenth centuries. In that way I have become part of Polish Hasidic life, and I also enter the world of my grandparents Dora and Josef. Today we go to Auschwitz. By the time we enter, I have changed from being a "surviving grandson" to being equal, arriving at the gates from the past in the past. Only now can I finally die with Josef, Dora, and my father Hans. Later as I walk back through the camp entrance at Birkenau, I am reborn, in my present life. As witness, not as survivor.[3]

A participant on the International Jewish Youth March of the Living wrote of seeing the piles of shoes in Majdanek:

I glance at my own shoe, expecting it to be far different than those in this ocean of death, and my breath catches in my throat as I see my shoe, though lighter in color, is almost the same style as one, no, two, three of the shoes I see: it seems as though every shoe here is my shoe. I wish I could throw my shoes into this pile, to grasp and feel each shoe, to jump into this sea, to become a part of it, to take it with me.[4]

If Eastern Europe is able to provide such a meaningful backdrop for staging Jewish rites, however, why has its value only recently been discovered? I think we need to consider a number of issues. One important factor must certainly be the genealogical fad which began with the airing of the American television series "Roots" and which continues unabated among various ethnic groups in the United States. Given the tendency of postmodern culture toward pastiche and nostalgia, as suggested by Fredric Jameson, this impulse should come as no surprise.[5] Another factor is the recent responsiveness, if not the very solicitousness of East European countries themselves. Floundering economically, and pressed for hard currency, they find that Western tourism represents a relatively simple way to generate income. Here, then, lies an obvious, if not entirely happy, marriage: the East European thirst for income, the Jewish search for roots, and, finally, the recent emergence of the Holocaust as a subject of popular Jewish discourse, indeed, as one of the tenets of what Jonathan Woocher refers to as American Jewish "civil religion."[6]

Although discussions of the Holocaust have long found their place in Jewish educational activities, and even in liturgical innovations, the subject itself has emerged from the confines of synagogue adult-education programs and is now addressed in university lecture halls and even on television. In the United States, the airing of the made-for-television film "Holocaust" and the annual showing of Holocaust-related documentaries on National Educational Television have undoubtedly made the subject less parochial and more an acceptable subject of popular and even ecumenical discourse. Furthermore, the response to the nearly ten-hour documentary "Shoah," made entirely of recent footage, simultaneously accomplished two things: it brought the Holocaust into the present by bringing victims and witnesses together in Poland, thereby demonstrating to millions of viewers that mythical time could be experienced even now; it also did what Joshua Meyrowitz has described as the impact of the media on social behavior in general since the 1960s: it realigned the sense of place. Poland ceased to be remote. Through repeated airings on public television of this and other films in which Poland is a backdrop, Poland has become a familiar place, encapsulated and contained both literally and metaphorically within the living room of each and every viewer.[7] This reconfiguration of time and space may explain how American Jews have come to focus "their imaginative energies upon the Holocaust," in the words of Jacob Neusner.[8]

The rabbi of the Montreal synagogue group wearing a March-of-the-Living jacket.

1   Hershel Shanks, "The Strange Enrichment of Seeing Auschwitz," *Moment* (February 1990): 4.
2   Sally Falk Moore and Barbara G. Myerhoff, *Secular Ritual* (Amsterdam: Van Gorcum, 1977), p. 7 (introduction).
3   Jeffrey Dekro, "First Time Home: Poland Leaves Its Mark on a Visitor," *Reconstructionist* 54 (October-November 1988): 11.
4   Dara Horn, "On Filling Shoes," *Hadassah Magazine* (November 1992): 16.
5   Fredric Jameson, "Postmodernism and Consumer Society," in E. Ann Kaplan, ed., *Postmodernism and Its Discontent: Theories Practices* (New York: Verso, 1988), p. 15.
6   Jonathan Woocher, "Sacred Survival: American Jewry's Civil Religion," *Judaism* 34 (Spring 1985): 151-62.
7   The same thing happened to Poles. "Shoah" was aired on Polish national television, and the film sparked a broad national debate on the Jewish view of Polish behavior during World War II. For the first time in more than forty years, Poles and Jews sparred with one another almost face to face, and yet they were really thousands of miles apart. The controversy seems also to have increased Polish curiosity about the Jewish place in the country's past: the American film *Fiddler on the Roof* was aired twice on national television, while a Polish traveling theater troupe performed it and received rave reviews throughout the country.
8   Jacob Neusner, "Can Judaism Survive the Twentieth Century?," *Tikkun* 4 (1989): 39.
9   Nathan Glazer's argument as cited in Herbert Gans, "Symbolic Ethnicity: The Future of Ethnic Groups and Cultures in America," in Herbert Gans et al., eds., *On the Making of Americans: Essays in Honor of David Riesman* (Philadelphia: University of Pennsylvania Press, 1979), p. 207.
10   Charles Silberman, *A Certain People: American Jews and Their Lives Today* (New York: Summit Books), pp. 182-220.
11   Judith Miller, *One, by One, by One: Facing the Holocaust* (New York: Simon and Schuster, 1990), p. 234.

The reason for earlier neglect of the Holocaust, however, was not just a more primitive technology. It stems, in part, from the lack of a literature of destruction in the years immediately after the war which could transform family trauma into history,[9] and also, in part, from the Jewish identification with hegemonic culture in the years during and immediately after the war, the result of two generations of rapid and self-desired Americanization. The Holocaust's recent emergence as a cornerstone of American Jewish civil religion is, as Charles Silberman suggests, generally connected to the rise of Jewish nationalism in 1967, immediately before and after the Six-Day War.[10] Mass media's sudden interest in the subject, however, also reflects, in part I think, the postwar emergence of American Jewry as no longer marginal but as a central group within American society and culture. This transformation is subtly apparent in the increasing prominence of Jewish characters in American television and film and the tendency of these characters to reflect on the nature of Jewish identity, but the change is even more apparent with the construction of a Holocaust memorial on the National Mall in Washington, D.C.[11] To some extent, it reflects the emergence of a postmodern ironic sensibility in which the mythic underpinnings of society are open to scrutiny. If there is anything that seems paradigmatic of this sensibility it is the spectacle of extermination that occurred during World War II.[12] Visits to the sites of mass death are for all people a way to experience the mythic birthplace of the postmodern, to witness cosmogonic time: Auschwitz, after all, is Poland's major tourist attraction.

Still, Auschwitz has special meaning for American Jews, and its current appeal may have as much to do with contemporary issues and beliefs as it does with those of the past. In this vein, Adi Ophir has even suggested the emergence of a Holocaust religion, with Auschwitz as the place of revelation of a new god of Absolute Evil.[13] But there are factors other than absence of traditional belief to generate the American Jewish interest in Poland and Auschwitz. These have more to do with the changing social structure than with the loss of cultural memory. Indeed, there are substantial sociological mechanisms at work here. Herbert Gans argues that the Holocaust has come to serve "as a need for the threat of group destruction . . . ." The need stems from increasing intermarriage, a decline in religious observance, and the fear that a lack of overt anti-Semitism has made the boundaries between Jew and non-Jew too permeable.[14] Charles Silberman argues that American Jews are extremely nervous about the degree of success they have achieved in America and that they are particularly afraid that the very security of their lives in the United States poses a threat to group survival, that without anti-Semitism Jews will lose their group solidarity. In the words of Jacob Neusner: "The central issue facing Judaism in our day is whether a long-beleaguered faith can endure the conclusion of its perilous age."[15] Seen within this context, it seems clear that the attraction of the Holocaust, in general, and of Poland as a place of pilgrimage, in particular, is that it represents a journey to a much simpler past. Moreover, given the fact that most tours begin by visiting Poland (thus entering the abyss of despair) and then conclude by touring Israel (thus experiencing redemption), we can read their underlying message as a warning against the danger posed by the Diaspora itself and the need to reinforce Jewish solidarity through the agency of a separate Jewish state. The ideological intent here is quite transparent, and it suggests not only the collaboration of Jewish organizations and Israeli officials in developing these "missions," but also why Israeli high school students are sent on similar tours.

Although pilgrimages to Poland began as inducements for securing donations from a wealthy and often nonobservant elite within the Jewish community, it is striking how common they have become. So much are they part of the lifetime of the Jew that, increasingly, Jewish children are sent on them as part of their religious or ethnic education,[16] and even fund-raising tours now promote multigenerational participation. Several years ago, an American Jewish family arranged to have their son's bar mitzvah in Kraków. The event was turned into the documentary film *A Spark among the Ashes*. In the summer of 1989, an American Jew married a Polish-born convert to Judaism at the Nozyk Synagogue, and the event was broadcast by the American television networks NBC and CNN. These examples point to two interrelated aspects of what Herbert Gans refers to as the emergence of "symbolic ethnicity": one is the heightened value placed on rites of passage in Jewish ritual, since they are generally less demanding than calendrical rites, the other the increasing tendency, in general, for ethnics to reinforce their identity by making trips to the "old country."[17] A problem with Gans's model, however, is that it lacks an underlying socio-political explanation. Cultural symbols, as Abner Cohen suggests, are often intricately tied to political and economic conflict.[18] The case I would like to make here is that the expansion of rites connected to the Holocaust, in particular the rite of pilgrimage to the death camps—the major focus of Jewish travel back to the Old World—has emerged

Participants in the March of the Living at the *Monument of Struggle and Martyrdom*, Majdanek, Poland, designed by sculptor Wiktor Tolkin and architect Janusz Dembek.

12 See, for example, Susan Sontag's impressions in *On Photography* (New York: Delta, 1977), pp. 19-20:
One's first encounter with the photographic inventory of ultimate horror is a kind of revelation, the prototypically modern revelation: a negative epiphany. For me, it was photographs of Bergen-Belsen and Dachau which I came across by chance in a bookstore in Santa Monica in July 1945. Nothing I have seen — in photographs or in real life — ever cut me as sharply, deeply, instantaneously. Indeed, it seems plausible to me to divide my life into two parts, before I saw those photographs (I was twelve) and after, though it was several years before I understood fully what they were about.

13 Adi Ophir, "On Sanctifying the Holocaust: An Anti-Theological Treatise," *Tikkun* 2 (1987): 63.

14 Somewhat the same process appears to be taking place among some young Armenians nearly eighty years after the Turkish slaughter. See Gans, "Symbolic Ethnicity" in *On the Making of Americans*, pp. 207-8.

15 Silberman, *A Certain People*, p. 24.

16 The March of the Living was organized to include thousands of Jewish school children from across North America. So successful was the event that rabbis who participated as group leaders have begun to take their congregations on similar pilgrimages, and the event has been repeated for other school children.

17 Gans, "Symbolic Ethnicity" pp. 204-5.

18 See the "Introduction" in Abner Cohen, *Urban Ethnicity* (London: Tavistock, 1974), pp. ix-xxiv.

19 The connection between Israel and the Holocaust is not accidental — indeed, it is used by various Jewish agencies to shore up support, both financial and moral, for the Jewish state. That connection has long been a cornerstone of Israeli public culture, a connection inscribed in the minds of new army recruits through visits to the Museum of the Jewish Diaspora and, more particularly, to the museum maintained by Kibbutz Lohamei Hageta'ot. Ironically, military occupation has caused problems, however. In an investigative article in *Ha'aretz*, Tom Segev reported that the Israeli army had stopped sending recruits to the Ghetto Fighters Museum when it was "found that, after exposure to the museum's exhibits, some soldiers were inclined towards even greater racism and brutality... [while] other soldiers were inclined to be sympathetic to the occupied populace... to the point of considering refusing to carry out orders, or even draft resistance schemes." See Israel Shahak, "History Remembered, History Distorted, History Denied," *Race and Class: A Journal for Black and Third World Liberation* 30 (April-June 1989): 80.

simultaneously with, and at least to some degree in response to, two conflicts with profoundly disquieting implications for American Jews: one is the Arab-Israeli conflict and the other is the rise in ethnic tensions in the United States.

One cannot help but think that the popularity of events such as the March of the Living, a pilgrimage to the death camps involving thousands of North American Jewish school children, is increasing in direct proportion to the ambiguousness of the Middle East situation: as long as Israel was perceived as a David against Goliath, there was no need for a ritual to convince participants and spectators of the vulnerability of the Jewish people. But with the increasing perception of Israel as Goliath — the use of stones by Palestinians is also a rhetorical strategy — there is increasing need for Jews to formulate a counterrhetoric of remembered victimization. Certainly, the Holocaust's attraction is its very lack of ambiguity.[19]

By evoking the Holocaust dramaturgically, that is, by going to the site of the event and reconstituting the reality of the time and place, American Jews are not only invoking the spirits of the tribe, that is, claiming their martyrdom, they are also making past time present. Moreover, in so doing, they are symbolically reversing reality: they are transposing themselves from what they are currently perceived as — in America as highly privileged and in Israel as oppressive — and presenting themselves as the diametric opposite — as what they in fact were. It is this image of the self which remains central to the Jewish worldview.

In stressing the political component of the ritual of pilgrimage, I do not mean to suggest that there is anything cynical at work here. On the contrary, those who perform these rites do so out of conviction because they offer a way out of a difficult moral dilemma and allow Jews to steer a course somewhere between hegemonic and oppositional culture. Moreover, these rites are performed primarily for fellow Jews. They are intra- rather than intertribal; they have the same agenda as all ritual, namely, to bridge fundamental discontinuities in life: those between American and East European Jewry, between postwar and prewar Jewry, between the living and the dead, and between power and powerlessness. They are an attempt to counteract fragmentation and the loss of belief that modernity itself has brought on and the possibility that such loss of belief will cause the complete demise of the tribe. They are also about memory, the attempt to retain some connection to a past, as if even the memory of loss could have a salutary effect upon contemporary culture.

The parking lot in front of the visitors' center in Auschwitz, 1989. The building was erected as a "reception hall" for the camp in 1941. From Reinhard Matz's series of some 200 photographs entitled "The Invisible Camps," 1987-92.

Paul Connerton makes a persuasive argument for the performative nature of social memory. Without the performance of physical ritual practices, he suggests, tribal memory cannot be maintained.[20] Perhaps, then, the direct, physical participation of marches to the camps constitutes the surest way for American Jews to remember the fate of European Jewry. If this is so, we ought to consider the emergence of these pilgrimages in the face of a growing discontinuity between actual memory, that of both the survivors themselves and American Jews who lived during and immediately after World War II, and social memory, that is, the meaning of these events for the Jews collectively. As time passes and the war becomes more distant, a crisis of continuity is bound to occur. How can those who themselves did not witness the war, yet who are convinced of its significance, pass the memory of those events and their consequences on to succeeding generations?

This crisis of memory is all the more acute given the general disregard for history within contemporary society or, perhaps more accurately stated, its appropriation by consumer culture through theme parks, docudramas, tourism, and related cultural activities. Pierre Nora writes that *lieux de mémoire,* "sites of memory,"

> museums, archives, festivals, and the like are fundamentally remains, the ultimate embodiments of a memorial consciousness that has barely survived in a historical age that calls out for memory because it has abandoned it. They make their appearance by virtue of the deritualization of our world—producing, manifesting, establishing, constructing, decreeing, and maintaining by artifice and by will a society deeply absorbed in its own transformation and renewal, one that inherently values the new over the ancient, the young over the old, the future over the past.[21]

As Nora argues, there are *lieux de mémoire* because there are no longer *milieux de mémoire,* or real "environments of memory."[22]

Although Nora's thesis is compelling, I think that he is wrong about society's deritualization. Perhaps the *lieux de mémoire* are a kind of reritualization made possible within the sphere of public culture and through the agency of state, academy, and other large and powerful groups. In his book *Zakhor,* Yosef Hayim Yerushalmi argues that for Jewish historians of the nineteenth century, because of "an ever-growing decay of Jewish group memory," history became "the faith of fallen Jews."[23] At the same time, the decline in Jewish memory should be seen not as the absence of memory. Indeed, Yerushalmi goes on to explain that his joining the rise of modern

Jewish historiography and the attenuation of Jewish memory was a reference to "a specific kind of memory of the past, that of Jewish tradition."[24] He admits, however, that most Jews have a memory of some sort of Jewish past and that the dilemma Jews face is not whether or not to know a mythical past but what kind of past to have.

It is here, it seems to me, that Yerushalmi's musings on historiography begin to border on anthropology. He quickly retreats, however, after suggesting some parallel between post-Holocaust Jewry and the generations that followed the expulsion from Spain, in that both prefer myth to history. But is it not a basic truism of cultural theory that peoples everywhere prefer myth to history? Is there not deep within Jews themselves a need to experience the great moments of the Jewish people directly as their own? The Passover *Haggadah* is a good case in point. Mass tourism has given that urge a dimension which was rarely possible in the past.

Still, myth and history are quite different, and if sites of memory are the means through which the modern era creates mythic structures, encountering them is particularly disconcerting, not only for historians, but also for anthropologists because of their tendency either to ignore or even to misapply the nuances of culture past and present. Indeed, during the pilgrimages, there is a clear tendency to place Poland and its people, both Jews and non-Jews, into a master narrative in which their cultural and historical specificity is completely removed. Moreover, it is extremely disconcerting that these rites only pay homage to the martyrdom of Polish Jewry without attempting to retrieve or recognize what their culture had achieved. Curiosity in the vitality of postwar Polish Jewry and its struggle to maintain itself in contemporary Poland is nonexistent. In the face of historical and social discontinuity, American Jewish memory culture has frozen Poland in time and turned its inhabitants into a vast *tableau vivant*.

I make these observations not to condemn American Jews. After all, given the plague of anti-Semitism in interwar, occupied, postwar, and even contemporary Poland, perhaps this is simply how things must be. If we object to the misuse of Poland's history and culture, then we are simply asking too much of American Jews. Ethnic groups are neither anthropologists nor historians; they do not remember for the sake of knowledge in the abstract but rather for the sake of group continuity. This

A United Synagogue Youth Mission reciting prayers and poems at Treblinka.

20 Paul Connerton, *How Societies Remember* (New York: Cambridge University Press, 1989).
21 Pierre Nora, "Between Memory and History: *Les lieux de mémoire,*" *Representations* 26 (Spring 1989): 12.
22 Ibid., p. 7.
23 Yosef Hayim Yerushalmi, *Zakhor: Jewish History and Jewish Memory* (Seattle: University of Washington Press, 1982), p. 86.
24 Ibid., p. 99.

Participants in the United Synagogue Youth Mission at Treblinka pose with a souvenir of their trip.

is the logic through which collective memory strips away nuance in favor of the grosser categories of experience, and the reason why some scholars of Jewish history find themselves not always in harmony with Jewish collective memory.

If collective memory and history are so much at odds then, perhaps stage rather than museum is the correct metaphor for explaining the relationship between Poland and its American Jewish visitors. Poland is filled with ready-made props — ruined synagogues, doorposts with impressions of *mezuzoth*, crumbling cemeteries, and death camps. These objects are deafening in their silence, for they are often scriptless: there is almost no one in Poland capable of writing texts and labels for the country's Jewish monuments. Moreover, Poland's viability as stage is enhanced by the fact that the country is nearly devoid of actors who might contest the presence of these foreign visitors or attempt to control the performance. What American Jews are doing is, if not searching for their actual identity, then at least attempting to piece together the icons of the past, in order to retrieve or reclaim them and reassemble them, albeit within a framework which inscribes their meaning through the present rather than through the past. Given the dimensions of the Holocaust and the challenge it poses to Jewish thinking to explain it, particularly nonrabbinic thinking, these rites have very special significance; they do what endless study and discussion cannot do nearly as convincingly. They create meaning: by shaping and systematizing otherwise abstract and diffuse cultural orientations[25] and by constructing them dialogically, that is, through the creative participation of those on such "missions" who interact with existing monuments through prayers, by reading poems and memoirs, or by visiting and photographing sites of martyrdom often overlooked by other visitors. But in whichever way they choose to consecrate these sites, the performance itself is meaningful.[26]

Although the same claim for a discursive thrust toward synthesis could be made for even the most nostalgic reflections, these rituals are unusual both because they are collectively formulated and therefore move much further than the nostalgic meanderings of individuals, but also because they are rituals and their underlying concern has to do with group continuity. Consequently, they are much less oriented to the pres-

A participant in the United Synagogue Youth Mission to Poland writes a note at the Janusz Korczak memorial at Treblinka.

25   Sherry Ortner, *Sherpas through Their Rituals* (New York: Cambridge University Press, 1978), p. 5.
26   See, for example, Edward Schieffelin, "Performance and the Cultural Construction of Reality," *American Ethnologist* (1985): 707-24; also James E. Young, *Writing and Rewriting the Holocaust* (Bloomington: Indiana University Press, 1988), p. 192.
27   Richard Schechner, *Between Theater and Anthropology* (Philadelphia: University of Pennsylvania Press, 1985), p. 51.
28   Horn, "On Filling Shoes," p. 21.

ent via the past than they are to the future via the past. Their work, to borrow a phrase from Richard Schechner, "is to 're-present' a past for the future (performance-to-be)."[27]

In part, a meditation on the past and, in part, a scripted play about the present, the rites I have described are also very much rehearsals of what American Jews are intent on becoming or, perhaps more accurately stated, intent on not becoming. After all, they emerge in the face of widespread intermarriage and assimilation, and they address explicitly or implicitly, the dangers the Diaspora poses for the continuity of the Jewish people. Little wonder then that the future of Israel figures so strongly as a subtext to these visits to the past.

> Tonight, we're going to Israel. Before I came here I had thought I was going on this trip to see Poland. I was happy about going to Israel, but I honestly felt that the time we would spend there wouldn't be very meaningful to me since I have been there several times before. But as everyone was running around the hotel, dragging suitcases and completely hyper, the thought of going to Israel began to lift my spirits, and pretty soon I was jumping out of my skin with excitement like everybody else.
>
> Every other time I've gone to Israel, I have simply visited as a tourist. But after being in Poland all week, I really wanted to go to Israel — because of a feeling I'd experienced the entire time we were there. Have you ever felt so unwelcome somewhere you could taste it in your mouth? Have you ever felt as though there was nothing left for you in a certain place, so much that everywhere you looked you could see only desolation? Have you ever walked through a graveyard and known there would never be anything else? I was excited to go to Israel because I needed to look around without seeing only death, to pull myself out of the ashes and out of my own despair. On other trips to Israel, I have always been only a tourist. This time, I was going as a survivor.[28]

How ironic. Poland, relegated to the past by American Jews, has emerged as a stage upon which to act out their future. How ironic, too, that the connection American Jews have to the State of Israel, even now, must rest so heavily upon this terrible past.

Author's note: This essay is part of a research project made possible by grants from the Memorial Foundation for Jewish Culture, the Lucius N. Littauer Foundation, Inc., and the Wisconsin Alumni Research Foundation of the University of Wisconsin in Madison. I would like to thank the Center for Jewish Research at the Jagiellonian University in Kraków and the following people, who read and commented on drafts of two larger versions of this essay entitled "The Rites of the Tribe: American Jewish Tourism to Poland": they are Michael Fischer, Kostek Gebert, Harvey Goldberg, Mark Kaminsky, Herbert Lewis, George Mosse, Peter Novick, and Frank Salomon.

Primo Levi

Revisiting the Camps

On many occasions, we survivors of the Nazi concentration camps have come to notice how little use words are in describing our experiences. Their "poor reception" derives from the fact that we now live in a civilization of the image, registered, multiplied, televised, and that the public, particularly the young, is ever less likely to benefit from written information . . . . In all of our accounts, verbal or written, one finds expressions such as "indescribable," "inexpressible," "words are not enough . . . ," "one would need a language for . . . ." This was, in fact, our daily thought [in the camps]: that if we came back home and wanted to tell, we would be missing the words. Daily language is for the description of daily experience, but here it is another world, here one would need a language "of this other world," a language born here.

Photographs . . . portray the camps, in particular Auschwitz-Birkenau, and the sinister San Sabba Mill, as they present themselves today to the visitor. It seems to me that they demonstrate what information theory claims: that an image, on parity of scale, "tells" twenty, one hundred times more than a written page; moreover, it is accessible to everyone, to the illiterate, to the foreigner; it is the best esperanto. These observations are not new; Leonardo already made them in his treatise on painting. But when applied to the ineffable universe of the camps, they acquire a stronger meaning. More and better than the word, they recapture the impression which the camps, well or badly preserved, more or less transformed into grand sites and sanctuaries, make on the visitor; an impression that is strangely deeper and more unsettling for those who have never been there than on us few survivors.

In many of us the old trauma, the scar of remembrance, still prevails over emotion, hence the need for distance. If, at the time of liberation, we had been asked: "what would you like to do with these infected barracks, these wire fences, these rows of toilets, these ovens, these gallows?" I think that most of us would have answered: "get rid of everything, raze it to the ground, along with Nazism and everything German." We would have said this (and many have by tearing down the barbed wire, by setting fire to the barracks), and we would have been wrong. These are not mistakes to efface. With the passing of years and decades, these remains do not lose any of their significance as a Warning Monument; rather, they gain in meaning. They teach better than any treatise or memorial how inhuman the Hitlerite regime was, even in its choices of sites and architecture. At the entrance to the camp in Birkenau, standing out in the squalor of the snow and the timeless barrenness of the landscape, one reads the Dante-esque inscription "Abandon all hope," and nothing better than the image could render the repetitive obsession of the spotlights illuminating the no-man's-land between the electric netting and the barbed wire. Different, but no less allusive, are the photographs of the Mill [of San Sabba]; it was nothing other than a mill, set up to refine rice . . . . In the very conversion of this factory into a site of torture, one discerns a theatrical and evil fantasy. Not by chance did they choose these very high walls, massive and blind. To visit it today . . . makes us remember that, aside from being a fanatical megalomaniac, Hitler was also a failed architect, that the staging of the vast parades was an essential part of the Nazi ritual (and its attraction for the German people), and that Speer, that ambiguous genius of organization and official architect of the Thousand-Year Reich, was the most intimate confidant of the *Führer* and the organizer of the savage exploitation of free manpower provided by the camps.

Editor's note: Primo Levi's remarks were originally printed in the catalogue *Rivisitando I Lager*, which accompanied an exhibition of photographs of the camps held at the Galleria San Fedele, Milan, in 1986 and was sponsored by the Associazione ex Deportati Politici nei Campi di Sterminio Nazisti. Reprinted by permission of the publisher.

Auschwitz-Birkenau in winter.

Holocaust Memorials and Monuments Mentioned in This Publication

Memorials at the sites of destruction: Poland, Germany, and Holland

Warsaw Ghetto Monument, Warsaw, Poland, 1948
Nathan Rapoport, sculptor (American, b. Warsaw, 1911; died New York, 1987)

Treblinka Monument, Treblinka, Poland, 1964
Franciszek Duszenko, architect (Polish, b. Grodek Jagiellonski, 1926); Adam Haupt, sculptor (Polish, b. Kraków, 1920)

International Monument at Auschwitz-Birkenau, Oświęcim, Poland, 1967
The Monument was built based on the combined finalist entries of three design teams. First team: Julio Lafuente, architect (Spanish, dates unknown, lived in Italy in the 1950s); Andrea Cascella, sculptor (Italian, b. Pescara, 1921); Pietro Cascella, sculptor (Italian, b. Pescara, 1920); Second team: Oskar Hansen, architect (Polish, b. Helsinki, Finland, 1922); Jerzy Jarnuszkiewicz, sculptor (Polish, b. Kalisz, 1919); Julian Palka, sculptor and graphic artist (Polish, b. Poznan, 1923); Lechoslaw Rosinski (Polish, dates unknown); Edmund Kupiecki (Polish, dates unknown); Tadeusz Plasota (Polish, dates unknown); Third team: Maurizio Vitale (Italian, dates unknown); Giorgio Simoncini (Italian, dates unknown); Tommaso Valle (Italian, dates unknown); Pericle Fazzini (Italian, dates unknown)

Memorial to the Warsaw Ghetto Uprising, Warsaw, Poland, 1946
Leon Marek Suzin (Polish, dates unknown)

Umschlagplatz memorial, Warsaw, Poland, 1946
Leon Marek Suzin (Polish, dates unknown)

Memorial Route of Jewish Martyrdom and Struggle, Warsaw, Poland, 1988
Hanna Szmalenberg (Polish), architect, and Wladyslaw Klamerus (Polish), sculptor.

Umschlagplatz memorial, Warsaw, Poland, 1988
Hanna Szmalenberg (Polish), architect, and Wladyslaw Klamerus (Polish), sculptor.

Monument of Struggle and Martyrdom, State Museum at Majdanek, Lublin, Poland, 1970
Wiktor Tolkin, sculptor (Polish, b. 1932); Janusz Dembek, architect (Polish, dates unknown)

Monument to the Deported Jews of Kazimierz, Kazimierz-Dolny, Poland, 1984
Tadeusz Augustynek, architect (Polish, dates unknown)

Monument Park at Buchenwald, Germany, 1958
Ludwig Deiters (German, b. 1921); Hans Grotewohl (German, b. 1923); Horst Kutzat (German, b. 1923); Karl Tausendschön (German, b. 1926); Hugo Namslauer (German, b. 1922); Hubert Mathas (German, b. 1929), architects.

Revolt of the Prisoners, Buchenwald Concentration Camp, Buchenwald, Germany, 1958
Fritz Cremer (German, b. 1906)

Winning entry in the competition for a memorial at the *Gestapo-Gelände*, Berlin, 1984 (not built)
Jürgen Wenzel, architect (German, b. 1935); Nikolaus Lang, artist (German, b. 1941)

Gypy Monument — Memorial of War, Museumplein, Amsterdam, Holland, 1978
Heleen Levano, sculptor (Dutch, b. Utrecht, 1941)

Homomonument, Westermarkt, Amsterdam, Holland, 1987
Karin Daan, designer (Dutch, b. Gennep, 1944)

Memorials in Israel

The Children of Exile, Kibbutz Mishmar HaEmek, Israel, 1947
Ze'ev Ben-Zvi, sculptor (Israeli, b. Ryki, Poland, 1904; died 1952)

Tower of Valor, Yad Vashem, Jerusalem, 1968-70
Buky Schwartz, sculptor (Israeli, b. 1932, lives in New York and Tel Aviv)

Children's Memorial, Yad Vashem, Jerusalem, 1987
Moshe Safdie, architect (Israeli, b. Haifa, 1938)

Valley of the Communities, Yad Vashem, Jerusalem, 1983-93
Lipa Yahalom, architect (Israeli, b. Poland, 1915); Dan Zur, architect (Israeli, b. Kibbutz Tel Yosef, 1926)

Mordechai Anielewicz, Kibbutz Yad Mordechai, Israel, 1951
Nathan Rapoport, sculptor (American, b. Warsaw, 1911; died New York, 1987)

Yad Mordechai Museum, Kibbutz Yad Mordechai, Israel, 1968
Arieh Sharon, architect (Israeli); Eldar Sharon, architect (Israeli)

Memorials in the United States

Memorial to the Six Million Jewish Martyrs, Battery Park, New York City, 1966-72 (not built)
Louis I. Kahn, architect (American, b. Estonia, 1901; died, 1974)

Liberation, Liberty State Park, Jersey City, New Jersey, 1985
Nathan Rapoport, sculptor (American, b. Warsaw, 1911; died New York, 1987)

Holocaust Memorial, Jewish Community Center of Tucson, Arizona, 1988
Ami Shamir, architect (Israeli, b. Tel Aviv, 1932)

Winning entry in the New England Holocaust Memorial Competition, Boston, 1990
Stanley Saitowitz, architect (American, b. South Africa, 1949)

United States Holocaust Memorial Museum, Washington, D.C., 1986-1993
James Ingo Freed, Design Partner/Pei Cobb Freed & Partners (American, b. Essen, Germany, 1930)

Beit Hashoah-Museum of Tolerance, Simon Wiesenthal Center, Los Angeles, 1993

Contemporary Art

Finstere Medine, Berlin, 1991
Shimon Attie, photographer (American, b. 1957)

Monument against Fascism, Harburg, Germany, 1986-1993
Jochen Gerz, artist (German, b. Berlin, 1940); Esther Shalev-Gerz, artist (Israeli, b. Vilnius, 1948)

2,146 Stones — Monument against Racism, Saarbrücken, Germany, 1991
Jochen Gerz, artist (German, b. Berlin, 1940)

Und ihr habt doch gesiegt (And You Were Victorious after All), Graz, Austria, 1988
Hans Haacke, artist (American, b. Cologne, 1936)

Denk-Stein-Sammlung, Kassel, Germany, 1989-1992
"Negative-form" Monument to the Aschrott-Brunnen, Kassel, Germany, 1987
Horst Hoheisel, artist (German, b. Poznan, 1944)

Memorial to the Missing Jews, Hamburg-Altona, Germany, 1989
Sol LeWitt, artist (American, b. 1928)

Extension to the Berlin Museum with the Jewish Museum Department, Berlin, 1989-1994
Daniel Libeskind, architect (American, b. Lodz, Poland, 1946)

Sonnenallee Memorial, Berlin-Neukölln, 1993
Norbert Radermacher, artist (German, b. Aachen, 1953)

The Holocaust, The Jewish Museum, New York, 1982
The Holocaust, Lincoln Park, San Francisco, 1984
George Segal, sculptor (American, b. New York, 1924)

Anne Frank Grave Marker, 1989
Doug and Mike Starn, artists (Americans, b. 1961)

Matthew Baigell is Special Professor in the Department of Art History at Rutgers University. He is the author of *A Concise History of American Painting and Sculpture* (1984) and coeditor of *Artists against War and Fascism: Papers of the First American Artists' Congress, 1936* (1986). His writings have been published in numerous magazines, books, and exhibition catalogues. His current projects include a book on Jewish-American artists of the twentieth century and, together with his wife Renee Baigell, a book of interviews with former nonconformist Soviet artists.

The German-born American architect, **James Ingo Freed** FAIA, a partner in the firm of Pei Cobb Freed & Partners, is the designer of the United States Holocaust Memorial Museum. As a young boy, he was a refugee from National Socialism and emigrated to the U.S. in 1939. Mr. Freed is the recipient of many architectural awards and has been the principal for design of the Jacob Javits Convention Center in New York; the Los Angeles Convention Center; the New Warner Building on Pennsylvania Avenue in Washington, D.C.; the 58-floor First Bank Place in Minneapolis; 499 Park Avenue, a 27-story office building in New York; and other noted structures. His current projects include the United States International Cultural and Trade Center, a 3.1 million-square-foot project which will complete the Federal Triangle in Washington D.C. Mr. Freed has taught architecture at the Illinois Institute of Technology, at Columbia University, and at Yale University. He is a member of the American Academy of Design, was architectural commissioner of the Art Commission of New York City, and is currently active in many other professional and advisory bodies.

Saul Friedländer is Professor of History and incumbent of the Chair of the History of the Holocaust at the University of California, Los Angeles and Professor of Modern European History at Tel Aviv University. He is the author of several works on Holocaust history and historiography, has written widely on historical memory of this period and on the "historians' controversy" in Germany, and is the editor of the journal *History and Memory*. His first book, *Hitler et les Etats-Unis (1939-1941)* was published in Switzerland in 1963, and appeared later in English as *Prelude to Downfall: Hitler and the United States 1939-1941* in 1967. Subsequent publications, which originally appeared in French, include *Pius XII and the Third Reich: A Documentation* (1964/1966); *Kurt Gerstein: The Ambiguity of Good* (1967/1969); *Arabs and Israelis: A Dialogue* (1974/1975), with Mahmoud Houssein; *History and Psychoanalysis: An Inquiry into the Possibilities and Limits of Psychohistory* (1976/1977); *When Memory Comes* (1978/1979); and *Reflections on Nazism: An Essay on Kitsch and Death* (1982/1984). He also edited *The Limits of Representa-*

tion (1992). His most recent book is *Memory, History and the Extermination of the Jews.*

Konstanty Gebert is a columnist at *Gazeta Wyborcza*, Poland's first legal independent daily. He has been active in the Solidarity movement in Poland and on Jewish issues and has written a book based on his experiences as an observer at the 1989 roundtable talks which led to the relegalization of Solidarity (1990). His other books include *Przerwa na myslenie* [A break for thinking] (1985), a collection of essays, and *Magia Slow* [The magic of words] (1991), an analysis of French policy toward Poland. He has also published many other books and articles and is a regular contributor to Polish radio and television, the BBC, National Public Radio, and other international media.

Jochen Gerz and **Esther Shalev-Gerz**, artists. Jochen Gerz has been exhibiting his conceptual, photographic, and text-based work extensively in Europe and North America since the early 1970s. He represented Germany in the Venice Biennale in 1976, was included in documenta 6 and 8 in Kassel in 1977 and 1987, and in the Sydney Biennale in 1980 and 1982. The Gerzes are highly regarded internationally as "new media" artists. Many of their conceptual wall pieces, installations, and videos, as well as their work in public spaces, conflate photography and texts, overlaying images with words. In their performances, they aspire to be "the painter, medium, paintbrush, and not just witness to a work." Jochen Gerz was Distinguished Visiting Professor of Art at the University of California at Davis in 1992. He has also taught at the Art Academy HBK Saarbrücken (1990-92). The Gerzes' disappearing *Monument against Fascism*, located in Harburg, a suburb of Hamburg, Germany, was installed in 1986 and lowered into the ground in November 1993. Jochen Gerz's invisible work *2,146 Stones—Monument against Racism* in Saarbrücken, located a short distance from the French-German border, was dedicated in May 1993.

Zvi Gitelman is Professor of Political Science and Preston R. Tisch Professor of Judaic Studies at the University of Michigan, Ann Arbor. He has lectured and written extensively on Soviet politics, Soviet Jewry, Eastern European politics, and Israeli politics. He has written or edited eight books, including *The Politics of Nationality and the Erosion of the U.S.S.R.* (1992), *In Quest of Utopia: Jewish Political Ideas and Institutions* (1992), *Developments in Soviet and Post-Soviet Politics* (coeditor 1990, 1992), *A Century of Ambivalence* (1988), and *Jewish Nationality and Soviet Politics* (1972). He has been awarded grants and fellowships from the American Council of Learned Societies, the National Council for Soviet and East European Research, and the Rockefeller, Ford, and

Guggenheim Foundations. He has been a Fulbright Professor at the Hebrew University and Visiting Professor at Tel Aviv University.

Hans Haacke, an internationally acclaimed artist, is Professor of Art at Cooper Union for the Advancement of Science in New York and is the subject of the monograph which accompanied a retrospective exhibition at the New Museum of Contemporary Art, New York, in 1986, entitled *Hans Haacke: Business as Usual*. A major exhibition of his work of the past decade was held in 1989 at the Musée National d'Art Moderne in Paris. Since 1962, Haacke has created compelling political works composed primarily of written texts and photographs that challenge conventional notions of artistic media. These "information" pieces deal with the connections between art, business, and politics and have targeted patrons of art, financiers, and multinational corporations.

Andreas Huyssen is Villard Professor of German and Comparative Literature at Columbia University. He has written three books, including *After the Great Divide: Modernism, Mass Culture, Postmodernism* (1986) and has edited five others. His writings on German literature and culture have been published in numerous academic journals. In 1974, he was a cofounder of *New German Critique: An Interdisciplinary Journal of German Studies* and now serves as coeditor. He is currently working on a collection of essays entitled *Memory, Amnesia, Simulation: Essays in Contemporary Culture*.

Claudia Koonz is Professor of History at Duke University. She is the author of *Mothers in the Fatherland: Women, the Family, and Politics in Nazi Germany* (1987) and has published several essays and articles exploring the role of women in both the Weimar Republic and Nazi Germany. Between 1990 and 1991 she held the Wallenberg Chair of Human Rights at Rutgers University. She has received grants and fellowships from the Rockefeller Foundation, the German Marshall Fund, the National Endowment for the Humanities, the American Council of Learned Societies, and the National Humanities Center. Her newest book is *Race, Eugenics, and Gender in Nazi Social Politics* (forthcoming).

Jack Kugelmass is Associate Professor of Anthropology and the Director of the Folklore Program at the University of Wisconsin-Madison. He is coauthor of *From A Ruined Garden: The Memorial Books of Polish Jewry* (1983), the author of *The Miracle of Intervale Avenue: Aging with Dignity in the South Bronx* (1986), the editor of *Between Two Worlds: Ethnographic Essays on American Jewry* (1988) and of *Going Home: How Jews Invent Their Old Countries*

(1993), and the author of *The Greenwich Village Halloween Parade* (1994). His most recent book is entitled *The Rites of the Tribe: The Public Culture of American Jews* (forthcoming).

Primo Levi, a survivor of the Holocaust and one of the preeminent writers on the subject, was born in Turin, Italy, in 1919 and trained as a chemist. His best-known book, *Survival in Auschwitz*, was first published in Italian in 1947. He continued to write books based on his experiences and gained an international reputation for his fiction. In 1982, thirty-seven years after Russian troops liberated the camp, Levi returned to Auschwitz as a tourist with a group of students, teachers, and other survivors. The visit was filmed for Italian television. His last novel *The Drowned and the Saved* was published in 1986. A year later, in April 1987, Levi committed suicide at his home in Turin.

Peter Novick is Professor of History at the University of Chicago. His major publications include *The Resistance vs. Vichy: The Purge of Collaborators in Liberated France* (1969) and *That Noble Dream: The "Objectivity Question" and the American Historical Profession* (1988). He was the winner of the Columbia University Clark M. Ansley Award and the American Historical Association Albert J. Berveridge Prize. He was also the recipient of a National Endowment for the Humanities Fellowship in 1990-91 and has been a Fellow at the Center for Advanced Study in the Behavioral Sciences in 1991-92 for research on the effect of the Holocaust on American culture.

Nathan Rapoport, sculptor, was born in Warsaw in 1911. His major commissions include the *Warsaw Ghetto Monument*, Warsaw, 1948; *Monument to the Six Million Jewish Martyrs*, Philadelphia, 1964; *Job*, Yad Vashem, Jerusalem, 1963; *Scroll of Fire*, Jerusalem, 1967; and *Jacob Wrestling with the Angel*, Toronto, 1980. Rapoport came from a Hasidic family in Poland. He began studying sculpture in Warsaw at the age of fourteen and began supporting himself and his family at an early age by working on architectural decorations for a local firm and, later, by taking portrait commissions. He attended the Academy of Art in Warsaw where he won prizes for work in architecture, sculpture, and metal. A scholarship enabled him to visit Italy and France in 1936, and then again in 1938, when he met Jacques Lipchitz in Paris. At the outbreak of World War II, he fled to the East, eventually reaching Novosibirsk where he began work on the *Warsaw Ghetto Monument* in 1943. He returned to Warsaw at the end of 1945 and continued to work on models for the project, which was finally unveiled in 1948. Rapoport lived in Paris, Israel, and Italy before settling in New York City, where he died in 1987.

Artist **George Segal**, a major figure in the American Pop Art movement, has had important solo exhibitions at the Museum of Contemporary Art, Chicago (1968), the Kunsthaus Zurich (traveled throughout Europe, 1971-73), the Walker Art Center (traveled throughout U.S., 1978-79), and the Seibu Museum of Art, Tokyo (1982). His *Holocaust* was first exhibited at The Jewish Museum, New York, in 1983. His works have been exhibited worldwide in group and solo exhibitions in museums and galleries. Numerous articles and monographs, including Sam Hunter's *George Segal* (1989), have been published about his work.

Jochen Spielmann, who lives in Berlin, studied Art History and Education. He received his Ph.D. in Art History, writing a thesis on the international competition for a monument at the former extermination camp Auschwitz-Birkenau. His thesis for his Education degree was entitled "The Corporate Identity of Non-profit Organizations." As an art historian and adult-education specialist, he strives for an interdisciplinary balance between these two areas of study and their practical application. At present, he is active as a lecturer in political science and cultural studies in an adult education program at the Pädagogisches Landesinstitut, Brandenburg. He has written numerous publications about the idea of creating monuments (see the references in his article) and is currently interested in adult education in eastern Germany and "cultural memory" in the twentieth century. He works with groups using the methods of living-learning on the basis of "Theme Centered Interaction" (TCI).

James E. Young is Professor of English and Judaic Studies at the University of Massachusetts at Amherst and curator of the exhibition "The Art of Memory: Holocaust Memorials in History" and editor of the book of the same title. He is the author of *The Texture of Memory: Holocaust Memorials and Meaning* (1993) and the critical study of Holocaust narrative, *Writing and Rewriting the Holocaust* (1988). Professor Young has written numerous reviews and articles on cultural history, documentary narrative, and memorials in the *New York Times Book Review* and the *New York Times Magazine*; in several journals, including *Critical Inquiry*, *Representations*, *Partisan Review*, *New Literary History*, and *Tikkun*; and in dozens of other publications and collected volumes. His books and articles have also appeared in translation in German, French, Hebrew, and Swedish. Professor Young has been the recipient of numerous awards and fellowships, including a Guggenheim Fellowship, grants from the National Endowment for the Arts, and a Yad Hanadiv Fellowship at the Hebrew University in Jerusalem.

Selected Bibliography

American Jewish Congress. *In Everlasting Remembrance: Guide to Memorials and Monuments*. New York: American Jewish Congress, 1969.

Amishai-Maisels, Ziva. *Depiction and Interpretation: The Influenco of the Holocaust on the Visual Arts*. Oxford: Pergamon Press, 1993.

Baigell, Matthew. "Segal's Holocaust Memorial." *Art in America* (Summer 1983): 134-36.

Beardsley, John. *Art in Public Places*. Washington, D.C.: Partners for Livable Places, 1981.

Berenbaum, Michael. *After Tragedy and Triumph: Modern Jewish Thought and the American Experience*. Oxford and New York: Oxford University Press, 1991.

Blatter, Janet. "Art from the Whirlwind." In Janet Blatter and Sybil Milton, eds. *Art of the Holocaust*. London: Pan Books, 1982. Pp. 22-35.

Bodnar, John. *Remaking America: Public Memory, Commemoration, and Patriotism in the Twentieth Century*. Princeton: Princeton University Press, 1992.

Boyarin, Jonathan. *A Storm from Paradise: The Politics of Jewish Memory*. Minneapolis: University of Minnesota Press, 1992.

Brenson, Michael. "Why Segal Is Doing Holocaust Memorial." *The New York Times* (8 April 1983): C16.

Burghoff, Ingrid and Burghoff, Lothar. *Nationale Mahn- und Gedenkstätte Buchenwald*. Berlin and Leipzig: VEB Tourist Verlag, 1970.

Bussmann, George, ed. *Arbeit in Geschichte — Geschichte in Arbeit*. Exhibition catalogue. Berlin: Nishen-Verlag, 1988.

Capasso, Nicholas. "Constructing the Past: Contemporary Commemorative Sculpture." *Sculpture* 9 (November-December 1990): 56-63.

Coffelt, Beth. "The Holocaust and the Art of War." *San Francisco Sunday Examiner & Chronicle Magazine* (23 October 1983): 12-15.

Connerton, Paul. *How Societies Remember*. Cambridge and New York: Cambridge University Press, 1989.

Council for the Preservation of Monuments to Resistance and Martyrdom. *Scenes of Fighting and Martyrdom Guide: War Years in Poland 1939-1945*. Warsaw: Sport I Turystyka Publications, 1966.

da Silva, Teresien and Stam, Dineke. *Sporen van de Oorlog: Ooggetuigen over plaatsen in Nederland, 1940-1945*. Amsterdam: Anne Frank Stichting, 1989.

Doezema, Marianne and Hargrove, June. *The Public Monument and Its Audience*. Cleveland: Cleveland Institute of Art, 1977.

Endlich, Stephanie and von Buttlar, Florian. "Über die Schwierigkeit, sich der NS-Geschichte durch Kunst zu nähern." In *Imitationen, Nachahmung und Modell: Von der Lust am Falschen*. Basel and Frankfurt: Stroemfeld/Roter Stern, 1989. Pp. 230-51.

Elsen, Albert. "What We Have Learned about Modern Public Sculpture: Ten Propositions." *Art Journal* 48 (Winter 1989): 291-97.

Erhalten Zerstören Verändern: Denkmäler der DDR in Ost-Berlin — Eine dokumentarische Ausstellung. Berlin: Aktives Museum Faschismus und Widerstand in Berlin und der Gesellschaft für Bildende Kunst, e.V., 1990.

Fenz, Werner, ed. *Bezugspunkte 38/88*. Graz: Steirischer Herbst, Veranstaltungsgesellschaft m.b.H, 1988.

Fenz, Werner. "The Monument is Invisible, the Sign Visible." *October* 48 (Spring 1989): 75-78.

Forgey, Benjamin. "In Search of a Delicate Balance." *The Washington Post* (23 May 1987): B1-2.

Frank, Volker. *Antifaschistische Mahnmale in der Deutschen Demokratischen Republik: Ihre künstlerische und architektonische Gestaltung*. Leipzig: Seemann Verlag, 1970.

Freed, James Ingo. "The United States Holocaust Memorial Museum." *Assemblage* 9 (1989): 59-79.

Friedländer, Saul. "Die Shoah als Element in der Konstruktion israelischer Erinnerung." *Babylon* 2 (1987): 10-22.

Friedländer, Saul. "The Shoah Between Memory and History." *Jerusalem Quarterly* 53 (Winter 1990).

Friedländer, Saul. "Martin Broszat/Saul Friedländer: A Controversy about the Historicization of National Socialism." *Yad Vashem Studies* 19 (Fall 1988): 1-47; also reprinted in *New German Critique* 44 (Spring-Summer 1988): 85-126.

Friedländer, Saul. "The 'Final Solution': On the Unease in Historical Interpretation:" *History and Memory* 1 (Fall/Winter 1989): 61-76.

Friedländer, Saul, ed. *Probing the Limits of Representation: Nazism and the "Final Solution."* Cambridge, Mass. and London: Harvard University Press, 1992.

Funkenstein, Amos. "Collective Memory and Historical Consciousness." *History and Memory* 1 (Spring/Summer 1989): 5-26.

Gedenkstätte KZ-Aussenlager Sonnenallee Berlin-Neukölln: Bericht der Vorprüfung. Berlin: Senatsverwaltung für Bau- und Wohnungswesen, 1989.

Geisert, Helmut; Ostendorff, Peter; and Spielmann, Jochen. *Gedanken und Denkmal: Entwürfe zur Erinnerung an die Deportation und Vernichtung der jüdischen Bevölkerung Berlins*. Berlin: Berlinsche Galerie, 1988.

Gerz, Jochen and Shalev-Gerz, Esther. "Das Denkmal gegen Krieg und Faschismus in Hamburg-Harburg." In Detlef Hoffmann and Karl Ermert, eds. *Kunst und Holocaust: Bildliche Zeugen vom Ende der westlichen Kultur*. Loccumer Protokolle 14 (1989): 201-12.

Gibson, Michael. "Hamburg: Sinking Feelings." *ARTnews* 86 (Summer 1987): 106-7.

Gintz, Claude. "'L'Anti-Monument' de Jochen & Esther Gerz." *Galeries Magazine* 19 (June/July, 1987): 82-87, 130.

Gittelman, Zvi. "History, Memory, and Politics: The Holocaust in the Soviet Union." *Holocaust and Genocide Studies* 5 (1990): 23-37.

Goldberg, G. and Persitz, A. "Monument commemoratif à Paris, tombeau du martyr juif inconnu." *L'Architecture d'aujourd'hui* 55 (July-August) 1954: 20-4.

Goldberger, Paul. "A Memorial Evokes Unspeakable Events with Dignity." *The New York Times* (30 April 1989).

Haake, Hans. "Und ihr habt doch gesiegt, 1988." *October* 48 (Spring 1989): 79-87.

Halbwachs, Maurice. *The Collective Memory*. Trans. Francis J. Ditter, Jr. and Vida Yazdi Ditter. New York: Harper and Row, 1980.

Halbwachs, Maurice. *Les cadres sociaux de la memoire*. Paris: Presses Universitaires de France, 1952.

Handelman, Don. *Models and Mirrors: Towards an Anthropology of Public Events.* Cambridge and New York: Cambridge University Press, 1990.

Hamer, Hardt-Walther, ed. *Zum Umgang mit dem Gestapo-Gelände: Gutachten im Auftrag der Akademie der Künste Berlin.* Berlin: Akademie der Künste, 1988.

Hartmann, Geoffrey H., ed. *Holocaust Remembrance: The Shapes of Memory.* Cambridge, Mass. and Oxford: Basil Blackwell Publishers, 1993.

Hartmann, Geoffrey H., ed. *Bitburg in Moral and Political Perspective.* Bloomington: Indiana University Press, 1986.

Hoffmann, Detlef. "Erinnerungsarbeit der 'zweiten und dritten' Generation und 'Spurensuche' in der zeitgenössischen Kunst." *Kritische Berichte* 2 (1988): 31-46.

Hoffmann, Detlef and Emert, Karl, eds. *Kunst und Holocaust: Dokumentation einer Tagung der Evangelischen Akademie Loccum* (Loccumer Protokolle 14). Rehburg-Loccum: Evangelische Akademie Loccum, 1989.

Irwin-Zarecka, Iwona. *Neutralizing Memory: The Jew in Contemporary Poland.* New Brunswick, N. J.: Transaction Publishers, 1989.

Kampf, Avram. *Jewish Experience in the Art of the Twentieth Century.* South Hadley, Mass.: Bergin and Garvey, 1984.

Koch, Heinz. *Nationale Mahn- und Gedenkstätte Buchenwald: Geschichte ihrer Entstehung.* Weimar, Buchenwald, 1988.

Koenders, Pieter. *Het Homomonument.* Trans. Eric Wulfert, Amsterdam: Stichting Homomonument, 1987.

Krajewska, Monika. *A Tribe of Stones: Jewish Cemeteries in Poland.* Warsaw: Polish Scientific Publishers, 1993.

Kugelmass, Jack and Boyarin, Jonathan, eds. *From a Ruined Garden: The Memorial Books of Polish Jewry.* New York: Schocken Books, 1983.

Lehrke, Giesela. *Gedenkstätte für die Opfer des Nationalsozialismus: Historisch-politische Bildung an Orten des Widerstandes und der Verfolgung.* Frankfurt and New York: Campus, 1988.

Liebman, Charles S. and Don-Yehiya, Eliezer. *Civil Religion in Israel: Traditional Judaism and Political Culture in the Jewish State.* Berkeley and Los Angeles: University of California Press, 1983.

Lishinsky, Yosef. "Yad Vashem as Art." *Ariel: A Review of Arts and Letters in Israel* 55 (1983): 14-25.

Litschke, Egon. *Nationale Mahn- und Gedenkstätte Ravensbrück: Museum.* Rostock: Ostsee-Druck, 1988.

Lurz, Meinhold. *Kriegerdenkmäler in Deutschland.* Heidelberg, 1985.

Mai, Ekkehard and Schmirber, Gisela. *Denkmal—Zeichen—Monument: Skulptur und öffentlicher Raum heute.* Munich: Prestel-Verlag, 1989.

Maier, Charles. *The Unmasterable Past: History, Holocaust, and German National Identity.* Cambridge, Mass. and London: Harvard University Press, 1988.

Marcuse, Harold. "Das ehemalige Konzentrationslager Dachau: Der mühevolle Weg zur Gedenkstätte 1945-1968." *Dachauer Hefte: Studien und Dokumente zur Geschichte der nationalsozialistischen Konzentrationslager* 6 (November 1990): 182-205.

Marcuse, Harold; Schimmelfennig, Frank; and Spielmann, Jochen. *Steine des Anstosses: Nationalsozialismus und*

Zweiter Weltkrieg in Denkmalen, 1945-1985. Hamburg: Museum für Hamburgische Geschichte, 1985.

Marcuse, Harold. "West German Strategies for Commemoration." *Dimensions* 3 (1987): 13-4.

Marrus, Michael R. *The Holocaust in History.* Hanover and London: University Press of New England, 1987.

Miller, Judith. *One, by One, by One: Facing the Holocaust.* New York: Simon and Schuster, 1990.

Milton, Sybil and Nowinski, Ira. *In Fitting Memory: The Art and Politics of Holocaust Memorials.* Detroit: Wayne State University Press, 1991.

Moore, Henry. "The Auschwitz Competition." Booklet published by the State Museum of Auschwitz, 1964.

Mosse, George L. *Fallen Soldiers: Reshaping the Memory of the World Wars.* New York and Oxford: Oxford University Press, 1990.

Muschamp, Herbert. "How Buildings Remember." *The New Republic* (28 August 1989): 27-33.

Nora, Pierre. "Between Memory and History: *Les lieux de mémoire.*" Trans. Marc Roudebush, *Representations* 26 (1989): 13-25.

Nora, Pierre. *Les lieux de mémoire,* Vol. 1: *La République.* Paris, 1984.

Plank, Karl A. "The Survivor's Return: Reflections on Memory and Place." *Judaism* 38 (Summer 1989): 263-77.

Rabinbach, Anson and Zipes, Jack, Eds. *Germans & Jews since the Holocaust: The Changing Situation in West Germany.* New York and London: Holmes & Meier, 1986.

Postal, Bernhard and Abramson, Samuel H. *The Landmarks of a People.* New York: Hill and Wang, 1962.

Postal, Bernhard and Abramson, Samuel H. *Traveler's Guide to Jewish Landmarks of Europe.* New York: Fleet Press, 1981.

Puvogel, Ulrike, ed. *Gedenkstätten für die Opfer des Nationalsozialismus: Eine Dokumentation.* Bonn: Schriftenreihe der Bundeszentrale für politische Bildung, 1987.

Rieth, Adolph. *Denkmal ohne Pathos: Totenmale des zweiten Weltkrieges in Süd-Württemberg-Hohenzollern mit einer geschichtlichen Einleitung.* Tübingen: Verlag Ernst Wasmuth, 1967.

Rieth, Adolph. *Monuments to the Victims of Tyranny.* New York, Washington, and London: Frederick A. Praeger, 1968.

Rosen, Jonathan. "America's Holocaust." *Forward* (12 April 1991).

Rosenblatt, Gary. "The Simon Wiesenthal Center: State-of-the-art Activism or Hollywood Hype?" *Baltimore Jewish Times* (14 September 1984): 62-74.

Rurup, Reinhard. *Topographie des Terrors: Gestapo, S.S. und Reichssicherheitshauptamt auf dem "Prinz-Albrecht-Gelände." Eine Dokumentation.* Berlin: Verlag Willmuth Arenhovel, 1987.

Safdie, Moshe. "Holocaust Memorial." In *Jerusalem: The Future of the Past.* Boston: Houghton Mifflin Company, 1989. Pp. 195-98.

Segev, Tom. *The Seventh Million: The Israeli's and the Holocaust.* Trans Haim Watzman. New York: Hill and Wang, 1993.

Sianko, Anna. "Quels monuments reconstruire après la destruction de Varsovie?" In *A l'Est, la mémoire retrouvée.* Paris: Editions la Découverte, 1990. Pp. 246-68.

Spector, Shmuel. "Yad Vashem." *Encyclopedia of the Holocaust.* New York: Macmillan, 1990. 4: 1,681-86.

Spielmann, Jochen. "Steine des Anstosses oder Schlussstein der Auseinandersetzung?" In Mai, Ekkehard and Schmirber, Gisela, eds. *Denkmal—Zeichen—Monument: Skulptur und öffentlicher Raum heute.* Munich: Prestel-Verlag, 1989: 110-14.

Spielmann, Jochen. "Steine des Anstosses—Denkmale in der Bundesrepublik Deutschland." *Kritische Berichte* 3/1988: 5-16.

Spielmann, Jochen. *Entwürfe zur Sinngebung des Sinnlosen: Zu einer Theorie des Denkmals als Manifestation des 'kulturellen Gedächtnisses': Der Wettbewerb für ein Denkmal für Auschwitz.* Ph. D. diss. Freie Universität. Berlin, 1990.

Szurek, Jean-Charles. "Le camp-musée d'Auschwitz." In *A l'Est, La mémoire retrouvée.* Paris: Editions la Découverte, 1990: 535-65.

Tolkin, Wiktor. "Die Denkmäler in Stutthof und Majdanek." *Zeichen* (March 1988).

Volkmann, Barbara, ed. *Diskussion zum Umgang mit dem Gestapo Gelände: Dokumentation.* Berlin: Akademie der Künste, 1986.

Webber, Jonathan. "The Future of Auschwitz: Some Personal Reflections." Oxford Centre for Postgraduate Hebrew Studies, 1992.

Wenzel, Hans. *Ein kurzer Wegweiser zu den Stätten des Gedenkens an die Zeit des Faschismus im Zentrum Wien.* Vienna: Presse und Informationsdienst der Stadt, 1988.

Yaffe, Richard. *Nathan Rapoport: Sculptures and Monuments.* New York: Shengold Press, Inc., 1980.

Yerushalmi, Yosef Hayim. *Zakhor: Jewish History and Jewish Memory.* Seattle and London: University of Washington Press, 1982.

Young, James E. *The Texture of Memory: Holocaust Memorials and Meaning.* New Haven and London: Yale University Press, 1993.

Young, James E. "The Veneration of Ruins." *The Yale Journal of Criticism* 6 (October 1993): 275-83.

Young, James E. "The Future of Auschwitz." *Tikkun* 7 (November/December 1992): 31-33, 37.

Young, James E. "The Counter-monument: Memory against Itself in Germany Today." *Critical Inquiry* 18 (Winter 1992): 267-96.

Young, James E. "The Biography of a Memorial Icon: Nathan Rapoport's Warsaw Ghetto Monument." *Representations* 26 (Spring 1989): 69-106.

Young, James E. "When a Day Remembers: A Performative History of *Yom Hashoah.*" *History and Memory* 2 (Winter 1990): 54-75.

Young, James E. "Die Textur der Erinnerung: Holocaust-Gedenkstätten." In Loewy, Hanno, ed. *Holocaust: Die Grenzen des Verstehens.* Reinbek: Rowohlt Verlag, 1993: 213-32.

Young, James E. *Writing and Rewriting the Holocaust: Narrative and the Consequences of Interpretation.* Bloomington and Indianapolis: Indiana University Press, 1988.

Zachwatowicz, Jan. "The International Memorial at Auschwitz." *Poland* (January 1965): 11-13.

Zum Umgang mit dem Gestapo-Gelände. Berlin: Akademie der Künste, 1989.

Zum Umgang mit einem Erbe. Berlin: Aktives Museum Faschismus und Widerstand in Berlin, 1985.

Lenders to the Exhibition

Archiv Internationale Bauausstellung Berlin 1987

Beit Lohamei Hageta'ot, Asherat, Israel

Professor Franciszek Duszenko, Gdansk

Facing History and Ourselves, Brookline, MA

Anne Frank House, Amsterdam

Renee and Chaim Gross Foundation, New York

Professor Adam Haupt, Sopot, Poland

Horst Hoheisel, Kassel

The Jewish Theological Seminary of America, New York

Louis I. Kahn Collection, Architectural Archives of the
University of Pennsylvania, Philadelphia

Luna Kaufman

Kultur Behörde, Hamburg

KZ-Gedenkstätte Dachau, Dachau-Ost, Germany

Heleen Levano, Netherlands

Sol LeWitt

Büro Libeskind, Berlin

Reinhard Matz, Cologne

New England Holocaust Memorial Committee, Boston

Pei Cobb Freed & Partners, New York

Buky Schwartz

Robert J. Stein/STEIN Architects, Inc.

Cornelis Suijk, Anne Frank Center, USA

Tucson Jewish Community Center, Tucson, AZ

United States Holocaust Memorial Museum, Washington,
D.C.

John Weber Gallery, New York

Hali Weiss, New York

Nina Rapoport-Wolmark

Yahalom and Zur Architects, Tel Aviv

Library, YIVO Institute for Jewish Research, New York

James E. Young, New York

Photograph Credits